*The **Folly** and the **Madness***

The Folly and the Madness

The Civil War Letters of Captain Orlando S. Palmer,
Fifteenth Arkansas Infantry

Edited by Thomas W. Cutrer

Voices of the Civil War • Michael P. Gray, Series Editor

The University of Tennessee / Knoxville

The Voices of the Civil War series makes available a variety of primary source materials that illuminate issues on the battlefield, the home front, and the western front, as well as other aspects of this historic era. The series contextualizes the personal accounts within the framework of the latest scholarship and expands established knowledge by offering new perspectives, new materials, and new voices.

Copyright © 2023 by The University of Tennessee Press / Knoxville.
All Rights Reserved. Manufactured in the United States of America.
First Edition.

Images are from the Library of Congress unless otherwise indicated.

Frontispiece: Capt. Orlando Stutts Palmer, 1862. FindAGrave.com.
Enhanced by the author.

Library of Congress Cataloging-in-Publication Data
Names: Palmer, Orlando S., 1839–1865, author. | Cutrer, Thomas W., editor.
Title: The folly and the madness : the Civil War letters of Captain Orlando S. Palmer, Fifteenth Arkansas Infantry / edited by Thomas W. Cutrer. Other titles: Civil War letters of Captain Orlando S. Palmer, Fifteenth Arkansas Infantry
Description: First edition. | Knoxville : The University of Tennessee, [2023] | Series: Voices of the Civil War | Includes bibliographical references and index. | Summary: "In 1860, Orlando S. Palmer left his home in north Alabama to study law in Tennessee and the following year went into practice in Des Arc, Arkansas. With Arkansas's secession, Palmer joined what would become Company H of the First (later Fifteenth) Arkansas Infantry and soon became his company's captain and brigade's adjutant. As such, he was closely associated with William J. Hardee, Thomas C. Hindman, and Patrick R. Cleburne, the latter of whom he served from the day that the First Arkansas was organized until Palmer and Cleburne both sustained fatal wounds at the battle of Franklin, November 30, 1864. The letters, almost all of which are addressed to his sister, "Missie," are divided equally between military and social concerns. Cutrer argues these letters offer a clear and entertaining window into the life and times of a junior officer serving in the Army of Tennessee"—Provided by publisher.
Identifiers: LCCN 2023031431 (print) | LCCN 2023031432 (ebook) | ISBN 9781621908418 (paperback) | ISBN 9781621908425 (pdf)
Subjects: LCSH: Palmer, Orlando S., 1839–1865—Correspondence. | Confederate States of America. Army. Arkansas Infantry Regiment, 15th. Company H. | Arkansas—History—Civil War, 1861–1865—Personal narratives. | United States—History—Civil War, 1861–1865—Personal narratives, Confederate. | Arkansas—History—Civil War, 1861–1865—Regimental histories. | United States—History—Civil War, 1861–1865—Campaigns. | Soldiers—Confederate States of America—Correspondence.
Classification: LCC E553.5 15th .P35 2023 (print) | LCC E553.5 15th (ebook) | DDC 973.7/467—dc23/eng/20230727
LC record available at https://lccn.loc.gov/2023031431
LC ebook record available at https://lccn.loc.gov/2023031432

To the memory of
Randolph B. "Mike" Campbell,
colleague and friend

Contents

Introduction
1

Chapter 1. 1860:
"All Will Yet Blow Over"
11

Chapter 2. 1861:
"The Flower of the Chivalry of the South"
21

Chapter 3. 1862:
"We Can Whip Any Army They May Send Against Us"
55

Chapter 4. 1863:
"This Dark and Troublesome Time"
99

Chapter 5. 1864:
"Bone and Muscle Could Not Endure"
135

Afterword
151

Notes
155

Bibliography
213

Index
223

Illustrations

Photographs

Following page 90

Albert Sidney Johnston

Braxton Bragg

Sterling Alexander Martin Wood and Staff

Patrick Cleburne

Flag of the 1st/15th Arkansas Infantry

Joseph Johnston

John Bell Hood

Mark Lowery

William Hardee

Thomas Brown Winston

Thomas Brown Winston, c. 1900

Oliver Sylvester Kennedy

The Battle of Mill Springs

The Battle of Nashville

Maps

Map 1. Bowling Green, Kentucky
20

Map 2. The Battle of Stones River
54

Map 3. The Battle of Chickamauga
98

Map 4. The Battle of Franklin
134

Introduction

Orlando S. Palmer, although orphaned at the age of eleven, was an idealistic, romantic, irrepressible, and relentlessly optimistic young attorney from Green Hill, Alabama, and, by his own assessment, "of a hopeful disposition" and "as merry and lighthearted a soldier as we have in our army." He was also more than a bit of a Lothario. "Do not censure me, for I cannot avoid loving a pretty woman," he wrote to his sister in March 1864. "Love is the weakness of my nature."

He was the son of Martha Person "Patsy" (Kennedy) Palmer, who was born in Mechanics Hill, North Carolina, on March 8, 1821, and Paschal W. Palmer, born November 21, 1815, in Franklin County, Georgia. The couple were married on October 26, 1837, at Martha's parents' home at Green Hill, Alabama, and were to have two children, a son, Orlando, and a daughter, Artimisia, known to her family as "Missie."[1]

Paschal Palmer died on November 4, 1844, in Tippah County, Mississippi, and the widowed Martha Palmer and her children moved back into the home of her parents, Hiram and Mary (Spinks) Kennedy, where she died only six years later.

The village of Green Hill, located on the Tennessee state line in Lauderdale County, Alabama, was, according to instructions that O. S. Palmer wrote on an envelope, "15 miles from Florence, ½ miles from the road leading to Nashville"—Andrew Jackson's Military Road.

The Kennedys and Green Hill were closely associated. The family had resided in Philadelphia, Pennsylvania, prior to the American Revolution, where Orlando Palmer's great-great-grandfather, John Alexander Kennedy, had designed and produced the famed Kennedy long rifle. When the British occupation of the city disrupted the weapon's manufacturing during the American Revolution, he removed the factory and his family to what became known as Mechanics Hill, Moore County, North Carolina.

From there, during the War of 1812, Kennedy expressed his willingness to manufacture such rifles as the United States government might require. "Tho I am not ancious to under take the bisness, as I am content with my present imployment, which a fordes me a cumfortabel livin . . . when I think on the blessings we injoy in our much beloved country, it makes my hart glo with the love of the same and makes me willin to incounter almost any hardship in defence of our rights."²

The Kennedys' factory, inherited by John Alexander's son David, was highly profitable and was said to have been the largest in that part of the South. One contemporary account reported his profits to have been approximately $15,000 annually and those of his brother, Alexander, "about 1,000 per annum."³

A period of a general economic decline beginning in 1825 and culminating in the Panic of 1837, however, saw a decrease in the factory's profitability, and, when Alexander Kennedy's general store failed, creditors demanded that David Kennedy repay his brother's debt, for which he had provided surety. He liquidated his North Carolina holdings—according to one source, one 300-acre tract of Kennedy's land sold for only four dollars—and sold the rifle mill at auction. Then, in 1828 he and his wife, Joannah, relocated the Kennedy Gun Factory to their son Hiram's cotton plantation at Green Hill, Alabama, where he continued to operate it until his death in 1837. Its ownership was then passed down to his son, Hiram Kennedy, who, in the 1850 census, identified himself as a "gunsmith."

In addition to the rifle factory, in 1830 the Kennedys of Green Hill were founders of the Milner and Kennedy Wool Factory, which was to produce cloth for Confederate uniforms and "slave cloth" for plantation use, and, as part of the firm of Baugh, Kennedy and Co.—later known as Kennedy, Baugh, and Leftwich—they operated a textile mill on nearby Shoal Creek. In the decade prior to the Civil War, the mill operated 2,200 spindles, 70 looms, employed 125 people, and had an annual production of nearly $90,000.

During the war, Federal troops burned all these establishments, but, according to *DeBow's Review*, "they enriched their worthy and enterprising proprietors. These gentlemen are not only in easy circumstances, but they are gratefully remembered as public benefactors, in having provided remunerative employment to hundreds of needy laborers."⁴

Orlando Palmer was graduated from Wesleyan University in Florence, Alabama, and, like his uncles Johnathan Spinks Kennedy and Elias Windsor Kennedy, entered the law, having attended the Cumberland School of Law in Lebanon, Tennessee. Although he found it to be "a bitter struggle for me to tear myself away from the home of my boyhood's happy days," early in 1861 he moved to Arkansas, then a raw frontier state, and entered practice in the burgeoning town of Des Arc.⁵

Although he claimed not to have "much interest in political affairs" he was an intense admirer of the fire-eating secessionist, "the glorious"

William Lowndes Yancey, as well as an ardent Breckinridge Democrat in the election of 1860. So much so, in fact, that his grandparents admonished him to cease "spouting politics."

As secession neared, Palmer enlisted as a private in Prairie County's militia company, the "Rector Guards." Although he informed Missie that he had volunteered "not for position, not for a name, but from patriotic motivation, to fight the battles of truth, of justice, and of my country," no sooner had his regiment become part of Maj. Gen. William Joseph Hardee's division than Palmer gained appointment as the general's personal secretary and quickly rose to become his regiment's sergeant major, his company's first lieutenant and then captain, and, concurrently, his brigade's adjutant, first under Brig. Gen. Sterling Alexander Martin Wood, a Lauderdale County neighbor to whom he referred familiarly as "Sterling," and then under Brig. Gen. Mark Perrin Lowery.[6]

Palmer's letters, all of which he addressed to his sister, "Missie," contained "all the news both of a private and public character." Of military interest, he offers a top-down view of operations, unusual in soldier letters that generally report only what could be observed at the company level because, as he wrote, "it is not the policy of the Generals to allow us to know anything about what is going on." As his brigade's adjutant, however, Palmer wrote, "I can learn all about the expected movements of the army and have a better opportunity to become intimately acquainted with military science than I could have in the army."

Generally, this means that his vision and his communications were more strategic than tactical. "I am not prepared to give you a general description" of the battle of Missionary Ridge, he wrote, "not being sufficiently informed to do so with any satisfaction." He did more than once, however, personally experience "the dread shock of war," and offers a soldier's-eye view of, for example, the battle of Perryville, where he "had a gun and have the satisfaction of knowing that I repaid the wounds they gave me at Shiloh." He also comments on the guerilla and partisan activity in southern Missouri, Kentucky, east Tennessee, and northern Alabama. Palmer's participation, however, was minimal because, as was typical of irregular warfare, the foe "decamped in hot haste when they learned that we were coming in force."[7]

As a staff officer, he often sent home evaluations of the high-ranking officers with whom he served and in whom he had boundless, if not always entirely warranted, confidence. On first meeting, he thought William J. Hardee was "a perfect gentleman, an intelligent, high-toned man in every respect," but soon found him to be "as touchy to us as a sore headed bear."

William Preston, on whose staff he served briefly, he found to be "one of the most agreeably entertaining, intelligent, and fine men I have ever yet had the good fortune to meet with. He is so excessively clever that you soon become easy in his company and are drawn to him by such a charm that you cannot resist it." The "indomitable" John Hunt Morgan, wrote Palmer, "has never met with a reverse but always comes off with triumph, victor in every battle. Destiny has surely pointed him out as the great partisan warrior of the Revolution. If all our generals were as successful as him, we would soon drive the vandals from our soil." Twenty thousand men under Albert Sidney Johnston, he believed, "can whip a 100,000 of the enemy." Of Simon Bolivar Buckner he wrote, "I have more confidence in him than any of them. I had rather fight under him than any other General in the service." Palmer had the highest respect for "the immortal" Patrick R. Cleburne, whom he thought to be "one of the bravest officers in the Army and a General of the very first character." His opinion of Braxton Bragg was, perhaps, less insightful. "I was well satisfied with Gen. Bragg," he wrote, and was "not disposed to join in the clamor against him. I think he is all right and will prove it." Joseph E. Johnston, one of "the great Captains of this age," he informed his sister, "is quite a military looking little man," and the men of the Army of Tennessee had the greatest confidence in him, he assured Missie. "We can safely trust our cause in his hands. He will act wisely and gallantly under all circumstances and, I think, will lead us to triumph over the vandal horde."

He could not, however, write about everything to which he was privy, explaining that military security required confidentiality. "As to the strength of our army," he wrote from Tupelo, Mississippi, on June 9, 1862, "I am not informed, and if I were it would not be proper for me to say." And when Missie Palmer inquired as to why their friend and neighbor, Sterling Wood, had resigned his command, her brother discreetly replied that "I ought not to write the facts fully and cannot, for reasons that will be apparent to you, do so in this letter." He did, however, promise to give her the full particulars "at some future time."

In addition to sharing his knowledge of the thoughts of the Army's high command, Palmer offers detailed descriptions of such mundane minutia of soldier life as the procedure for applying for a furlough, the quality and quantity of his daily rations, the construction of winter quarters, and a thorough description of a staff officer's uniform, of which he was inordinately proud.

But his letters were also highly personal, reflecting, as Walt Whitman wrote, "not chiefly the facts of battles, marches, what-not but the social being-ness of the soldiers." This young man, away from home, friends, and family, complained bitterly of the woeful soldier's lot of not receiving mail. Although he was well aware of "the derangement and uncertainties" of the mail— "the mails and Yankees are so irregular," a kinsman wrote—Palmer nonetheless lamented that he had "written home so often and can get no response that I am discouraged to so great an extent that I do not feel much like writing."[8]

His letters also express his grave concern for family members either in an area raided or occupied by Federal troops or, later in the war, suffering the depredations of "tories," loyalists unrestrained by the absence of Confederate authority. "I know that the good and loyal people of Lauderdale must have suffered heavily from the presence of the hated foe in such large numbers for so long a time in their midst," he wrote on December 12, 1863. "They have now felt the dread realities of war and I sincerely hope they may henceforward be far from the inroads of the enemy."

Less common is his extreme concern for what the modern reader might identify as his sister's chronic depression: "the same old monster," he calls it, or more simply, "the blues." Throughout his letters he admonishes her to "struggle against this lowness of spirit, this bitterness of thought" that seems to have beset her for years. His distress over her condition, he wrote, "sometimes renders me sad, very sad, and disqualifies me from the prompt and efficient discharge of my duties."

He constantly encouraged Missie to improve her mind and cheer her spirits with reading, and recommended to her such books as he thought best for her—those of Walter Scott and Washington Irving, for example. He pressed upon her "the importance of constant steady reading of choice works," and confessed that he longed for the war "to bring itself to an end so that I can seek some fair companion as fond of books as I," then to "hunt some lonely, secluded spot full of romance and beauty and there enjoy the happiness of literary pursuits."

In fact, Palmer and his sister, having been orphaned at an early age, were remarkably close. "You are the only being in whom my heart's purest, warmest, and entire feeling is all concentrated. I have no fair lady love with whom my affection for you is divided."

Although he claimed that he "would not willingly or knowingly influence your mind in any way," he advised his sister on her marriage prospects. "Ponder well before you decide" upon a husband "is the only advice I can give you in this, your trouble." Likewise, although he did not always agree with her negative assessments of his candidates to become her sister-in-law, he often requested that she advise him as to his choices among marriage prospects, and he "exactly followed," her advice "about a certain matter with a certain young lady who shall pass without a name."

Although his soul and his letters were marbled with a deeply engrained Calvinist fatalism—"a wise Providence rules all things," he counseled, and "trials are intended for your ultimate good"—by and large Orlando Palmer was a likable young man with a young man's foibles, and he sought to "snatch joy and happiness from the very clutches of fate." His high spirits and frolicking nature sometimes clashed with his somewhat Puritanical personality. "We should not murmur at the decrees of fate. It is our duty cheerfully and patiently to submit to every inconvenience, hardship, privation, and suffering which follow in the pursuit of and obedience of moral obligation," he often intoned. "Patience under suffering and trial are the highest attributes of a refined and enlightened Christian civilization." But when he was not expressing concern over his sister's melancholia or Federal troops occupying Lauderdale County, the tone of his letters was generally playful, bantering, and teasing, and full of self-deprecating humor. He admitted to a penchant for language that was "romantic, high-sounding, and, in my humble opinion, pretty." Brimming with mid-nineteenth century rhetorical and romantic panache, Palmer's letters echo and imitate the style of Byron, Poe, and Scott, with whom, in his fancy, he went wandering "through the ruins of ancient castles." He was in love with words, never using one when several struck his more poetic fancy.

And although he claimed to "think it best at all times to tell the simple truth" and to believe that "an unvarnished tale is always the safest," he often exaggerated for the sake of humor. He facetiously refers to himself as "a bashful, silent, retiring boy" and laments that "I am but a plain, simple boy who has not wit nor worth nor power of speech with which to charm fair maiden's ear," when, in fact, his letters reveal a continuous train of girlfriends . . . virtually a new one every month and sometimes two or more at a time . . . and he seems to have been constantly "head and ears in love."

His letters, therefore, reveal much about courtship customs and relationships between young men and young women during the Victorian era. "You know I never was very indifferent to the society of the dear ladies," he admits, and he delighted in "the refining influence of lovely and accomplished women." Like Romeo, Palmer was in love with love, admitting that "I am in love with several dozen of them and am having a huge time generally."

"I am not without a sweetheart, no matter where I am," he wrote from Triune, Tennessee, in December 1862, but on another occasion, not long afterward, he grieved that he had "no fair lady love. . . . No; I have no sweetheart, no fair creature of whom to dream and to whom to dedicate my whole thoughts and affections."

For all his political conservatism, Palmer's opinions sometimes ran counter to accepted Victorian social mores. At least somewhat progressive regarding women's rights, he suggested that his sister borrow a horse from their uncle in order that she might "go anywhere you desire." If she must ride unescorted and unchaperoned, he advised her, "just go on by yourself. Be as independent as any of them. Do not stand back for slight inconveniences."

On another occasion, he stated his opinion that he saw "no impropriety in any young lady traveling in company with a young gentleman acquaintance," and "any one who would be disposed to make disparaging remarks about a young lady who should have the boldness of mind to do so is a vain meddler whose soul would stoop to any depth of degradation."

Slavery is never an overt issue in Palmer's letters but is a recurrent undertone. Four days after the bombardment of Fort Sumter, for example, he gives voice to the persistent nightmare of the white South, slave rebellion. "If an insurrection or anything of the sort should be feared or anticipated," he wrote to his sister, "you must send me a dispatch informing me there of, and I will instantly leave for home and stand by those who are nearest and dearest to me." Although he mentions individual enslaved people only seldom and the general subject of slavery not at all, he did have as many as three bondsmen with him from time to time during the war. He only alludes to the nature of their servitude, saying that they were "hired out," but his letters frequently include information regarding the state of their health and conveying their love to their mothers. When one of them, Marion, contracted an unspecified disease, Palmer took him to a doctor in Decatur, Alabama, to effect a cure and told him to "go home when he got able and remain there until he entirely recovered."

Palmer never doubted the rectitude of the cause for which he was fighting and therefore accepted without hesitation "the imperative necessity of every man remaining steadily and contentedly at his post" and remained loyal to the secessionist cause to the last. In this, he echoed the sentiments of his cousin Oliver Sylvester Kennedy who wrote of his "imperative duty to go forth into the army to vindicate my country's honor—to battle for rights dear to us all and which involve the existence of our infant Republic, and, loved one, to defend you from rude insults and taunts of hessians should they reach our Southern homes."

"Our cause is just," Palmer intoned, "and a just God will deliver us from the hands of our enemies." Ever conscious of his patriotic duty—and often quite exhilarated by military life—"I like the soldier's life very much—the activities, the adventure, and the excitement are really charming," he wrote, "and I become more attached to this sort of life every day"—Palmer was nevertheless eager for the war to cease. He was an admittedly ambitious young man and believed himself to "have as fine a prospect for happiness as heart could wish," and, with peace, "with will, energy, and luck my most ardent expectations might be more than realized."

The Letters

Unlike the majority of mid-nineteenth century letter-writers, Palmer practiced remarkably good penmanship and was a fine speller. As a staff officer, he had access to good writing materials and, generally, to a desk upon which to write, a luxury denied to most Civil War-era correspondents. His writing was, however, largely innocent of punctuation and almost entirely destitute of paragraph separation. These, the editor has largely supplied, and where the author's use of abbreviations and style of capitalization are at odds with modern usage, the editor has also, to a degree, standardized them.

Interspersed with Orlando Palmer's letters are those of his first cousin, Oliver S. Kennedy, to his fiancée and wartime bride, Georgia Cheatham Foster, also of Florence. Oliver Kennedy was born on January 24, 1841, in Lauderdale County, the son of Cynthia Palmer and William Wesley Kennedy. As a child he moved with his parents to Tippah County, Mississippi, but returned to Lauderdale County at the age of eighteen when he enrolled in the Wesleyan University in Florence, graduating in 1861. Kennedy enlisted as a private in Company C, Sixteenth Alabama Infantry, and was elected as his company's third lieutenant when the regiment was organized. He was said to have arisen "out of a sick bed" to command his company in the battle of Fishing Creek, on January 16, 1862, "the captain being absent." In March he was appointed as his regiment's adjutant and promoted to the rank of captain. At Shiloh, Kennedy wrote, he "commanded left wing of regiment as Lieutenant Colonel, the colonel absent and major wounded" and was said to have "acted his part well." In his application for membership in the United Confederate Veterans, Kennedy says that he was offered command of the Sixteenth Alabama in May 1862 but "declined it because Colonel W. B. Wood was then the colonel, being wounded, and I prevented his removal on account of prolonged absence." Soon thereafter, Kennedy was left sick or wounded at Carthage, Mississippi, and was absent on sick leave for some months until he resigned from his regiment in June 1863. Although his service record does not mention it, he seems, from internal evidence in his letters to his fiancée, that he was captured during this period. Twice he served in the commissary department under his uncle Jonathan Spinks Kennedy, but both times was forced to retire due to ill health. Of this service, Kennedy merely wrote, "Health failed, and joined commissary department." On January 27, 1863, Kennedy married Georgia Cheatham Foster in Florence, Alabama.[9]

Sadly, the Kennedy letters lack the legibility of those of Oliver Kennedy. As he confessed, he often wrote "under embarrassing circumstances . . . endeavoring to prove interesting while there is a continual noise around." On the eve of battle he attempted, "amid wild confusion and noise," to write to his fiancée, and, he admitted, "I guess it is a great scribble." His penmanship was not so fine as that of his cousin, and time has not been so kind to the letters themselves, many of which are faded, damaged, and pages of some have gone missing.[10]

※ ※ ※

The editor of this volume would like to extend his thanks to Christopher Thrasher, professor of history at National Park College and the author of *Suffering in the Army of Tennessee: A Social History of the Confederate Army of the Heartland from the Battles for Atlanta to the Retreat from Nashville*, and to Michael P. Gray, professor of history at East Stroudsburg University and author of *The Business of Captivity: Elmira and Its Civil War Prison* and *Crossing the Deadlines: Civil War Prisons Reconsidered*; to Evan R. Spencer, Archivist, Special Collections, University of Texas Arlington Libraries and to Jamie A. Simmons, curator of the Wilbur Smith Research Archives. These individuals have made invaluable contributions to this volume.

Chapter 1

1860

"All Will Yet Blow Over"

In August 1860, Orlando Palmer entered the Cumberland School of Law, in Lebanon, Tennessee, which he left before the end of the year, presumably without a degree.[1] As well as displaying a keen interest in the law, his interest was captured by the hotly contested presidential election of 1860, in which he was a fervent supporter of the Southern Democratic candidate, John C. Breckinridge, as well as an ardent admirer of secessionist William Lowndes Yancey.[2]

* * *

Lebanon, Tenn.
Aug. 22nd, 1860

Dear Sister,

I arrived here safe, sound, and in good health Saturday morning, 9 o'clock, without anything strange or wonderful transpiring on the way. Being rather worn down with travel and the many changes of scene and incidents of the trip, I did not write immediately as I should have done but will now endeavor to make amends by writing more at length than it would have been possible for me to have done sooner.

To begin at the first and give you a succinct account of my trip is the object of this epistle, and if you think you will weary with the narration, you had better throw it aside and exercise your imagination instead thereof. The trip to Lawrenceburg was very lonesome. No passengers and nothing to divert my mind from the sad thoughts which naturally forced themselves upon my notice upon leaving the dear ones at home and going, "a stranger in a strange land."

However, there must be a terminus to all things, so to my sad thoughts. They flee before the smiles and greetings of those estimable young ladies, viz., Misses Hortie, Ada, Isabel, and last and least, (but not least in my affections,) Anna Dear. They collected in a crowd of celestial beauty, dazzling with the brilliant flashes of their houri-like eyes at Mr. [William?] Simonton's gate, anxiously awaiting my appearance. They seemed very happy to see me, and I know I was transported with joy to spread my optics upon them all (but most of all) Miss Anna.[3]

After exchanging greetings with them at the gate, we adjourned Florence, Alabama to the house and passed off the time very pleasantly until a very late hour in the night. But I could not banish from before my gaze the lovely form of the sweet Anna. Bright visions of her were floating through my mind and figuring extensively in my dreams.

Next morning, we all, with the exception of Miss Ana [Allis?], went to Giles County. Mrs. S[imonton], Misses R [H?] and Anna and myself went in Mrs. S's superb carriage and Miss H and her servant (Lover) in a buggy. I had a fine time in the carriage. The ladies were more charming and interesting, if possible, than ever before, and time sped by on rosy pinions. But, as I am a bashful, silent, retiring boy, I would have much preferred a seat in the buggy with _____ by my side.

We reached the neighborhood of Mayfield at noon, went around to see Grandpa and c. Then came back to one of my dear old uncles where we sojourned for the remainder of our stay in the neighborhood. I sat on the front porch with Miss Anna and watched the movements of the heavens and made many conjectures. I don't know how long we were there—had no idea of the lapse of time—and was only brought back to a sense of things terrestrial by Miss Harriet coming out and inviting Anna to her room.

Next morning, we went to Pulaski [the seat of Giles County], Miss Anna and I having the buggy, and lest I might weary you, I will say nothing of what I said to her, and c. and leave you to fill up the blank just as it suits your taste.

Pulaski is very pretty town, about the size of Florence. There are several fine residences there. Altogether it is a prettier place than Florence.

We put up at Mr. Rose's, a mile from town, for dinner.[4] Went into town in the evening and drove all around, showing off the fair creatures by our sides to the wonder-stricken denizens of P____, returning to Mr. R's for tea. Had a glorious time with the young ladies till late at night. Had a long conversation with Miss Anna, but did not make a speech to her, and right here I must inform you of a fact which might not sound very harmoniously to you, viz., she is a dangerous rival of yours. She speaks very highly and frequently of Lee Rogers, how much she thinks of him and how pretty and good he is.[5] In order that she may not succeed in her attempts to seduce him from his loyalty to you, I made some advances myself, and you know I am not a half-way man in that line. You know if I can cut him out, you will owe me a debt of gratitude not easily cancelled.

More of this anon. I left Pulaski Thursday morning and reached Columbia at 8 o'clock where I expected to meet my trunk, which I sent through by the stage from Lawrenceburg, but it was not there, and I was obliged to get a horse and buggy and go down to Mt. Pleasant after it. Found it there and got back to Columbus time enough to meet the evening train for Nashville. Arrived in N____ Thursday. Was very much disappointed with the general appearance of the city. Instead of coming up to my expectations, it fell far short. Is a nasty, filthy, disagreeable, disgusting place with very few if any fine buildings or anything to render it attractive.

Did not look around much the first night. Was tired and went to bed early. Hearing that Yancey!! was to speak there Friday, I determined to remain to hear him.[6] Whilst running around next morning, I struck up with some friends and felt more at home but was disappointed in hearing that Yancey would not be there. However, I consoled myself as much as possible by going up to examine the Capitol and was walking around through it for some three hours [*Ink splatter. Word illegible*] went in the Library room and found it to contain the finest collection of books I ever saw. I ascended to the topmost step of the cupola and had a splendid view of the city and its environs. The sensation produced by such an exalted position was very peculiar and exciting. The city, however, did not improve in appearance in the least.

Porter Weakley was with me, and he seemed very happy to see me and conduct me through the magnificent structure.[7] It is beyond doubt or cavil the most splendid pile I ever saw. Every particle of it, from the base to the top is finely polished limestone. The floors, steps, and banisters, and c. are all rock. As to how such an immense building could be constructed, and to stand when it is all rock, is one of the mysteries of architecture I have not yet been able to solve. I wished frequently while wandering through its large and spacious halls and rooms that you were with me, sharing with me the rapture which everyone must feel on going through such magnificent buildings.

I did not visit any other places of note except the residence of Mrs. James K. Polk and the grave of Pres. Polk. I saw the place where rest the bones of the greatest and best President the United States ever had, but saw no monument that would correspond with his fair fame and character. It is a very ordinary monument and unworthy of the great man.[8]

I left Nashville at 2 o'clock, A.M., Saturday and on a crowded stage of about twenty boys. In consequence of such a crowd, I was very tired when I landed at the hotel. I found the town to be much nicer than my most sanguine hopes could warrant. It is about such a place as Florence or perhaps not quite so pleasant. There are some very nice residences, but as for the inhabitants, I cannot speak, for I know nothing of them and care less.

I found Cooper awaiting my arrival at the hotel. He had not been able to secure us a boarding house. Could not find one worth staying at, all the first-class houses having been engaged for months and we did not desire putting up at a starvation establishment. By dint of continued and laborious exertion of two or three days, we finally succeeded in renting the back room of Capt. Jos. Anderson's law office and procuring eating at Mr. Thompson's, who keeps a very fine table, good provender, well cooked and dressed. I think we will be pleased with it.[9]

Our room is back of the street, a tolerably quiet place and a very nice room. We give ten dollars per month and ten dollars each for eating, and one dollar and fifty cents for washing, making, in all, sixteen dollars per month, leaving out servant hire, lights, and fuel. The charges at the regular boarding houses around town are from $17.50 cts. to $18.00 per month, so you perceive we will not lose anything by the operation. Board is tremendous high, the people say, in consequence of the scarcity of provisions and the difficulty of procuring the same. There will be nothing scarcely made in this country. Corn is completely burned up as it also is in Giles, Lawrence, and Maury. A general starvation is staring these good people in the face, in anticipation whereof their faces are powerfully elongated, but they can send on for a supply from their beloved "brothers of the North!"

Tell Grandpa and Grandma I have so far complied with their advice and left off spouting politics except when the name of the glorious Yancey is mentioned, and then I would be unworthy of Alabama if I did not raise my voice in his defense. Everything here is for Bell and Everett, the most corrupt and rotten place politically in the South. The majority of the students are for Breckenridge and Lane. There has been speaking twice since I have been here, such as it was.[10]

Well, dear Sis, I suppose you are long since weary of this and wish I would stop. I will do so after asking you to inform me what the contents of Miss Jennie's letter were. One came for you from her the evening I left. Please give me an analysis of its contents as I am somewhat anxious to know which way the wind blows. Also how are "Cotton Plant" and "Canton"? Write and c.

Give me all the information you have about the "Star" women. Present my very best respects to any of them who may inquire, and especially to Miss B, anyhow.

Excuse the many blots and mistakes in this letter. My love to Grandpa and Grandma and all the dear people and consider this line freighted with my love for you.

Your brother,

Orlando S. Palmer

Write immediately on receipt and don't cross your letters.

Lebanon, Tenn.
Sep. 30th, 1860

Dear Sister,

Your two letters were duly and thankfully received. The first came in the midst of an interesting trial in the Circuit Court which I was regularly attending and hence did not have time to respond as soon as I could have wished. The second came a few days since whilst I was buried in my week's work and could not exhume myself long enough to reply then.

This, as you perceive by the caption, is Sunday. The solemnity of this day is forced upon my mind by the deep-toned merry peals of the many church bells that swing their glad calls over this quiet Christian village. But as it is a damp day, I shall not peril my good health by venturing out to hear a good sermon or even to feast my optics on the budding beauties of this burg. On the contrary, I shall remain with closed doors and endeavor in some slight degree to repay you for your two excellent and kind epistles.

However, you must not expect me to write fine, polished, and entertaining letters as some other of your correspondents do, for I am but a plain, simple boy who has not wit nor worth nor power of speech with which to charm fair maiden's ear or captivate her roving romantic fancy.

I was quite happy to know that all were well, that Grandma contemplated a trip to Florida and Grandpa one to Ripley. I hope Grandma will keep up her courage and go to see Uncle David and that her fear of the cars may blow away and she will cheerfully and confidently make the attempt and go on her way rejoicing, willing for a time to deprive herself of the sweet pleasures of looking up her chickens and turkeys and waiting on the poor black ones who are not able to wait on themselves. I am of the opinion that the trip would be highly beneficial to her as well as gratifying and joyous. Anyway, it could by no possibility do her any harm and she will have the pleasure of seeing Uncle David, his wife and children, and then she could be better satisfied after learning how they were situated.

She could then locate them in her mind, which, you know, is a great consolation of itself. Persuade her to go by all means.[11]

You and Delia can keep house while she is gone, and this should be strong inducement for her to go since it would greatly benefit you thereby in all your domestic qualities and qualify you for the situation which you are both so anxious to procure, viz., mistress of your own houses.[12]

I am surprised to hear that Grandpa is going to Mississippi. I did not think he would ever manage to get that far from home again. I am glad he is going. It will be a great pleasure to him, and he ought not to deprive himself of it when he can go so easily and quickly. You failed to inform me of what induced him to think of going. Surely something caused him to take the notion. Why did you not tell me, for you know I cannot but wonder at his taking such an unexpected determination.

The information that I had a "new cousin" born at Uncle Jesse's was very pleasing. Since you know that I have such a scanty supply of the same and am always glad to hear of any accessions to the list. That Aunt Olive would ask me to name my dear, sweet little cousin was very unexpected to me, for I am proverbially fond of ugly names, my various and numerous sweethearts having such names as Kate, Sue, Jane, Ann, Add, and Bet and c. Since she knows I admire such names as those, it is something wonderous strange that she should call upon me for a name. But if she wants one, I suppose I must supply one out of my list of favorites, and if she is not pleased therewith, she need not accept it.[13]

My especial favorite for a name is "Eugenia Anabell." This is something rare: romantic, high-sounding, and, in my humble opinion, pretty, and if her and Uncle Jesse should take a fancy to both or either of these names, I will make it a present some of these days when I marry rich.[14]

Give my very best love to and kiss a thousand times the dear little creature. May health and gentle peace perch upon its cradle, innocence and youthful joy attend its wanderings, and beauty and happiness and gratified conquest of gallant young swains be with her in the lovely years from sixteen to twenty, and when the hour of the shady side of twenty shall come, may some kind, affectionate and worthy man be joined to her in the bonds wholly.

My well wishes to Aunt Ollie and Uncle Jesse and tell them I will write sometime soon.

I do not suppose that other young cousin of mine will ever know there was ever such a chap in existence as myself except it knows me but to curse and scorn and loathe me, for it is to be expected it will be trained up in the way in which its parents think it should go. I would be sorry if this were the case, but it is not in my power honorably to prevent the same or to drive away from their minds the sovereign contempt they entertain for my unworthy self. Peace be with them.

Your advice about a certain matter with a certain young lady who shall pass without a name had been exactly followed in anticipation. I did as you counseled before I knew what it was or would be. After I wrote you, having duly deliberated on the affair in its every phase and long debating with myself some very nice and subtle question which I occasionally stalked upon, long doubting as to the propriety of my former course, I at last—all doubts and misgivings as to the proper conduct for the future having been dispelled by a faint glimmering of reason—concluded that the true and only honorably line of policy to be checked out and then followed was to write to her, to explain the uncertain events of the last 8 months, clearly and explicitly state the true sentiments that still held their high courts in my bosom (gloomy region), and leave it to her to determine as to what the relation between us should be.

Acting upon this decision, I wrote her a long letter giving her a plain, simple narrative of everything relating to our former connection and then requested her, after mature deliberation, to decide as her heart and good sense dictate. I cannot imagine what her answer may—nay, cannot hope she will deign to notice my communication at all—further than to scoff at its contents and scorn its author. If she thinks proper to reject me as an unworthy offering at the shrine of her vanity, it shall all be well with me. I shall not rave, tear my hair in deep despair, commit suicide or do any other extravagant act at which the world might grow sad, but will go on the even tenor of my way, yea, verily, I will even smile, talk, act, and think as other mortals do who may not have sorrowed or pondered in moody silence over the ruins of their once majestic hopes. I shall even banish from memory's kingdom the unpleasant thoughts that have roamed at ease through the wild wastes and brought agitation and distress to every other peaceable inhabitant thereof.

No more in pensive silence will I ponder the loved face and call to mind the graces of her person and the perfection and power of her intellectual graces. Never will my fancy go roaming and dwell upon "her softness and sweet attractive grace."[15] But I will be, as I should be, forgetful of the emotions that once stirred the deep, pure waters of my soul at the sound of her name or the tread of her nimble feet.

However, I shall hope for the answer that would bring into realization the cherished thought of days gone by.

I will inform you of the result of my negotiation as soon as I, myself, am cognizant thereof.

So, no more of this.

I do not know that I can render you any assistance in coming to a conclusion on the very difficult and important question that now puzzles your brain and makes your nights sleepless(?) Your own good sound sense and judgement, aided and controlled by your feelings, are the best and, in fact, only safe adviser in such a case, for it is a subject more materially concerning your own welfare than that of anyone else.

Let them guide you in the task of forming a decision, not neglecting at the same time to take into consideration everything calculated to throw any light on the question and enabling you to come to correct conclusions. I would not willingly or knowingly influence your mind in any way by any expression of mine, for you might be misled thereby and then accuse me of giving you the wrong advice. It is always best in such cases for the party most deeply interested to determine for themselves as to the proper course. Then they can attach no blame to anyone. I have such confidence in your discernment and sound judgment that I do not fear but you will come to that decision best calculated to ensure your own happiness and that of your brother who cannot but be happy when he knows you are. Then, whatever be the result of your ponderings and deliberations, I will rest satisfied, for I am certain that your choice will be the only proper one.

Ponder well before you decide is the only advice I can give you in this, your trouble.

I am glad to learn of Joe Milner's success in the line matrimonial, and hope that he may have a happy time. He was getting almost old enough to marry and has acted the part of a wise man. Tell Elias to follow the example of his old brother and roommate [at LaGrange College] and procure him a roommate.[16]

Miss [Margaret A.] Woodell and Miss Annie [Davidson] did not stop to see you? They promised most faithfully that they would. If I were you, I never would speak to them any more for treating you so shamefully. I wouldn't have D___! No, I wouldn't, and I am tempted to say I won't have Miss Annie, that is, it has always been understood that I can't get her, no how.

I forgot to mention in my former letter the fact that I had bought "Waverley Novels." I purchased them in Nashville . . . gave $13.50 for them. What little spare time I have, which is only when I become worn out and sated with Law, I put over perusing about in them, wandering with Scott through the ruins of ancient castles.[17]

If I have money enough when I go through Nashville on my way home, I intend to buy "Irving's Works," and make you read every one of them. How do you like that? Will it be as hard as it was to study "Logic" last winter? Ha ha.[18]

I have answered Elias's letter at length and will give Oliver's due notice in a few days.

Politics run high here though it is all most one way, like the man's jug handle: all on one side and that on the wrong side. The "Belleveretts" will carry this county by 1200 majority or more. However, there are a great many Democrats here, and they are striving gallantly. They are going to have a "Brecklane" rally here next Wednesday.[19] Several distinguished speakers are expected: Senators Johnson and Nicholson and Andrew Ewing of Nashville.[20]

I do not take much interest in political affairs . . . scarcely ever read a newspaper and never talk Politics, which I think is quite small business for a student. I have, however, a splendid photograph of Breckenridge over my mantlepiece at which I often look and admire very much.

I have written now until I am tired, and I know you cannot be otherwise in deciphering it.

Give my love to all and write immediately to
Your Brother,
Orlando S. Palmer

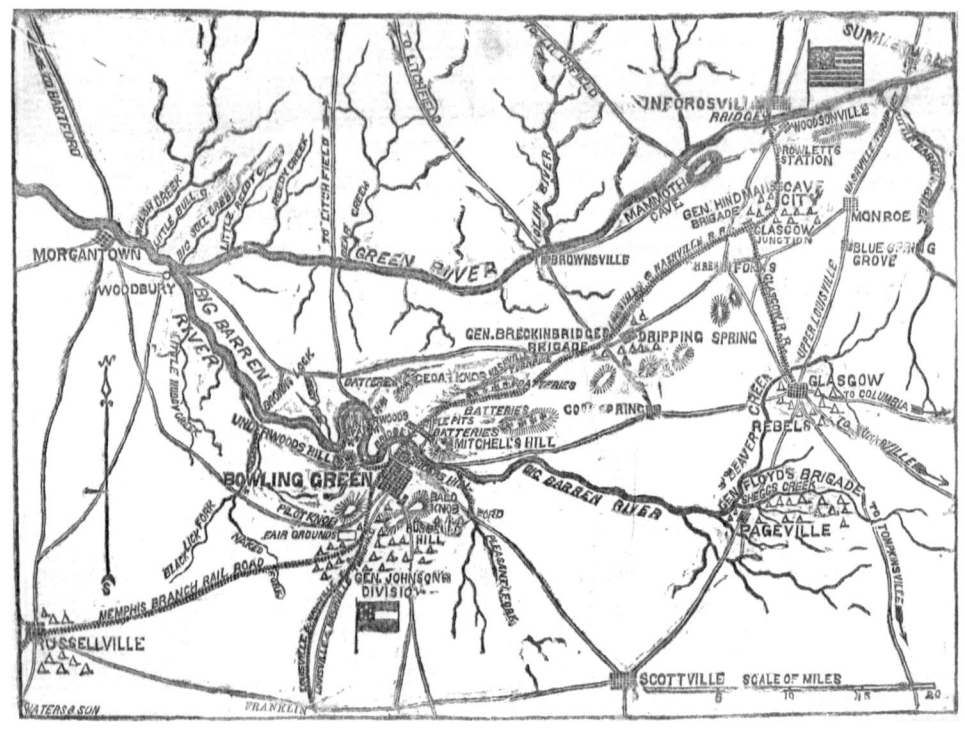

Bowling Green, Kentucky.

Chapter 2

1861

"The Flower of the Chivalry of the South"

Madison, Ark.
Jan. 15th, 1861

Dear Sister,

When I wrote to you a few days since, I was tolerably well pleased with this little town and thought I would remain here. Since then, I have become very much dissatisfied with the town and will leave here tomorrow for Des Arc. This town, as I told you before, is in a low, flat, wet place and I do not think I could possibly have my health here. But this is not all that determined me to leave. This is quite a small town. Very few inhabitants and from the great number of outlets for the produce of the county, I do not think it can ever be much of a place. Besides, it is one of the muddiest, wettest places you ever saw. This is not very inviting. Further, there is no society here, no refinement. In fact, nothing to make it pleasant, and I cannot be contented to settle down in such a country though I might make something here after a while.

Des Arc is a growing place some six or seven times larger than Madison and the prospects for its being a large place are very bright. It stands fair for being one of the first cities in the state and hence it is I prefer going there. There certainly is some society, some respectability there, and I would prefer perishing there to living in this charnel house. I want to go to a place that will someday be a place fit to live in, and I greatly fear me this never will.

It is true, Des Arc will be a little farther from home and my sweet sister, but I can soon go home from Des Arc with very little more expense, and then, if you should ever want to visit me, you could come to a place worth visiting where you would enjoy yourself and not be disgusted with the place where your brother was.

After considering the thing in every light and aspect, I think I am acting for the better. I am going to a young city and can grow up with it and if I do anything whatever will do much more than I could ever do here. I flatter myself that I can do anything here I can do just as well there, if not more, and then I will have the pleasure of living in a place fit for white men to live in. Do you not think I am doing right in going there? It is only sixty miles from here, but I shall go to Memphis and take a boat as it is cheaper, much pleasanter, and just as quick. In fact, the roads are so very bad, it is almost impossible to go by stage.[1]

Tell Grandpa I saw Mr. Dunn the other day. He and family were well and he sends his best respects to Grandpa.[2]

Mr. Shefield still treats me very finely. His wife is still sinking very rapidly. She is in the last stages of consumption. Mr. Beard and Lady reached here Saturday. Were well and c. I have not time to write any more at present, but when I get settled will give a long letter. Tell Delia to write to me. I shall expect a letter from you in a very few days. You must write to me immediately and direct your letter to Des Arc.

My love to all and Miss Jennie [Kendrick]!

Your brother

O. S. Palmer

P.S. If any letters come to Green Hill for me, send them to me.

Your Brother

Des Arc, Ark.
Feb. 14th, 1861

Dear Sister,

I have just received your letter of the 2nd inst. and was perfectly frantic with joy at hearing from you at last. It seemed I was never going to hear from you in Alabama except Uncle Elias.[3] I had not heard one word from home since I left there, and you can easily imagine my anxiety to hear from you and learn the joyous news that all were well. I had almost given up to have a severe attack of the blues and become sick with disappointment, since you know "hope deferred maketh the heart sick."

I was sorry to learn that you were not very well and trust this will find my precious sister well and enjoying herself. I was saddened to know you were giving way to desponding thoughts which I have so often guarded you against. What good does it do to yield to such unpleasant reflections? Why should we thus allow ourselves to become the sport of every wayward thought? It is wrong. We must not, and I hope my courageous, strong-hearted sister will henceforth brace herself against them and snatch joy and happiness from the very clutches of fate.[4]

It was a bitter struggle for me to tear myself away from the home of my boyhood's happy days. The friends of my early days and, more than all, the good kind relations who have so long sheltered and protected the lonely orphan and to go "a stranger into a strange land." But necessity demanded it and I had arrived at an age when it was no time for consulting the dictates of affection.

I had a name and fortune to carve out of the wide world and it was high time I was "up and doing." Now that I am here, I sometimes allow myself to revert to the places where my heart is, the home of my sister, and a sadness unawares comes over my heart and I feel as if I could give up everything and fly to the roof where all would rejoice to see me. But I do not submit to such emotions. I know it will not do for me to thus render myself miserable, and I plunge more vigorously into the investigation of some point of law to escape from the spirits my fancy has called around me. I am contented and could be satisfied with my lot were I certain, my sister, that you were contented and happy and did not grieve over the absence of one whose spirit is ever with you. If you were happy, I could not be otherwise, for what constitutes your happiness has a reflective influence over me and my sentiments partake of the nature of yours. Dear Sister, throw off these gloomy thoughts, drive away these dark specters, and look upon the sunny side of life.

You are something "more than a trouble to Grandpa and Grandma." You are not intruding. You are a blessing forever, a joy and a comforter to them. You cannot imagine how great a pleasure you are to them. In every respect instead of being a trouble to them, you are a pleasure to them. You can smooth their journeys down the declining hill of life—the thorns and stumbling blocks—your young, loving, willing hands can remove and render them happy in the ministering service of so sweet a creature as yourself.

You are right when you say, "very few orphans have fallen in such kind hands as we have." They have, indeed, in every respect been to us as parents and treated us with the same love and kindness as it we were their own children. And would that I could find some way to repay them for it, the best energies of my nature should not be wanting to perform the labor of love. You have an opportunity and I know you will use it, and you can and will render yourself happy and cheerful in accomplishing this service.

Yet again I entreat you not to give way to your thoughts. Pick up some book, determine to read it to shake off your thoughts, and do not lay aside the book until you succeed. Do this once, the next time it will not be as difficult, and very soon you will get rid of your gloomy thoughts without an effort. I have tried the plan and I know you can as just as I have said. The plan has always been successfully carried out by me, whenever I resolutely set my head to do it. Will not my sweet sis make one long determined effort to gratify me and benefit herself in this respect?

Political excitement out here is very high. Our elections come off next Monday. The State is certain to go for secession. I am taking no part whatever more than keep posted.

I belong to the "Rector Guards" of Prairie County. We have a very fine company and hold ourselves in readiness to defend our soil from the pollution of Black Republicanism and c.[5]

[*No formal ending to letter*]

Des Ark, Ark.
March 11th, 1861

Dear Sister,

Yours of the 27th inst. was received a few days since, and I should have answered immediately had I been at home, but I was not, being compelled to go to Austin, some thirty miles from here. I was happy in knowing that all were well and that nothing more serious than colds was prevalent. I was pleased to learn that you had had a merry time out at home amid the dear old halls, now much dearer to me than ever before, since I can now see how dear they really are to me.

Why can you not be joyous and lighthearted there all the time? It seems to me if I were there, no trouble would mar the completeness of my happiness. You have everything there that heart could crave, so why should you permit sorrow to cast its gloomy shadow around the soul and shut out the pure sunlight of pleasure? You must not do it. If you are happy and contented at home amid the loved ones there, your brother cannot be otherwise, for in the knowledge of your joys consists the only thing that can render him resigned to his situation. Will you not, then, look upon the sunny side of life?

You asked me earlier a hard question as to who I would prefer to get the first honor. It is not proper that I should make any invidious discrimination on this question, and I leave it to your heart to tell you where my preferences are. I know of no young man who I would rather call brother than T[homas] B[rown] W[inston], noble, pure, and honorable. There is none more worthy of the hand of my sweet sister than he and to none would I more willingly commit the happiness of my loved sister. I told Oliver to make him a present of a very valuable work which I have on anatomy. I hope he will accept it.

Aunt C[ynthia], I think, treated you most shamefully.[6] She ought to have treated you with more respect and courtesy than she did. You ought to have gotten after her with a vengeance for such an unpardonable act of impoliteness.

I did go to Little Rock but saw nothing worthy of your attention. The country from here to there is one continuous plain, the road passing through a region timbered very much like the land around home. The only difference is there is no rocks on it, and it produces very finely and is being rapidly settled upon and subdued. Little Rock is an old, dingy, dirty, rickety looking town of some five thousand inhabitants. There is nothing at all attractive about it. The Capitol is a very ordinary concern. The buildings all small and decaying and not at all worthy of the State of Arkansas. They ought no longer to disgrace the state with their insignificant appearance.

I saw W. C. Ratcliff. He is here studying Law. Is well, doing well, and c.[7]

I had but a short time to look around the city and not stay but a sort time, only four or five hours. Whilst there I went before the Supreme Court to stand an examination. The honorable Judges gave me a very thorough examination which, with credit to myself be it said, I passed very well and was highly complimented by their honors.

In going to Austin on Friday last, I was caught in a very hard rain and had got very wet but felt no inconvenience from it. I had quite an adventure when I arrived there. Riding out to Mr. Neely's (who has just moved out here from about Rogersville) the man I was going to see, I caught the glimpse of a very pretty girl standing in the door. All at once, she came darting out of the house, hurled the gate aside, and came with the tread of nimble feet towards where I was, her arms extended and her lips fixed up for kissing, and I thought surely I would get a sweet kiss on somebody's credit. But alas! When she got within some three paces of me, she discovered her mistake and recoiled as if from a snake and said she thought I was her brother-in-law.

I merely remarked I was sorry she discovered the mistake before I got the big salute. Was not that a very provoking disappointment? I soon found out that it was Miss Mollie Neely who perhaps you saw at the camp meeting last fall. I had quite a nice time with her.

By the way, there are several quite interesting ladies in our town. My landlady (a widow) is a very fine woman. Several young ladies are in the habit of coming around to see her (?) frequently and we boys have a good time generally.

I do not recollect whether I have written to you since I formed a copartnership with Mr. Simpson. If not, it will not be amiss to now say something of it. I do not think I could have a better. He is getting a very fine practice, is quite popular, very clever, a fine Lawyer for a young man, has a very fine library (a thing I did not), and, withal, is one of the best young men in the world. He reads his Bible and prays every night and morning. Do you not think, then, I did well to form a copartnership with him? He is so good I feel ashamed of myself and often wish I were as good as he. He sets me a very fine example if I could but follow it.[8]

Tell Aunt Mary [Mary S. Belk Spinks] I have not written to her because I have been so busy and had so much writing to do I could not conveniently do so. I am writing to Elias and Oliver every week and she can hear from me by that means. But if she will trouble herself so much as to write to me, I will most certainly answer. Tell her to write to me. I would be very much pleased to hear from her and c.[9]

I received a letter from Uncle Jesse last night giving me some very unpleasant intelligence as to a certain transaction about his Country. A certain young lady has my sympathies. I am sorry for her.

You do not tell me anything about what nor how much you are reading. How is this? Is it an oversight in you or done by premeditation? You must tell me all about what you are reading and c.

I am and have been quite well and think by care I can remain so.

Give my love to Grandpa and Grandma, Delia, and c.

You must write to me at least once a week and I will write as often as I can.

Your Brother,

O. S. Palmer

I send you the "Des Arc Citizen" and "Constitutional Union." Do you get them?

Des Arc, Ark.
March 27th, 1861

Dear Sister,

I have intended to answer your very interesting letter by the next mail after its reception, but time and opportunity was wanting to enable me to do so and even now I have but a very short time to write. I was very much pleased to learn that you had gotten out of the way you had of having the blues and was happy, contented, and well. Continue thus to drive away those gloomy thoughts which sometimes gather round your naturally lively heart, and sunshine and pleasure will meet you on every side.

I admire the purity, strength, and sincerity of your attachment for your newfound Lover and trust your brightest daydreams of the coming joyous future may be more than realized in the full fruition of a well selected marriage. You must be very devoted, indeed, if you can withstand the bold attacks of that most fascinating preacher upon the citadel of your affections. From what you and Delia both say of him, he must be indeed a dangerous rival and one who I would not like to come in competition with.

If you still prove true to your old love when such a noble conquest is made as he, I can but admire your firmness and superiority to most of the girls of this fickle-minded age. You know that most of them delight to boast of the number and character of their conquests, the number of noble hearts they have stricken down, and so soon as they have achieved one conquest they flit by, "conquering its conquest" no matter how noble, how worthy their last Lover may be. Still, this natural propensity to swell the list of their admirers renders them forgetful of everything except the gratification of this criminal desire. I always knew you were above it, and in this instance, you act as yourself. I do not think you could have made a selection more acceptable to me than Mr. W[inston]. I think a great deal of him and feel confident your trust will never be betrayed.

It is true, two years seem to lovers' eyes almost an eternity, but with happy hearts the intervening time is passed quickly and before you can imagine it real you are brought suddenly to the long-wished-for time.

In the meantime, you can speed the time very properly in preparing yourself for the realities of life and in storing your mind with such solid knowledge as will render your Lord proud of his Lady, make you an ornament to society and a source of never-failing pride to your brother. You do not say anything about what you are reading or, in fact, whether or not you are reading anything. How is this? You promised me to study ever so much and keep me thoroughly advised as to what you were doing, and I now remind you of your promise and ask of you the desired report of your progress, etc.

As for me, I do not have any time scarcely for miscellaneous reading. I have been and am very busily engaged in studying the "Statutes of Arkansas" and in preparing myself for the practical duties of the Lawyer. This together with the time taken in entertaining the many loafers who think a Lawyer has nothing to do but to talk to them whenever they change to come (which is quite often) has almost taken up my entire time. I have formed the acquaintance of several of the young Ladies of the town and vicinity, but none of them have made any impression on my susceptible nature. Some of them are passably good looking but not the smartest creatures in the world.

Has the great fears entertained by some of you as to me and Miss Sue's marrying subsided? Or are they still entertained? I have not seen her lately, but think I shall go out to Charley Smith's (who married Miss Babe Perry) Saturday night to get some good milk and honey, the former of which I almost famished for since we never get any at our boarding house, and perhaps she will be there.[10]

I was sorry to hear of Miss Fannie C's going back north. I know Oliver must be in a sad condition, his friends flown and he all alone. He surely will not fly himself with his usual energy or success would have been certain as always heretofore. I am sorry she has gone. I wanted to see her once more. Perhaps I might have fallen in love with her. Who knows? She was so interesting, how could I resist the fascination of her laugh? Miss J.[Jennie?] E., I trust is flourishing, pretty as ever and sweet as she looked like she was when I saw her. Mind, say as looked, for I cannot from experimental knowledge say she was really sweet since I never tried her.

I am glad that Miss Bet is still flourishing and hope with returning spring she will resume her gaudy colors and come forth in her matchless charms to consume the hearts of young men like stubble. Who is the object of her affection now? She, of course, has at least one sweetheart, and who is the happy fellow? All success to him.

You seem to be particularly partial to Miss Mollie H., and I am very near ready to follow in your footsteps. She is truly a sweet girl, and no doubt some nice young man worthy of so charming a girl will claim her as his own before I see her again.

Who is Delia's bright particular? Or has she so many she cannot choose "whom she will serve."

There is considerable political excitement here now and will be more between now and August next when our vote on secession or union comes off. We do not entertain any fear as to there being a war between the two governments. All will yet blow over without any bloodshed. So think we, and we are drilling here every evening—have two fine companies. I will not go off to war before seeing you if I can help it. However, I do not think we will have to go at all.

Tell Delia I will write to her as soon as I can. Give my love to Grandpa and Grandma and tell them I am in very fine health and c.

Do not forget to write to me once a week. You have plenty of time and must write.

Your Brother
Orlando

* * *

"We, the undersigned, (citizens of Lauderdale County, State of Alabama) hereto subscribe our names for the purpose of organizing ourselves into a military company to be called the Florence Guards. Said company shall be a rifle company or, as the Governor shall direct. Said company shall be organized in accordance with an act entitled "an act for an efficient military organization of the State of Alabama." Said company shall consist of not less than forty nor more than eighty men, all of whom shall be more than eighteen years of age. Said company shall be well uniformed, perfect and complete the style of the uniformed to be hereafter determined hereafter [sic] by the Governor of the State of Alabama."

This company was to become Company A, Seventh Alabama Infantry. Among the signatories of this document were Orlando S. Palmer, his first cousin Oliver S. Kennedy, his uncles Jonathan Spinks Kennedy and Elias Windsor Kennedy, and Sterling A. M. Wood, later to become his brigade commander.

Des Arc, Ark.
April 17th, 1861

Dear Sister,

As Mr. Simpson leaves here this evening for Florence, I will write you a short note informing you of my good health and what will be my course in these warlike times. There is great excitement here now ... more than we have ever had before. The news of the fight at Fort Sumter with other hostile developments has fired us up, and we are a united people on the question of the opposition to Lincoln. A great many are anxious and willing to go off to the war. Several vain attempts were made to raise a company for the purpose of tendering their services to President Davis, but the men had, all too many of them, lately married and cannot think of leaving the sweet creatures so soon.[11]

I would like very much to come round with Mr. Simpson. Nothing would please me better than to see the dear ones at home, and then off for the war. But we have business entrusted to our fidelities and care and cannot both leave and do justice to our clients. I cannot get off from here until the 10th of June, after our Supreme Court. If the war is then raging and men are needed, I shall come home and join any expedition that may be on foot. Till then, I am necessarily compelled to stay here. I cannot do other men such gross injustice as to leave their business unattended to. Hence, I shall try to reconcile myself to remaining here.

I do not think there will be much fighting done until the first of July no way. Hence, you see, I can get there in time to go into the war regularly.

However, if anything should turn up that my presence at home was needed, I can probably make arrangements to come. Anyway, I will come whenever you think I would do any good there in any way. If an insurrection or anything of the sort should be feared or anticipated, you must send me a dispatch informing me there of, and I will instantly leave for home and stand by those who are nearest and dearest to me. Do not hesitate to dispatch to me at any time, and I shall come without delay.

I was not at all surprised when I heard Uncles Spinks and Elias were gone to war. I knew they would go at a moment's warning to the defense of their native South. Though we may fear for their safety, we cannot but bid them God speed and admire their spirit. Tell Aunt Mary and Grandma to be of good cheer, for they are nobly doing their duty and the prayers of the good and loyal will ask for their protection and success and safe return to their homes and loved ones.[12] Grieve not over their absence, for we must hope for the better and anticipate their safe and quick return.

Tell Vernon and Delia I received their letters a few days since and will answer as soon as possible. They must bear with me. I will answer when it is convenient.

I will be very busy now for some six or seven days and Mr. Simpson is going off and we have several cases to get ready for court. You all must write to me immediately and cheer me up, for I will be very lonesome here all alone. Tell me what all the news is, what are our friends doing, and when you heard from Uncles Spinks and Elias, how they were getting along and all you have heard from and about them. Do not forget this.

Give my love and sympathies to Aunt Mary, Grandma, Grandpa, and c. and tell them my heart is with them in this trouble over the departure of those they hold so dear.

Your Brother,
Orlando S. Palmer

Des Ark, Ark.
May 9th, 1861

Dear Sister,

I received your letter on yesterday. Was very glad to hear you were well and c., but sorry to see that you were in much trouble and were so low spirited. I have often cautioned you against yielding to gloomy feelings that I think it useless to again harp upon the same topic, though I trust you will remember all the excellent counsel I have given you on the subject and cheer up in this, your hour of darkness. Brave-hearted sister, I beg of you not to yield to these desponding fits you will they render yourself miserable when you ought to be happy. It is true, it is a bitter struggle for you to give up Mr. W[inston] and bid him go forth to fight the battles of Liberty, but then duty commands that you should yield cheerfully and cheer him on to the contest if he thinks he ought to go.[13]

I do not know now what I will do. I wrote you a letter by Mr. Simpson, but, as you said nothing about it, I suppose he neglected to deliver it. In it I told you I was undecided and did not know what to do or how I would act and that I was so situated that I could not leave here until the May term of our court, which comes off on the 27th inst. After that time my course will be determined by circumstances altogether. If they are fighting anywhere and I think my services are needed, I shall tender them willingly instantly. However, I do not wish to go into camp until I am certain there is going to be a war. I do not now think there will be any war of any consequence. I cannot think the Northern people are so utterly devoid of sense as to wage an unholy war against us when there is no chance of their conquering us. I think both sides will see the folly and madness of the war, and peace will be declared.

However, I may be mistaken. War may come with all its horrors, and we may suffer the consequences of it. If so, I shall certainly come home to see you, my sister, before going upon the tented field. But you need not look for me until you see me coming, for, situated as I am, I cannot say positively when I can come.

I dispatched to Oliver a few days ago that I would be home the last of this week, but I soon saw it would never do for me to leave here now. I have been so busy all this week that I could not write to you by last mail as I had intended. I was employed on Monday to prosecute a man for stealing a watch. Two of the best Lawyers in the town were employed to defend it. The trial lasted two days. The courtroom was crowded all the time, and a great deal of interest was manifested in the trial. One of the Lawyers on the other side was the oldest and best one in the county. He is a proud fellow . . . had been in the habit of running over all the other attorneys and gaining the cases anyhow. He had a good many enemies and they were anxious to see him defeated. He made a tremendous effort to clear the man, but did not succeed. I gained the case.

The day afterward, I prosecuted a man for perjury. The same attorneys, with another to assist them, were on the other side. They were mad because I defeated them the day before and exerted themselves to the utmost to get me down and retrieve their characters. But they were defeated more signally than ever. Everybody is perfectly delighted at the result, and some of them think of your brother as a pretty good Lawyer. One man who was not at all interested in the case was so pleased that he gave me five dollars and another one presented me with a six-dollar hat.

From all this, my sister, you will perceive at once that I am not friendless out here and that my prospects are very bright. I think I can do very well here if the war will cease and things go on quietly again. I have assurances from the best citizens here that I shall have their business and influences.

From what I can learn, our convention, which is now in session, will pass a stop law, which will prevent any suit being brought. If so, there will be not litigation for some time, and I shall come over home and stay till it is over.

Our convention passed the secession ordnance last Monday, so we are now under the same government and the same gallant President. Huzzah for the Southern Confederacy.[14]

I am now boarding in one of the nicest families I have ever met with anywhere. I am perfectly delighted with them, they treat me so kindly.

You never have as yet told me whether you get the paper which I had sent you. Do you? If so, how do you like it?

Give my love to Grandpa, Grandma, Aunt Olive and Uncle Jesse, Delia, Vernon, Oliver Spinks, Willie, and c., and c. Write soon and often. I want to hear from you once a week, anyhow.[15]

We have had very severe rains here lately. Crops very much injured thereby. It is raining very hard now and has been all day.

Give my respects and well wishes to Mrs. B. F. Crittenden.[16]

Your devoted
Brother

Des Arc, Ark.
May 24th, 1861

Dear Sister,

Your two letters of the 13th and 17th inst. came to hand yesterday and I hasten to reply. You upbraid me for not writing oftener and I, of course, must give some reason for so long a silence. If you will think for a moment, you will recollect that some two or three or four weeks since, I was in a great hurry to get off home and was expecting to go every day or two. I did not then write because I expected soon to answer your letters in person. With this explanation, I trust you will forgive me and no longer entertain the idea that I have forgotten you.

Your advice and that of Uncle Elias and Grandma is very good. Whether or not I shall follow it, or how far, I am not now able to say. The developments of a day or an hour may change in these troublesome times the most wisely lain plans. I cannot now make any calculations on the future with any hope of being able to fulfill them in the least.

Our convention, which is now in session, has just passed a "stay law," the provisions of which are that no executions shall be issued upon any judgements heretofore or hereafter rendered in any of the courts of the state until the convention in their wisdom see fit to remove this restriction upon the collection of claims by legal process. This, of course, precludes the necessity of remaining here all summer as there will not be any litigation of any consequence, at least not enough to pay me to remain here. It is not yet entirely certain that the convention has passed the said stay law, but from all we can gather it is barely doubtful.

Our circuit court comes off next Monday. As I have several cases on docket, I shall be compelled to attend and get judgment on them. My determination now is to shut up my office as soon as I return from court and go over home, then my course will be shaped entirely by circumstances. I cannot say what I will do. I will not, however, return here until the stay law is repealed as I cannot afford to remain here on expenses when there is no probability of making anything. However, our convention is such a wayward, changeable body that they my repeal the aforesaid law at any time before they adjourn.

I am sorry to see you write in such a desponding strain and sorry that my sister's sunny nature should ever be overcast with even the shadow of a cloud, but glad that you unburden your heart fully to me as I think I can cheer you up when I see you, so that the same old monster will not soon visit you.

You must cheer up and struggle against this lowness of spirit, this bitterness of thought. The best remedy for the blues is to take up some interesting book and sit down with the determination to cut loose a while from those from those bitter thoughts which trouble you so much and let you mind be absorbed in the book on which you are engaged.

Try this and see what will be the result. Resolve that you will forget your gloomy thoughts and that your buoyant nature still shall surmount the troubles and difficulties with which you are surrounded and, my word for it, you will succeed.

I can sympathize most fully with your grief at parting with your intended, but then, you must not grieve over parting from him, for were it not for the sorrowful parting, there would not be the pleasure of a joyous meeting after a brief absence.

I hope to be over in the course of two weeks, however I may not be able to get off that soon. Look for me in 3 weeks, anyhow. I may get there sooner and I may not.

Give my very best respects to all the girls (Misses Bet, Jennie, Mollie, and c.). I trust soon to spend some happy, happy moments with them.

My love to Grandpa, Grandma. Tell Oliver I will come over as soon as possible.

I have not time to write more.

Your Brother,

O. S. Palmer

P.S. Mama M[ary] was so anxious to hear from Orlando I broke open your letter.

H[iram] Kennedy

* * *

On 1 June 1861 "a large number of citizens of White River Township" met at Des Arc, and Orlando Palmer was appointed to a committee of five to draft a preamble and resolutions "expressive of the sense of this meeting." The committee quickly produced the document, which declared that "the Black republican government has inaugurated a war of conquest against the Confederate States of America, and is now marshalling its warriors by thousands and tens of thousands, with the open and avowed purpose of invading our country, crushing our liberties by reducing us to subjection to its wanton power and tyranny, laying waste our fields, our towns, cities, homes and firesides for *'booty and beauty,'* marking their pathways through our country with fire and smoke, death and devastation, and placing our women at the rude mercy of a corrupt and licentious soldiery—and whereas, from the extent of our border, and the neglect of our government to sufficiently provide for its defense render us particularly exposed to the dangers of a brutal and bloody foray into our own noble State, by the cringing sycophants and heartless hirelings of a despotic government, which has discarded all the rules of civilized warfare, and scruples not to murder our women and children, with circumstances of barbarity and horror, which must bring upon it the condemnation of an enlightened world and the wrath of a just God."

The committee therefore offered the resolution that the citizens of the township form two companies of volunteers, in addition to the two already mustered, to "hold themselves in readiness to march at any moment to any quarter of our State to repel invasion" and that the citizens provide "the necessary means for thoroughly equipping the aforesaid companies."[17]

On 28 May the *Des Arc Semi-Weekly Citizen* reported that "all the forces have been removed from Camp Rector to Bearfield Point, which is in the extreme northeast corner of Arkansas, and about 120 miles below Cairo by water. This is the highest point on the river occupied by Confederate troops."[18] One week later, under the screaming headline, "Bradley Proves Himself an Idiotic Coward," the paper set off a firestorm of consternation when it reported that Brig. Gen. Thomas H. Bradley, the commander of a brigade of Arkansas state troops, had fallen back before a superior force of advancing Federals.

According to "COP," a member of the Rector Guards and an anonymous correspondent of the Des Arc *Semi-Weekly Citizen*, at 1:00 A.M., 26 May, "the whole camp was aroused by the officers and told that 30,000 Abolitionists were in a few miles march of us," and that they must leave immediately for Randolph, Tennessee, where, with the Tennessee state troops they would "make a stand against their encroachments on our soil."[19] "COP" claimed that every man in the camp was in favor of remaining where they were and resisting the reported Federal advance. "But no, Bradley's order was out and must be obeyed, and no one was allowed to express an opinion, which would in the least conflict with that of his supreme dictatorship."

On 4 June 1861 the citizens of White River Township met again to consider Bradley's "the unwarranted retreat" from Bearfield, "taking his men two miles below Randolph on the Tennessee side: Also the conduct of said Bradley was disgraceful to himself, and calculated to disgrace the regiment under his command." Palmer was appointed to a committee of five to "draft suitable resolutions and report to an adjourned meeting" at nine o'clock the following morning.[20]

On 5 June the committee met again to read the report, gleaned from "sources which we deem perfectly reliable," that stated that Bradley "did ignominiously order a precipitate retreat from Bearfield's Point, on vague rumor of an intended attack by the enemy, without consultation with the officers; leave scouts sent out the day before, without making any provision for their safety; abandon many valuable articles belonging to the companies, and in various other ways behaved in an unsoldier like manner; and desert a position, which from its commanding military advantages was of the greatest importance to our State.

. . . The officers of the expedition of which he was in command did meet and bring various charges against him for forcing upon them such a shameful retreat, and removing them from the post of honor and danger, to the soil of another State, thus compelling them to forsake their own State which they were sworn to defend."

Bradley was then at Little Rock to have his officers court martialed for "mutiny." The citizens of Des Arc commended the actions of the brigade's officers in "refusing longer to serve under an officer who so signally proved himself to be totally unworthy of the high position which he occupied" and expressed their admiration for "the noble courage and manliness" demonstrated by the Rector Guards "in standing forth and refusing to move until their scouts were cared for."[21]

Des Arc, Ark.
June 7th, 1861

Dear Sister,

Yours of the 27th ult. was received yesterday, and I hasten to reply so that you will not have occasion to upbraid me any longer for not writing oftener. I wrote you sometime last week explaining why it was I had not written in so long a time. I trust the letter has been received and the apology satisfactory.

I am glad to hear that you are well and in such good spirits under the circumstances and sympathize most heartily with you. I know well what your feelings must have been after parting with Mr. W[inston], but, my brave-hearted Sister, you must not give way to your desponding thoughts or grieve over your lonely situation, for a wise Providence rules all things and these trials are intended for your ultimate good. Wait patiently, bear up bravely. There is a good time coming. Such love as yours was never intended to be disappointed. It must and will be rewarded.

I am glad to learn that you have finally determined to resort to your books as a guard and shield against the blues. Continue so to do and you will soon see how much benefit you will derive from it in several important ways. You will forget your gloomy thoughts, cultivate your mind and powers of endurance, and acquire a taste—a love—for reading which you can ever fly to as a stronghold in the time of trouble and disappointment.

I know with your naturally buoyant disposition you can bear up against troubles and trials far worse than any you have yet experienced if you will but arouse yourself and exert your will which I know you will when you think of yourself properly and acquire confidence in your ability to be cheerful.

I would be very much pleased to know that you were happy and trust to hear so in your next letter.

I was in hopes Vernon had broken up housekeeping and was with you. She ought to have done so. It is wrong for her to keep house and go on to such an extent as you state. Her Pa and Ma should know of it. Why do you not write to them or get Grandpa to inform them of her carryings on? Either of you can do so without her knowing anything of it and you would do them and her a great benefit by so doing. My advice is to write to them immediately and they will stop her and send her out to you all.[22]

What is Oliver doing? It seems to me he ought to come out to Grandpa's and stay a while with you all. He is doing nothing in town and I think you deserve his services some as well as Vernon. I shall write to him this evening to know of him why it is he does not carry you around some.

What did Uncle Elias do with his horse? If he is in town, you ought to send and get him. Then you can go anywhere you desire. If you have no one to go with you, just go on by yourself. Be as independent as any of them. Do not stand back for slight inconveniences. I know Uncle E. would just as soon you had his horse as anyone else. So, take him no matter who has him.

I expect to be home somewhere about the middle of July, however I cannot say positively at what time I can get there. Look for me when you see me and not before, for you might not see me when you looked, and that would be a disappointment to you. I will come around as soon as I well can, but cannot tell what may detain me nor for what length of time.

I am still well and gaining friends every day. Every public meeting we have here I am called for and cannot get around making a speech.

I sent you two papers by this mail in which you will see an account of two meetings being held, committees appointed to draft resolutions. I was on both committees and had the honor of drafting the resolutions in both instances. So, you see, if the war will cease there is some probability of your Brother doing something after a while. I do not think I could have found a better place in the state to locate in than this. I am surprised to find so many substantial citizens so very friendly towards me.

But I must stop all this or you will think your Brother is becoming vain. I do not, however, speak of these things from vanity but to let you know that I am doing well and c.

Write soon and often.

Give my love to Grandpa and Grandma and c. and c.

Your Brother

O. S. Palmer

What is the news from the Tippaholites? [i.e., friends from Tippah County, Mississippi] Has Miss K[atie] P[ate] come up yet? If so, how long does she contemplate remaining? What has become of all the girls? Who of them married and who engaged and who would like to be?

Pitman's Ferry, Ark.
July 26th, 1861

Dear Sister,

I reached this place this morning and, according to my promise, I write to you at every opportunity. I was so fortunate as to get a very fine position here, which was altogether unexpected and unsought for by me. I am General Hardee's private secretary.[23] The position is a very fine one, which throws me with the refined, intelligent, and gentlemanly class of the army. It is one of ease, honor, and comfort, and one that suits my former habits better than any other I could possibly have gotten anywhere. Colonel T. C. Hindman procured me the position at the solicitation of Major Glenn of Des Arc, the brother of the gentleman with whom I have been boarding. You can now rest easy. My position is one of perfect safety and in which I will not be more exposed than when at home in my office. There is about three thousand troops here, and they are being thoroughly drilled and equipped for the hard service which is before them.[24]

General Hardee is a fine, portly man of military bearing and manner, about forty-five years of age, a perfect gentleman, an intelligent, high-toned man in every respect, and I have no doubt but that my association with him will be most pleasant and profitable to me.

The country here is very hilly, and of course cannot be otherwise than healthy. I entertain no fears as to my health. So, sweet sister, you see I have a pleasant position in which I will not be exposed in the least, and you must not grieve over my absence or any imaginary danger in which you may suppose I may be placed. Be cheerful, be brave for your brother in safety and in the discharge of his duty. I will come home to see you just as soon as I can get off, though my duties will be so constant and continuous that I cannot well get off without losing my position. However, look for me when you see me.

Give my love to Grandpa and Grandma and c and c, and write to me immediately, giving me all the news and c.

Direct your letter to me at Pocahontas care of Col. Cleburne, First Arkansas Regiment.

Your devoted Brother,

O. S. Palmer[25]

> Camp 20 miles North of
> Pitman's Ferry, Ark.
> [no date]

Dear Sister,

As we are resting today and I have time to write, I eagerly avail myself of the opportunity. I left Pitman's Ferry August 1st and reached the regiment which had started two days before on the 2nd. I did not have to walk but got a traitor Missourian's horse and rode him 20 miles without saddle or bridle, which you know must have been very pleasant. After getting with my company, I left the horse and walked on for six miles to the camp. Was not much tired and slept finely on the ground for the first time in my life. Next morning we rose before day, cooked our breakfast, ate, and crossed Black River and marched some 3 miles, and struck our camps to rest and wait for the rest of the army to come up. I wish you could have seen me yesterday evening.

The first thing I done was to help my messmates (by the way, one of them is Miss Hays Dunn's cousin—a nice fellow, too) get dinner. It was my first experiment, and I made a very good cook considering all things. At least our dinner eat well. After that, as most all my clothes were needing washing very badly, I gathered them up, got some soap, and started for the branch. Went into the water with my sleeves and pants rolled up and started in to washing. I tell you, it was a fine sight. Along the branch as far as the eye could see were men fixed just as I was. All laughing, singing, whistling, joking. All merry and all washing like they cared nothing for it. It would have been a sight never to be forgotten if you could just have passed along and got a view of the interesting sight.

What sort of a cook and washer, think you, your brother will make when I come home? I will cook a meal for you all just to show you what I can do. I feel very well and think that I shall be fat as a bear before the campaign is over. I never enjoyed anything so much and c.

I wrote to you the other day that I was Gen. Hardee's private secretary. I retained the position ten days. Our company was then on and off, and I could not come with them until the Genl returned from Pocahontas. When he returned, he was as touchy as a sore headed bear, and no one could remain with him with any degree of satisfaction. I was anxious to get on to the regiment before they had a fight, and threw up the place of private secretary and came off. The Genl would not treat me with the respect due from one gentleman to another, and I will not stay in any position, no matter how honorable, where I cannot be treated with proper respect. I first thought the Genl was one of the most pleasant of men to associate with, but I soon discovered that I was widely mistaken and left him immediately. I am now a high private and feel proud of my position. I have nothing to trouble my mind and am perfectly satisfied. And since so many men are seeking position and go to war for nothing else, I think it is an honor to go into the ranks and fight purely from patriotic motives. After all, a soldier's life is not so hard as most people imagine. We never march more than ten or fifteen miles a day, and after we become somewhat accustomed to walking it is not a hard thing to walk that distance. I shall get along finely. I feel better now than I have for several days heretofore and think I am gaining strength every day.

I have several very warm friends in the company and if any vacancy occurs in the company and I wish it, I have no doubt it will be given to me. However, I care not. I had just as soon be in the ranks with a minie rifle and have the satisfaction of knowing that I was doing the enemy some harm as to flourish a sword five hundred yards from the enemy and never hurt one of them. I came to the war, not for position, not for a name, but from patriotic motives to fight the battles of truth, of justice, and of my country. I let the result be what it may. I shall never regret that I came.

We have about 1000 men here. Other regiments are coming up and we will soon have a force strong enough to march on Ironton, which is about 200 miles from here. I think that there are 4000 men there and we will have to strengthen ourselves before we attack them. However, I do not think they will await our coming. When we advance, the probabilities are that they will retreat, and thus it will be until we get to St. Louis where we are going and where we anticipate a big fight. I cannot, of course, tell anything about the plans of the campaign, but think it is to go to St. Louis.

The news reached here sometime since of the great battle of Manassas and of the success of our arms. The news was received with the greatest enthusiasm by all the soldiers. It was, if our report is correct, a most splendid battle as well as destructive and an important victory for us. It will have a tendency to shorten the war and many there are that will rejoice over the news of the cessation of hostilities.[26]

We are in a fine country—hills very rocky and well-watered and thought to be healthy, and I have no doubt but what it is. It is rather unpleasant to walk over the rocks, and very destructive to shoes, but we cannot expect to have everything just as one could wish. We must have some bitter with the sweet. I had rather have the water with the rocks then no rocks and no water.

Captain [George Washington] Glenn was discharged on account of ill health. Our company was sorry to see him leave and were anxious for him to remain, and yet he was compelled to go and we could not help ourselves.

It is almost impossible to get letters, either to or from here, so if you do not hear from me often do not be uneasy but attribute your not hearing from me to the derangement and uncertainties of the mail in the country. Almost all the lines going along here are stopped, and we have to send our letters by hand to Arkansas, and then have them mailed, so you see, everything in the mail line is uncertain and in confusion.

My sister, you must be bold and cheerful. Never yield to gloomy thoughts and give way to the sorrows which you, in common with everybody else, must have.

Write to me at Hicks [i.e., Hix] Ferry, Randolph County, care of Colonel Cleburne. I may get your letters.

My love to all,
your devoted brother,
Orlando S. Palmer

Pitman's Ferry, Ark.
Aug. 12th, 1861

Dear Sister,

I have just returned from Greenville, Mo, some sixty miles from here, where we went to whip out six hundred dutch who were there playing havoc with the people, generally. But they did not await our coming. They fled from before us to Lesterville. We sent out a detachment to catch them there, but they again took to their heels and left the town. We have about 2000 men out there, well-armed and equipped and anxious—begging—for a fight.[27]

I am still with Gen. Hardee and like my position much better than when I wrote you last. He is to furnish me with a horse and c., and I think I shall get along finely hereafter. He treats me very kindly now and says that I suit him very much and he is pleased with me.

I have not heard from you since I left Des Arc, but I hope to hear from you soon and to hear that all are well and that you are in fine spirits and c. I am improving my health very much and think I shall continue to improve so long as I take so much active service. It is really pleasant to sleep on the ground at night with no covering but the broad canopy with its myriad bright stars shedding their sweet influence over you and calming the troubled spirit. I have enjoyed it several nights, and it is really pleasant. I like the soldier's life very much—the activities, the adventure, and the excitement are really charming, and I become more attached to this sort of life every day.

I occasionally write for the Des Arc Citizen, which I direct the editor to send you. I sign myself "Remlap," as you get the paper, if so, preserve the papers which contain my letters. I will want them when the war is over.[28]

I am anxious to see you all and nothing would please me better than to spend a few days, but I cannot come now. I will come when my time is out, and, Oh!, what a joyous, happy time we will have. What pleasant days will they be when we meet around the old hearthstone.

Give my love to all and tell them I am well and doing finely.

Write to me at Pocahontas care of Col. Cleburne, 1st Regiment, Ark. Vols.

God bless thee, sweet sister.
Your devoted Brother.
Orlando S. P.

Pitman's Ferry, Ark.
September 12th, 1861

Dear Sister,

Your two letters of the 8th and 28th ult. received a few days since, and, as they were the first I have gotten since I left Des Arc, you can imagine the joy I experienced in reading those charming, heart-strengthening, encouraging letters. The information that all were well, and you were in fine spirits was very acceptable in as much as I had been very much troubled because I could not hear from home by any means, and imagination conjured up a thousand dark pictures to wound and agonize the soul. But now that I have heard from you, I am more at ease. I can more patiently submit to the stern fate that has cut lose so many tender ties which were so tightly wrapped round the soul.

Your letters found me well and installed in my new office, discharging its light but rather pleasant duties, and getting along as well as the soldier could desire. I trust that I shall hereafter continue to get your letters and that no one of them will contain any information which will place a feather's weight upon the already sorely tried heart, but on the contrary that they bring joy and cheer the spirit of the soldier and render him happy though far away from home and kindred and the comforts of life.

Doubtless you were very pleasantly surprised by the unexpected visit of Mr. T[homas B. Winston] and that you spent some happy hours together. I heartily sympathize in the struggle it cost you to part with him and the sorrow which his absence has cast over your heart and sincerely wish that you may be many times surprised by his arrival as before that he will often render you as happy as he did that time, yet before his term of enlistment has expired.

I did at one time entertain the hope that he and I would meet anywhere in this quarter. There is not the most distant probability or possibility of Hardee and Pillow uniting their force, and, of course, until this is done, there is not much probability of he and I getting together.[29] However, if we do meet, rest satisfied that he shall be as dear to me, yes, and dearer, than any man, and that if it ever comes in my way to serve him, my best blood shall be shed to save him from harm and return him in safety home to you to render you blessed and happy. This I should do, as well, on account of my real feeling towards him and the innate merit of the man. As you suggest, he is a man of many sterling qualities which would make him respected and liked wherever he was known and render him an acceptable brother to anyone.

I was sorry to learn of the death of Charlie Banks[30] as also of Prof.[?] Briggs, Posey[?], and c., but their murder is but another incentive to nerve us, to urge us on to avenge the death of so many brave and gallant spirits. Their blood calls to us from the ensanguined field and demands that we should never lay down our arms or waver in the conflict until the last enemy has been driven in consternation from our soil, and death, fire, and sword and one universal conflagration carried on to the country that sent out the murderers who have invaded our Government.

I received intelligence yesterday of the death of some of my very best and most intimate friends who were among the list of the glorious dead at Springfield.[31] Several of them had pledged their devotion to their Country and her Cause with their lives, and now they sleep the last long sleep beneath the soil wet with the blood of the best men of our Country. Thus it is. Fresh information is constantly pouring in from every quarter of the death of some cherished friend, the flower of the Chivalry of the South is being offered up to appease the wrath of the King of the Storm and bear aloft the proud and as yet triumphant banner of imperiled liberty. But that must be. Our country demands it. Our loved ones at home urge us on, and the promptings of Patriotism alike render us willing to suffer all, endure all, and give up all in the great cause for which we are battling.

For this reason, I do not think any movement of importance or activity will be undertaken before next spring unless the volcano, the premonition signals of which we have even now heard, burst forth in its wild terror in Kentucky and East Tennessee and we are ordered there as more fuel for the bursting flames.

If the war does open in good earnest in either one of those places, we may probably go and bear our breast to the storm. All here are anxious to be transferred to some active service and doing the Government some real substantial good and not lie here in camp, a drag to ourselves and a heavy drain upon the Government. Of course, I would prefer being somewhere we could get a glimpse at the foe, but I am but an instrument in the hands of others and hope when called upon to do my duty I shall be at my post, ready to discharge that duty no matter what it may be.

We are in a good, healthy location, and I am in good health. I will not deceive you at any time as to how I am, for I think it best at all times to tell the simple truth, an unvarnished tale is always the safest. I thought I had written about having a chill, and think yet that I did, however if I did not it was an oversight. Bill [William Cummins] Ratcliff and H. H. Hicks are here. I see them occasionally. They are both well.[32]

I shall remember your advice and will now assure you that you need not entertain any fear as to my morals for they are now better than when I left Des Arc, and they were then better than when I left home. So, you see, I am not in much danger of being corrupted.

Sister, you must by no means fail to write me often hereafter. I think I will get all your letters, so you need not fear they will be written in vain.

Kind angles guard thee, Sister dear.

Your affectionate brother

O. S. Palmer

Direct your letters to Pocahontas care Col. Cleburne.

Bowling Green, Ky.
November 4th, /61

Dear Sister,

Your very kind and consoling letter was received this evening and to show you how highly I appreciate it and how anxious I am for the reception of another, I hasten to reply. It is always a source of pleasure, of encouragement, and of happiness to read one of you heart-breathing sisterly letters, and I always look for them with a great deal of anxiety. You cannot write too often if you were to write every day. Each succeeding letter would be looked for with increased anxiety.

I was rejoiced to learn that you were in such good health and fine spirits and were getting along so well with all the relations. My greatest source of trouble was the fear that you would not be able to please them all, that something would occur to disrupt the harmony of your intercourse with each other, and that unpleasantness would arise which would render you dissatisfied and unhappy. But your letter removes all fear on this subject, and I can now rest satisfied that you are in good keeping and can enjoy the moments as they pass. Let things come true thus. Tell them that for my sake and yours, two lonely orphans, to let nothing shake their love for you or change their conduct towards you.

I am sorry that your wishes in reference to my health do not correspond with the reality. I have had chills for about 6 or 7 days and missed it today for the first time. I think that by observing the proper precautions, I will now get rid of them. If I can escape them, I think I will then get along well enough.

Aunt C[ynthia] is anxious for Oliver or I to do something to "crown our brows with immortal honors." As far as I am concerned, I will say this much. I have been Sgt. Major nearly 3 months. Today the adjutant resigned and the colonel of the regiment, having been pleased with the manner in which I discharged my duties, offered me the position of adjutant of the regiment. I could not hold the office until I was a lieutenant, which I will be in two days, one of the lieutenants in the company having resigned today, and there is no doubt that his resignation will be accepted. The captain of the company (with the unanimous consent and petition of the members) will recommend me to the vacant lieutenant's place, so you perceive I will soon flourish the very uncommon title of 2nd lieutenant.(?)[33]

You want to know why I did not accept the office of adjutant? In the first place, the duties of the office are so various and so arduous that I fear the discharge of them during the severity of the winter would be too much for me. It is the most laborious office in the regiment, but were it not for another and more serious objection I should certainly have accepted the position anyhow.

Colonel Cleburne has been detached permanently from the regiment and put in command of the brigade, and that placed the lieutenant colonel [Archibald Kennedy Patton] in command of the regiment. He is not the man I would like to hold the position of adjutant under. He is a man of very unpopular manners, very negligent in the discharge of his duties and a great drunkard in the bargain, characteristics not at all calculated to make him popular with the regiment or even respected by the privates.[34]

The odium that falls to him would extend to a greater or lesser extent to his adjutant. I do not desire to share his shame or do his labor and get no credit for it, hence I very properly, in my opinion, refused to accept the position of adjutant. Think you I acted wisely or foolishly?

There is a plan on foot by the officers of the regiment to get him out of office and place in his position Major Glenn, the friend I have so often written to you about. If this is done, I can then get the appointment of adjutant and will accept it, for under him I would gain honor and get along pleasantly. When I get to be a lieutenant, I will not have much to do, and I can write you more respectable letters than I have been doing heretofore.

I propose to myself the pleasure of spending a few happy days with you all sometime this winter, when I can't say, whenever I can get a furlough.

Tell Aunt C[ynthia] I left Des Arc the 16th of July, and my term of service will be out the 14th of May, next.

We went on an expedition the other day to meet a body of the enemy supposed to be advancing on this place. Were gone three days but saw no enemy. They ran as soon as they learned we were coming. I don't think we will have any fighting to do here at all. We will not attack the enemy and it is a dead moral certainty that they will not attack us, so will go into winter quarters without a fight.

Give my love to all. What luck had Uncles John and Roe [Griffin] in their bear hunt? Write to me immediately and address it thus:

O. S. Palmer, Sgt. Major
1st Regt. Ark. Vols.
Bowling Green,
Ky.
Care Col. Cleburne
Your devoted Brother,
O. S. Palmer

Bowling Green, Ky.
Nov. 21st, 1861

Dear Sister,

I have not written to you for several days because I have not been here. I have just returned from a march of over one hundred and fifty miles. We were sent out in search of some roving bands of abolitionists who were going through the country laying waste to everything as they went. We left here with about 1500 men on last Saturday was a week ago and reached Scottsville on Sunday. Here the enemy's scouts had been a day or two before but decamped in hot haste when they learned that we were coming in force. From there we marched to Jamestown where we learned the enemy was to make a stand.

The boys were all anxious for a fight and confidently expecting one, but when we got in town, we found it deserted. Not a living soul. Not one idle loiterer. Not even a woman urged by curiosity was to be seen anywhere. Nothing was heard save the echo of the heavy tramp of trained bands of soldiers who, with downcast looks and disappointed expectations, marched wearily through the town. Wearied and sore with heavy marching, I was in hopes that we would not have to go any farther but would rest a few days and come home again, but no. Col. Cleburne could not relish the idea of coming back without a fight, and a fight he must and would have.

So, we took up our line of march for Tompkinsville where he thought certainly to measure arms with the cohorts of Lincoln. Every house on the road from Jamestown to Tompkinsville was deserted, the doors shut and barred, and horses and stock generally driven into the woods. No one was to be seen anywhere. When we reached Tompkinsville, we found it almost entirely deserted. Stores, groceries, hotel, and dwellings all being equally deserted. None had the courage to stand the approach of hated Southrons. There was no enemy there.[35]

We remained there until noon next day when, not yet satisfied that he could find no fight, he started off in the direction of Columbia. That evening our scouts fell in with about forty of the enemy who fled in the greatest consternation, leaving in their consternation two fine cavalry horses, fully equipped. That night the Texas Rangers captured some fifteen cavalry horses with their accoutrements.[36]

Next morning, Col. C., satisfied that he could get no fight unless he went to Columbia, where there was about 4000 of the enemy, strongly posted, thought that discretion was the better part of valor and concluded not to go into certain destruction, but to come back home content with having driven them before us from every point.

We reached home without anything of interest occurring in the way on last Sunday might. The men, a great many of them, were almost completely broke down. The trip did me good. I improved every day. I had been having chills for several days before starting, but the exercise cured me, and now I am in perfect good health and have suffered no inconvenience from the long and tiresome march over a very rough country except a sore foot. The last day on the return, we marched 20 miles, and my boot rubbed the instep of my right foot from which the artery was swollen and the foot inflamed. I have kept my tent all the time since we got in camp and my foot is now considerably improved and will be well in a few days.

The troops here now are very busily engaged fortifying the town. An attack by the enemy is, I think, expected and we are preparing for them. The natural advantages of this position are as great as any I ever saw and 2 weeks from now 20,000 men under [Gen. Albert Sidney] Johnston can whip a 100,000 of the enemy. I don't think they will ever attack us though they may, and if they do, we will give them a glorious drubbing.[37]

Was Tom in the fight at Columbus?[38] How is he? Tell him I will write to him soon, not to think hard of me for not doing so before, for I have been running around so I could not.

My love to all.
In haste,
Your devoted Brother
O. S. Palmer
Write immediately

Bowling Green, Ky.
December 1st, 1861

Dear Sister,

I have written and written and waited daily hoping and expecting to hear from you until I have lost all hope and now make a final effort to hear from you. The last letter I received from you was dated the 3rd of November, and with the almost daily mail communication between this place and Ripley, it seems that I might hear from you at least once a week, and why it is I have not heard from you for near a month I cannot for the life of me conjecture. I fear that something is wrong, that you, perhaps, may be unwell or some other cause operates to prevent you from writing.

I received a letter from Grandpa dated the 21st ult. He says he heard from you. That you were well and anxious to come home, but then he did not say what date your letter was, and of course I am left to conjecture whether or not it was later than the one I got. I wrote to you on the 7th November in reference to sending my clothes to Corinth by the 20th of November, and I have not heard a word in reply. The young man who I expected to bring me the clothes returned the other day and said that he inquired particularly for them and did not hear anything of them. From this I infer they were not sent there because no one would do you the favor to carry them or you did not receive my note in time. The latter, I fear, is the case. I am sorry I did not get them for they would have come in in very good time. You could send them to me by express if I were certain that we will remain here long enough for them to reach here. But in the present state of doubt and uncertainty in the minds of our Generals, I cannot say that we will remain here long. We may leave here tomorrow, or we may remain here for the expiration of our term. It is impossible to form an intelligent or reliable opinion any way about the matter.

From daily accounts we see in the papers of the movements of the enemy in the West, it is undoubtably his purpose to make a desperate attack on Columbus or Bowling Green. Regiment after regiment is pouring into Louisville and the most of them, it would seem, forwarded from there to Cairo and Paducah. This would seem to indicate their policy to attack Columbus and not Bowling Green. But it may be, and the general impression is that they will attack both places at the same time, with the further object of getting possession of both Memphis and Nashville before the winter campaign closes in this section.

I know nothing of the number of troops at Columbus or the number that can be thrown there in case of an attack, but from the natural advantages of the position and the impregnability of the hill, which is thoroughly fortified, I do not think one hundred thousand of the enemy can take it from thirty or forty thousand of the gallant defenders of our young Republic.[39]

As to this place, I think we can whip a force three times as large as ours. There is not more than 20,000 effective men here, but we have batteries erected on commanding hills, which will sweep every avenue to the town for three miles. These batteries, it is true, are not yet complete, but if we hear of the approach of the enemy in any force, we can make them spring into completeness and terror in a moment. I entertain no apprehensions as to the safety of this place. We can check the career of any force and send them howling back to the bosom of Father Abraham for succor and consolation.[40]

It may be that we have to leave here to defend the Mississippi Valley, for my humble opinion is that the enemy is determined to concentrate his entire available force here in the West at Cairo and descend to river and bend all his energies to work the downfall of Columbus. If I am correct in this supposition as to the intention of the enemy, I think my second supposition well founded and undoubtedly correct.

If they attempt to descend the Mississippi River, they will, of course, leave this place alone, put forth all their strength to get possession of the Mississippi Valley with its immense wealth. Then, with enough troops to garrison this place, only be left here and the others sent to form a breastwork of glittering steel to stop the progress of the trained hirelings of Abraham II.

We have not yet gone into winter quarters, nor is there the least probability of our doing so for some time yet to come. We are still in our tents, and if the weather continues as it has been for the last four or five days, I do not see how we can stand it in our tents. During the last week we had heavy, drenching rains for three or four days and snow and sleet which melted as fast as it fell to render it almost impossible to get about. My foot has gotten well, but I continue to sit by the fire in our good old camp kettle which renders our tent tolerably comfortable.

I do not know that I will be able to get a furlough to come home this winter. I learn from Grandpa that Uncle Elias is very anxious to have me as an assistant. I wrote to him about it yesterday. If I can get a transfer I would prefer to be there, both because it would be much more pleasant to be with my kind Uncles and more comfortable there than in this land of north winds and heavy snows. If I get the transfer I will, of course, come by to see you. As soon as we go into winter quarters or know that we will remain at any one place long enough for you to send me some clothes I will write to you.

Remember me to all the relations and tell me what is Oliver's address.
Write to me, Dear Sister, immediately.
Your devoted Brother,
O. S. Palmer
Lieut. O. S. Palmer
1st Regt. Ark. Vols.
Bowling Green,
Ky.
[*in margin*]
Where is Uncle Mose? Where is his wife? Where and how is Miss Jennie Kennedy, Miss Katie Pate, Miss Kittie H, and all the girls? Miss Annie Davidson, also. I want to know all the news—especially of interest.

[The envelope in which the following letter was mailed was postmarked Bowling Green, Kentucky, 16 December, and although identified as a "soldier's letter" was stamped "Due 5[¢]." It bore the return address "O. S. Palmer, Lieut., Co. G, 1st Regt., Ark. Vols."]

Bowling Green, Ky.
Dec. 15th, 1861

Dear Sister,

Yours of the 29th ult. and 7th inst. respectively were received in due time, the latter yesterday. I should have answered the first sooner, but I had just written and did not deem it necessary to write so soon again. I am glad that you have gotten my clothes started and trust they will arrive safe and soon. I am sorry you did not send them by Uncle Mose, for he came within 60 miles of this place and could have then have forwarded them to me without so much delay or risk and I could then have had the benefit of them during the cold weather.

If, however, be this as it may, they will soon be here, and, oh!, what a happy time I will have looking over them and calling to mind the loving hearts and willing hands that was so thoughtful as to send them and thus protect me from the severities of the coming winter.

I am glad to hear that you are well, and I trust that the orphan's God will continue to throw around you His strong arms of protection to shield you from harm and render you happy and contented. I wish that I could come home on furlough, even if I could not get off any longer than to carry you home. However, it is impossible for me to come. No furloughs, not even sick furloughs, are granted under any circumstances, so, you see, the utter impossibility of my coming home. I hope you will find someone passing so that you can get home without troubling anyone. Be satisfied no matter what occurs. Let the reliance and trust you repose in Him who rules above sustain and comfort you on every trial and bereavement of this dark and troublesome time.

I have had another spell of chills but have got rid of them again and am up now and fit for duty! I have some bitters made out of persimmon bark, carbonate of iron, and c., and am drinking them before each meal. I am getting fat fast and gaining my strength rapidly. I trust that I shall not have them any more and I think by proper care I can escape them.

My foot has recovered and now able to go into its accustomed pace. So, my understanding is now all right and in good condition to be encased in the good, warm socks you are sending me.

Miss K[atie] P[ate] has married, whether wisely or not. She perhaps has by this time discovered to her joy or sorrow. She knows best which. I trust she has done well, but from my knowledge of his character in other days, I fear me she has not done so well as I could have wished she would do. However, I can assure you of one thing—her marriage has not seriously affected my peace of mind or wrenched many of the strings of my heart. Peace and happiness to her.

I would have like very much to have been at the concert and feasted my gaze for a while on the beauty of the lovely creatures that were there in powerful array. Oh, how happy I would be to see the young ladies you wrote of and have a few short hours converse with them. It would be doubly dear to me since I have been so long deprived of the delightful refining influence of lovely and accomplished women. I could relish their society now more than ever at any time before, and you know I never was very indifferent to the society of the dear ladies.

I received Delia's letter, also the note of Uncle W[esley] and Aunt C[ynthia] and will answer as soon as I have convenient opportunity. Tell Uncle Wesley that there are no gun barrels here and I do not know of any I could get anywhere.[41]

We have moved three miles from town and commenced putting up huts. We have been here over a week. A good many of the boys have got their little houses up at fitted out entirely and are quite comfortable. We have not finished ours yet but will get it done in a very few days, and then we will live quite comfortable, almost as much so as you are at home. If they will permit us to remain here all the winter, we can stand the winter very well and suffer but very little from the heavy snowstorms which I have no doubt we will have here.

Col. Cleburne is commanding the 2nd Brigade of Hardee's Division and Lieut. Col. A. K. Patton is commanding our regiment. You need not direct my letters to the care of anyone. If to anyone, to the care of Col. A. K. Patton.

I saw William H. Cook the other day. He enquired particularly of you. He has been sick with the chills.[42]

I also saw Cousin William L. Spinks, Cousin Tennie's[?] brother. He called to see and spent the day with me. He says Cousin Tennie married very badly. All the family was opposed to it.[43]

I know nothing of the movements of the troops here or of the enemy in front. We can learn nothing of what is going on here. We are as much or more in the dark than you are. It is not the policy of the Generals to allow us to know anything about what is going on here.

I have not been out much lately and do not know anything of the fortifications that have been recently thrown up here. I think they are very nearly completed.

Give my love to all and Miss Jennie K[indrick] in particular.

Write to me immediately.
Address
Lieut. O. S. Palmer
1st Regiment, Ark. Vols.
Bowling Green, Ky.
Your devoted Brother
O. S. Palmer

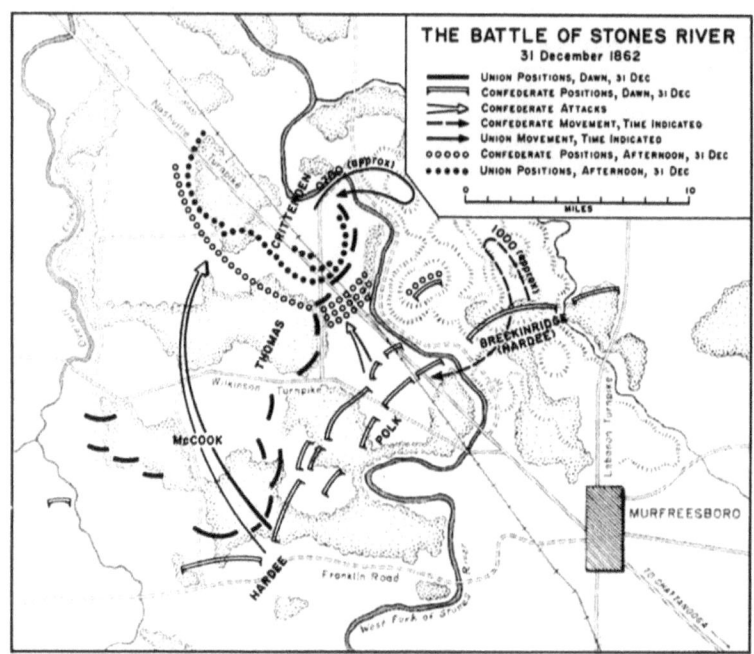

The Battle of Stones River.

Chapter 3

1862

"We Can Whip Any Army They May Send Against Us"

The Union capture of Fort Henry on February 6, 1862, opened the Tennessee River Valley to invasion, and soon afterward Flag Officer Andrew Hull Foote, the commander of the Union flotilla, dispatched the gunboats *Lexington*, *Tyler*, and *Conestoga* under the command of navy Lt. Seth Phelps "as far up the river as the stage of water will admit." Phelps arrived in Florence, situated on the north bank of the Tennessee at Muscle Shoals, Alabama, on 8 February where he reported destroying "considerable quantities of supplies" and everything of strategic consequence including the Kennedy family's mills.[1]

"They have ascended to Florence," Rebel war clerk John Beauchamp Jones recorded in consternation and dismay, "and may get footing in Alabama and Mississippi!" This was the deepest incursion to date into Confederate territory and the ease with which the heartland had been penetrated demoralized not only they local population but the entire South. In Richmond, Jones lamented that "three of the enemy's gun-boats have ascended the Tennessee River to its very head of navigation, while the women and children on the banks could do nothing more than gaze in mute despair."[2] Lieutenant Phelps, however, assured them that he and his sailors "were neither ruffians nor savages and they were there to protect from violence and enforce the law."[3] According to the New York Times, the citizens of Florence were "so delighted at finding the Stars and Stripes once more giving protection to them that they prepared to give a grand ball to the officers of the gunboats, but they could not remain to accept their courtesies."[4]

A correspondent to the *Charleston Mercury*, however, in a letter from Florence dated 22 February, rebutted the *Times*' claim, declaring that it was a "point blank, jet-black abolition lie." Rather, he avowed, "not a lady of Florence went to see them, or desired to go, or had any communication with them. They were held in utter detestation by every soul."[5]

Pvt. William Cowan McClellan, then serving in Virginia with the Ninth Alabama Infantry, feared that his family would be vulnerable to danger during the enemy's stay. On 15 February 1862, McClellan reported to his father, Thomas Joyce McClellan, a state representative, that "there is a gooddeal [sic] of excitement in North Ala about the Yankees coming up to Florence.... Our Regi[ment] was on its head to go down to Flo[rence] and clean out the yanks."

After its capture of Fort Donelson on 16 February, Grant's Army of the Tennessee continued up the Tennessee River, establishing its headquarters at Savannah, Tennessee. From there Grant planned to attack Albert Sidney Johnston's Confederate army camped at Corinth, Mississippi. Johnston and Beauregard moved first, however, striking the Federals at Pittsburg Landing on the Tennessee River.[6]

Bowling Green, Ky.
Jan. 7th, 1861 [i.e., 1862]

Dear Sister,

Your two letters have been joyfully received, the first on the 3rd and the latter today. I thought I would not answer the first until I learned whether you had gone home or was still at Ripley. I was quite happy to hear from you that you were well, and c.

As to the question you proposed in reference to the propriety of your going home with Mr. L for an escort, I have simply to say that I see no impropriety in any young lady traveling in company with a young gentleman acquaintance, and anyone who would be disposed to make disparaging remarks about a young lady who should have the boldness of mind to do so is a vain meddler whose soul would stoop to any depth of degradation.

What is it that a young lady should travel with a young man whom she knows and recognizes as a gentleman? I am sure I can see no objection to it, and had you gone with Mr. L to Florence, no one could have cast any reflection on your action. But it seems you did not go, and that Uncle W[esley] will take you whenever you are compelled to go. So, I can now rest easy, satisfied that your kind uncle will see you safely home when you want to go.

If you conclude to remain there until May, I will then come by for you as I will be free again either the 27th of April or the 13th of May. I do not know positively which. It will not, therefore, be very long until I can be with you, and, oh! how happy I shall be to see my sweet sister!⁷

Tell Uncle W. that I have not yet been able to see any of our military men here who are acquainted with our members of Congress, but if I do, I shall certainly use my best endeavors in his behalf. I think if he were to get the members from Mississippi to present his claims to the Department it would be better and more certainly insure him the position he desires. I hope he will get it and that without any trouble.

Aunt C[ynthia] is going to Holly Springs[, Mississippi,] to keep boarding house, is she? What is to become of her children in the meantime? Surely she doesn't intend carrying them with her and going thus to the enormous expense of boarding them, that is, buying everything they get to eat when they have plenty for them at home. Then what, in the meantime, is to become of the farm? Surely they do not intend to forgo the certain profits of a crop for the uncertain and doubtful gains of a boarding house, which is generally more trouble than profit. However, I trust whatever they do will be for the best and that happiness and prosperity may be combined.

We have had some of the strangest weather I ever saw. We have had some rain every day for the last week, and it has been cloudy and warm all the time. Up to this time the winter has been very mild, uncommonly so. We have had no snow and but very little ice. I expect we will have a mild winter.

We have no war news of interest or importance. Still working on batteries.

I saw Mr. Rogers the other day. He had a very bad cold. Was coughing almost all the time.

I have not seen any of the Florence boys for a week or two. I went over to see them twice and none of them have called over to see me. I have not seen Bill Chisholm at all. He was out of camp. I hope I will see him soon.⁸

I send you ten dollars on the bank of Tennessee. I trust it will reach you safely. If you get it, write to me immediately and I will send you ten more . . . that is, if you want it. I can spare it very well.

I have no time to write more now. I wrote to T[om] W[inston] the other day. Write to me immediately after you receive this letter. Let me know all the news.

Give my love to all and remember me kindly to all the young ladies.
Your devoted Brother,
O. S. Palmer

Bowling Green, Ky.
Jan. 24th, 1862

Dear Sister,

I received your letter of the 13th a few days since. I was glad to hear that you were well and had received my letter with the ten dollars. I was glad, too, that you were going home. I thought that you ought to go home, for there you can be of more benefit than at any other place.

Jan. 26th: (I had not time to finish this letter the other day and will try to do so now.) I received your letter written at home today. I was very glad to know that you arrived safely, but was quite sorry to learn that Grandpa had met with such an accident and trust that he may soon recover from the fall.

I hope that you and Aunt O[live] will have a nice time. You will have a good opportunity to read, thus to cause the hours to fly more swiftly by and store your mind with such useful knowledge as will be greatly to your advantage and fill your mind with such rich gems of thought as will cause you to be admired and respected and shine where the most highly cultivated are assembled.

I take this opportunity to press upon you the importance of constant steady reading of choice works. You can have the choice of both Uncle Elias's and Spinks's libraries, and out of them you can get such, and as many, works as you may desire, and it is my desire that you do so.

It may be hard at first to confine your thoughts and keep them from brooding over this horrible war and the ones who are so dear to you, but then, if you will make a strong, continued effort, with the high resolve to conquer your own thoughts and render them subservient to a strong and determined will and concentrate them upon some gem of literature, you will succeed.

I know that you will encounter many difficulties at the outset, but after a time you will find how completely the mind is under the control of a strong and determined will. I have in days that are gone made the experiment, and after a while succeeded, and I know that you are as capable of anything of this kind as I am. You have only to trust, as I did when I was at home reading Law and regretting certain affairs of the heart, to find that every word I tell you is true.

Commence with Waverly novels, then *The Spectator*, and then history and general literature. I wish you and want you to restrain your thoughts from brooding too much over the troubles incident to a state of war. Submit willingly to the dispensations of Providence and murmur not.[9]

Everything is going on here as usual. We are drilling and working on batteries, preparing for the approach of Gen. Buell and his grand army.

We have strange and startling news here. It is reported that the enemy in strong force is advancing upon Paris, Tennessee, and Fort Henry on the Tennessee River—both these places are said to be in great danger. Columbus[, Kentucky,] is also said to be greatly threatened and in some danger. How true these reports are, I cannot say.

We also have startling news of an unaccountable and disastrous defeat suffered by our forces under Zollicoffer at Somerset. It is said that our forces were completely routed, retreating in such perfect confusion and terror as to lose all their wagons, tents, clothing, artillery, a great many small arms, and all their commissary stores.[10]

This news comes to us fully confirmed, and there seems to be no doubt that we have suffered a great and terrible defeat and the ultimate consequences of which no one can tell. If the army there is in the condition it is reported to be, there is a great probability of it being utterly destroyed or at least so badly whipped as not to be of any more service to our cause.

I was quite sorry to hear of the sad news, but trust it is not near as bad as it is represented to be, that our loss and rout was not so terrible as first accounts give of it.

I understand from Sterling (now Gen.) Wood that Col. W. B. Wood's regiment did not arrive on the field of action until the last moment, that they fought bravely and lost but few men, and that Col. Wood and Oliver were safe.[11] I hope soon to hear the full particulars of the fight and that we have heard an exaggerated account of it.[12]

Some 8 or 10,000 men have left here within the last week on the cars in the direction of Nashville or Memphis, one. No one, of course, knows where they are gone. Some think to Fort Henry, others to Paris, whilst others say they are gone to East Tennessee. I, myself, think they have gone to defend Paris and Fort Henry.

I hope, yes. I know they will strike some blow that will counteract the evil influence of the battle at Somerset and shed lustre upon our arms and change the mourning of our people to rejoicing over a brilliant victory.

Whether or not we will have a fight here, I do not know. Some think we will advance upon Paris, Tennessee, and Fort Henry on the Tennessee River. Both these places are said to be in great danger. Columbus is also said to be greatly threatened and in some danger. How true these reports are, I cannot say. Whilst others think differently, no one can form an intelligent opinion about it. I confess that I cannot comprehend the plans of the enemy or our own.[13]

We may have a fight before June and we may not. No one can tell what a day or an hour may bring forth. If we do fight here, I feel confident we can whip any army they may send against us. This is the best fortified place in the Confederate States, and no force can take it.

I got my suit of clothes from Capt. Price and am delighted with it. Everyone likes it so much and say they had rather have it than any they have seen. Capt. Murray (my Capt.) likes it so well that he would like one like.[14] If Grandma has any more like it, he would be glad to get it, and if she has any opportunity to send it to do so. I will collect the money for it and send it to her. He can have it made here if he has the cloth. I would like very much for you to send me something good to eat if you have a chance.

Give my love to all—to the young ladies, Missies Jeanie, Mollie, Bettie, and c.—and write immediately and often.

Your devoted Brother,

O. S. Palmer

[page missing]

You asked me in your letter with the one from Aunt C[ynthia] and Cousin D[elia] if I was in love with or engaged to anyone? The answer to the first question is also an answer to the last. I am in love with—*no one*, and I congratulate myself that I am not. To be in Love and in the army at the same time would be more than I could stand. Human nature could not endure so much. If I were in love, I could not stay in the army. I would have either to desert the service or My Love, either of which would be followed by the most serious consequences.

By the way, how comes it that in your last letters you say nothing of Mr. W[inston]? Have you and him fell out, quit, or anything of the sort? It seems strange to me that you said not a word about your lover true when in every letter before there was something about the dear one. I promised him I would write to him when I got settled down here, but I have not found time or chance to do so yet. Please tell him this in your next and that I shall certainly write in a few days, anyhow.

How are all my lady friends around and in Ripley? I hope they are all as sweet and pretty as ever and well supplied with gallant soldier boys for sweethearts. Remember me to them all very kindly and present them with my best wishes for their happiness and the safe return of their lovers from the horrors of "wrinkle fronted war."[15]

Is Miss K[atie] P[ate] engaged? If so, to whom? I ask not from any particular interest (?) but from sheer curiosity, which you will do me the pleasure to gratify.[16]

Delia and Mr. Little are getting on finely, I trust. I hope that nothing may occur to ruffle the current of their love. Success to their love.[17]

Pick me out a "Duck" and keep her heart disengaged until I return. She must play on both the piano and guitar. Remember, these two are indispensable requisites. Who, think you, fills the bill?

I can write no more now. I have written enough anyway to worry you all and must close by begging you to take a breathing spell after so long a detention.

Goodbye and God bless you.

Your Brother,

O. S. Palmer

[*in margin*]

I am in fine health, weigh 150 pounds. I get $90.00 a month—have since 23rd Dec. I can't get change to pay the postage on this letter. Excuse me for not doing so.

Decatur, Ala.
March 6th, 1862

Dear Sister,

I reached here Tuesday evening at 5 o'clock. Nothing of interest occurred on the way. Capt. Murray had gone to the country. He was quite sick. Could not stay out in the Camp and would not stay in the Hospital. So, he found a good place a mile and a half from town and went out there to remain until he recovered. I went out yesterday morning to see him and remained until the morning. He is quite sick. Threatened with typhoid pneumonia. I took him a bottle of cordial and some cake. He was glad to receive it but could not use any of it now.

I had quite a pleasant time out there with two very nice and sprightly young ladies. They were very talkative and interesting. I never spent a day more pleasantly at a strange place, and I would not object to staying out there all the time.

I have good news for you all, which I hope will relieve you all from anxiety. I missed my chill yesterday evening, and I feel very well this morning. Much better than I have for some time. I am not deceiving you in this. It is all true with no exaggeration, and I have some medicine which the doctor says will keep them off entirely, and I trust it is true.

It is quite cold and snowing this morning. I fear we will have some very bad weather, but it will not last long.

My mess was very proud of the box I brought, and they all return many thanks and drink your and Aunt Olive's health. None of us has or will get tight on the cordial brandy.

Columbus is certainly evacuated. I don't know where the troops are. General [Albert Sidney] Johnston's army is moving on down this way. Where it is going, I cannot learn. I have not time to write more.

My love to all. Write immediately.

Your devoted Brother,

O. S. Palmer

[Oliver S. Kennedy to Georgia C. Foster[18]]

Decatur, Ala., March 10th, 62

I have just arrived at Camps and embrace the earliest opportunity to fulfill my promise to write you on my arrival. I write under embarrassing circumstances, too, as I am now at Gen. [Sterling A. M.] Wood's Headquarters, endeavoring to prove interesting while there is a continual noise around the General's Aides, Adjutant, and Orderlies, making details, writing orders, and sending them. However, all this cannot stop my pen or for a moment keep memory from carrying me back to the few days which have been the most pleasant of my life. I do assure you, dearest Georgie, that the greatest possible change has taken place in my feelings. Since I've found again you love me, I have with different emotions moving me onward to the great goal of distinction and renown and glory. I feel happier and that I live also to promote the happiness of the one that loves me.

I cannot tell you how I felt ere now. The gloom and despondency that rules my heart entirely since I am not by my Georgie's side. But then I know although it is the purest pleasure to be with you and hear you say you love me still—although it delights me to know I could promote your happiness by being with you—yet at the same time I know it to be my imperative duty to go forth into the army to vindicate my country's honor—to battle for rights dear to us all and which involve the existence of our infant Republic, and, loved one, to defend you from rude insults and taunts of hessians should they reach our Southern homes.

I have been thinking of you with melancholy and pleasant emotions. Melancholy because I am not able to marry you now and offer you a home in which you might be happy amid all this turmoil and stress of the outer world. Pleasure because I have the assurance that you love me better than anybody else.

It is rumored that we will go down the road tomorrow to Tuscumbia, Florence, or somewhere there. I know not whether there is any truth in it or not. I hope, however, it is true. Frank Foster informs me of this.[19] Says we will go tomorrow. I will go to see General Wood and will try to find out the truth of it and make a note. I think it is exceedingly doubtful. I would write you a longer letter but could get no more paper and could not delay writing until tomorrow. I hope this will find you entirely recovered from your cold and in good health and spirits. This separation is very painful to me, but necessity forces much upon us and we must bear it as well as possible. Write soon a long letter to one that loves you well.

Yours,
O. S. Kennedy

[Oliver Kennedy to Georgia Foster]
Camps near Iuka, Miss.
Camp near Iuka, Miss.
March 18th, 1862

My Dear Georgie,

My promise to write to you immediately on my arriving at this place has not [*illegible*]. . . .[20]

. . . circumstances surrounding them. For three years our hearts have been estranged and we have been separated. This was a sad misfortune for us, but fate seemed to decree thus it should be. Although I was the cause of this, yet I did not know it then [*several words faded to illegibility*] all.

. . . left behind with the 2nd Battalion. Now I know you will forgive me for not writing until this morning. The 2nd Battalion arrived last night about two o'clock and slept without stretching tents. So, I am glad I did not remain with the [*illegible*] as . . .

. . . more than that, to see you even now although it has only been one day since I saw you. It is not very strange that all other conversation than yours proves uninteresting no matter what theme discussed? That your presence creates happiness and your absence. . . .

I [*illegible*] to [*illegible*] in each patriot's bosom a feeling of [*illegible*] which tells him, "fear nothing, but brave all for your country's sake!" The feelings on any on the battlefield where nothing is heard but the whistling of balls and thundering roar of the cannon are far different from what you would suppose would [*illegible*] it.

There is no continuing and overpowering fear which one would suppose would fill the mind of the [*illegible*] soldier. He banishes all such thoughts and thinks of nothing but destroying the enemy and of gaining a victory. Hence, I think this feeling is a principle implanted in us by the

Devine Being, and this [*illegible*] us the right of fighting, especially in a just cause. I have been in one . . .

I know we will finally succeed, for our cause is a just one. [*Illegible*] has thus far favored us [*illegible*] and hope to continue [*illegible*] fight with us [*illegible*] what we fight for [*illegible*]. And will it not be a proud day when the glorious Stars and Bars shall float in triumph over every battlefield and the praises of the infant Republic shall be sung by every tongue, both at home and abroad? Then we shall see happy and bright days will shine around us.

Georgia, although we will soon be on the way to the battlefield on which a glorious victory is to be won or a disastrous defeat to be suffered, be calm and contented. There is a sacred joy in the faithful discharge of duty, and if we should gain the day and drive the rude and heartless invaders from the soil of Mississippi, it will be one of the greatest prognoses of our final success and a brilliant triumph over the hessian soldiery.

Georgia, if I should go into a fight as soon as I think, I feel satisfied I shall come through it without a wound even. I pray for this. Oh, that we may prove victorious. If I <u>should</u> fall, which is possible and probable in such a contest as this, often [*word illegible*] to the memory of one who loved you as dearly as life and one who thought of you even in the last moments of life, for I shall think of you at every moment. Cherish the memory of one that loved you and died with the sweet consolation that this intense love was fully reciprocated. More, visit my grave and shed a tear over the earthly remains of him who loved you as <u>his Georgia</u>.

[Oliver Kennedy to Georgia Foster
Iuka, Mississippi, March 1862]

My Dear Georgie,

I wrote to you today, but I promised you I would be certain to write to you [*illegible*] before [*illegible*] into the fight. . . .

. . . battleground where men were dying and falling fast around me and know what I have said to be true. I thought all the while that those around me would fall next, but that I would remain safe, and so I <u>did</u>!

The same feeling is upon me while I write to [*illegible*]. Then I will feel when we reach the field and commence the bloody work of death and destruction, I know not, but believe there will be no change.

This will be a desperate and bloody conflict. Each side will go into it with a determination to conquer, hence the side that gains a victory will have to fight hard and long, in my estimation, before that victory is gained. If the Federals should prove victorious, it will be months before [we] will recover from the blow. . . .[21]

[Oliver Kennedy to Georgia Foster]
Head Quarters
16th Reg. Ala Vols
Corinth, Miss., March 24th, 62

My Dear Georgie,

I have written to you twice since we parted. I hope you have now received one of my letters as you only spoke of one in your letter, which I have just received and read with much pleasure and interest. I am glad you concluded to write me such a long letter. I could read one twice as long from you and then not be satisfied. Don't say again I waste time when perusing letters as interesting to me as yours always are, for you cannot imagine with what true delight it was read. It was a treat, indeed. The only regret is when I finished it that I have not another like it to cheer me with its sweet consolations in my hours of idleness around the campfires. Promise me now, Georgie dear, that you will write to me at least once a week when you know where to send your letters and oftener if you feel so disposed. I would feel ungrateful did I tax your patience to write to me oftener although it would gratify me exceedingly to hear from you every day. To know that each day you are enjoying good health, are in fine spirits, and are happy as circumstances will permit.

I wrote you a long letter the night we left Iuka. I remembered my promise to write just before going into battle and that night an order came round to prepare one day's rations and pack everything ready to march at a moment's warning. So, I was almost certain a battle would come off early next morning. So did all. I sat down and amid wild confusion and noise wrote to you and I guess it is a great scribble. But, dear Georgie, if I should be ordered into a battle without having an opportunity to you, keep that letter as containing my true sentiments. Just before such a trying time as that, I believe now, as others here do, that there will be no fight at this place. We learn nothing of the movements of the enemy, but I think they know our strength very well and will attack us at some other front, if at all, because they know we have a strong force at this point.

Uncle Spinks was out to see me yesterday evening. He says this is the best army he has seen anywhere . . . the finest looking men and he best armed and equipped men he has seen, and, more than that, it is impossible to whip such an army as this. He is about correct, too, for an army like the one here is almost invincible. They are large, strong, fine-looking fellows and are fighting for principle. It is not like the Northern rabble, fighting for pay, but their all is at stake, and they know and feel that when they submit to the iron will of the Lincoln despotism that they are ruined and forever. Hence, they will fight with a desperation unknown in military history and gain a victory the most brilliant of any army that ever fought or ever conquered. May this time soon come. I earnestly hope this year, this month. . . .

[after 6 April 1862] . . . that I will try by every means in my power to get a leave of absence and come to see you, Georgie, if it is but for one short hour, and I believe I will succeed as I have been closely at my post since the battle of Shiloh and have done more, by a great deal, than was my duty. Every officer and man in this regiment knows and will acknowledge that I have done more for the regiment by far than was required of me by law or orders. Hence, they are glad of my promotion. I have gone up gradually from 2 Jr. Lieut. to Captain, and now I command Co. C, Captain Coffee having resigned. The company are, or seem to be, much pleased with me as captain, so am I with them. . . .[22]

Tupelo, Mississippi
June 9th, 1862

My Dear Sister,

I have an opportunity to send you a note by Tom Sloss and I am quite happy to avail myself of it to inform you of my whereabouts and good health.[23]

We reached here yesterday from Baldwin. Tupelo is on the Mobile and Ohio R.R., some fifty or sixty miles below Corinth. What we are here for or where we are going and when are questions which we vainly ask or attempt to solve. Some think we will go to East Tennessee, others that we will await the enemy at this place. I cannot form any opinion as to the accuracy of any of the various rumors afloat as to the designs of our Generals. The Army is all here and in tolerable good fighting condition, ready to meet the enemy at any moment and battle manfully in our righteous cause. As to the strength of our army, I am not informed, and if I were it would not be proper for me to say. Suffice it that we have an army equal to any emergency, and I think we will soon hurl back the immense horde of Hessians that is congregated in our front.

I do not know whether the enemy is following us or not. Rumor says they are, but of course we can tell nothing of their movements. Yet I do not think they can follow us. If they do attempt it, they will subject themselves to enormous expense and great danger of being entirely overpowered. I do hope they will attempt to follow, for I feel the utmost confidence in our ability to repulse them and their splendid army.

Enough of this subject. I wrote you the other day, but I fear you did not get it. I wrote you that I wanted Marion sent me, but now I do not want him. I have Peter now and shall keep him, so you need to send him. I would rather he was at home as long as I can have Peter.[24]

I am in very fine health. My leg is entirely well but is weak yet, so much so that I cannot walk very far or fast. However, I have a very fine horse which I shall keep until I am perfectly well. Then I will send him to you if I can do so. It is one of the finest horses in the army, perfectly gentle and a very fine saddle horse. I want you to have him and you shall when we go by home on our way to Kentucky.[25]

I enjoyed myself finely whilst at Ripley. I did not suffer but very little from my wound and was going around to see all the young ladies. I found me a new sweetheart. She is very ugly, but the most intelligent young lady I have ever met with. I suppose you know of whom I speak. I refer, of course, to Miss Mattie Carter, a most interesting young lady. What do you think of her? Will she do for a sister or not?[26]

I saw Kittie H. and Annie Davidson and c.[27]

I received your letter of the 11th of May, the first I had heard from you since I left home. I was quite happy to hear from you and that you were well, and I trust to God you may keep well and in good spirits and free from every care and trouble. I would like so much to be with you. It would be a pleasure greater than any other that could be granted. I trust that peace will soon bless our land and we may yet spend a happy and joyous life together, far from care and sorrow.

Most persons think that the war will not last more than 60 or 90 days longer, that France and England will interfere and put an end to this destructive, this ruinous war. I shall rejoice when they do so, and so will all good persons.[28]

I saw Tom W[inston] the other day. He was very well and is getting along finely. He was in the battle of Shiloh and came out unhurt. He enquired of you and said he had heard from you, and c.

Uncle Mose is here, captain of a company. I saw him this evening and he is not very well—has been a little sick several days but is better now. He sends his love to you. Uncle John is at home sick. I do not know what is the matter with him nor how he is.[29] Uncle Elias is below here forwarding forage. He is well and will be here tomorrow.

I forgot to tell you I was Captain of my company. My old captain (Murray) is now lieutenant colonel of the Regt.

We have glorious news from Maryland. "Stonewall" Jackson has entered Maryland, routed Gen. Banks's command, and is advancing upon Washington. All Lincolndom is in consternation and the militia is rising in all quarters to save their Capitol from the impetuous young general. Success to him.[30]

We cannot hear any correct news from the battle at Richmond[, Virginia]. I fear it is no victory for us. Memphis is in possession of the enemy. The whole Mississippi is now in possession of the enemy.[31]

Sister, I will write you by every chance, and you must do the same. If you have a chance to send a letter to Uncle Spinks or Elias do so, and they will forward it to me.[32]

I have nothing more to write now except to say be of good cheer. Do not despair. There is a better time coming where all our troubles will be forgotten, and, oh, how happy will the hours pass away.

Give my love to Grandpa, Grandma, Aunt Olive, Uncle Jesse, and c.

Write me all the news the first opportunity, for I know nothing of what has occurred since I left home.

Goodbye, Sweet Sister, and may God bless and protect you is the constant prayer of your Devoted Brother,

Orlando

Address your letter thus: Capt. O. S. Palmer, 15th Ark. Regiment, Cleburne's Brigade, Hardee's Division

[Oliver S. Kennedy to Georgia C. Foster]
[spring 1862]

... drawing our enemy as far south as the Tennessee River increased his expenses to $5,000,000 per day, and is it not presumed if he follows us, it will be proportionately increased? More than that should we get them this far from the River and protection of his heavy siege guns. We will gain a signal victory and when once started back, that the whole army will be [*page torn*] and if not [*one line effaced by tear*] [there can be] no resisting to our march. If we once start for Kentucky we will go there, and once there, our Independence is as good as established, I think.

The news from Virginia is cheering—that General Johnston has gained a victory over McClellan and driven him back from Richmond and ....

.... letter as you used to, and I think it will cheer me considerably. It is the consciousness of having wounded your feelings that causes my depression of spirits. I am fully penitent and I know if you knew how I feel about it you would without hesitation forgive all. I believed I was doing justice to you and myself, but think now I was rather hasty.

We left Corinth at 10 o'clock [*page torn across. line effaced*] been on the most [torn] and fatiguing duties night and day for a week or ten days, marched all night and next day without halting but one night, a distance of 40 miles. Hence, we all feel worn out and exhausted, but a few days here in the [*page missing*]

... long enough for you to answer this, so I will look for it. Tell Miss Berta to be certain to answer my letter. Tell her I gave her love to Charley. He returns his and would like to see her. I believe he really loves her.

I saw B. Stainbach at Corinth. He came from home to see me and asked several questions about you and Miss Berta. Requested me to send you his love and c.[33]

[torn] you [torn] prosperity and [torn]essity is the prayer of one who loves you.

O.S.K.

[Oliver Kennedy to Georgia Foster]
Hd. Qrts., Co. C, 16th Regt. Ala. Vols.
Tupelo, Miss., June 12th /62

My Dear Georgie,

I was delighted on returning to camps yesterday to find a letter from you awaiting my arrival. I have banished all such feelings as the blues and now I feel in fine spirits and am in good health and cheerful as any soldier could be. I had been looking for a letter from you for a day or two, but I suppose Lieut. Brown was detained on the way by having to come such a circuitous route to get here safely.[34]

You write as though you have entirely recovered your health. I hope you have. I have been quite uneasy about you since I heard you were sick. You must take good care of yourself and your health. I think you are in better spirits than when you last wrote, too. That is right. Be happy and contented amid all troubles and trials—as much so, at least, as possible. Always look on the bright side of every picture. If you will submit to it, imaginary trouble will disappoint and pain you as much as real troubles. A great many of our troubles are imaginary. I have come to believe that if we allow every little trivial circumstance to ripple the smooth surface of our happiness, that we will become continually melancholy and moody. Sadness instead of joy will reign and rule us as a despot on his throne.

I am sorry of one thing, however, that a military necessity forced us this far south and you are all left to the tender mercies of the Federal mercenaries. You are now in the Federal lines and two sets of pickets between us, yet I hope you will get this letter safely and will have an opportunity of answering it soon. There is no telling when we will have an opportunity of keeping up a regular correspondence again. It may be when Gen'l Halleck advances on General Beauregard and Gen'l Beauregard learns [i.e., "teaches"] him to double-quick to the Tennessee River and we go into Tennessee with our army. When this occurs, which will be partly, if not fully accomplished should he advance. . . .[35]

* * *

In August, Maj. Gen. Edmund Kirby Smith invaded Kentucky from Eastern Tennessee, winning a small but impressive victory on the thirtieth over Maj. Gen. William "Bull" Nelson at Richmond, Kentucky. The battle of Richmond was, although on a small scale, as close to a total victory as the Confederacy ever achieved. In the fall of 1862, Braxton Bragg's Army of Mississippi and Edmund Kirby Smith's Army of Kentucky were advancing on converging paths into Kentucky. On the afternoon of 29 August, Cleburne's brigade, the vanguard of Smith's army, encountered Federal troops south of Richmond. Both sides were speedily reinforced, and by the morning of the thirtieth both were in line of battle and prepared to attack.

Palmer, at the head of his company and "under the eye of General Cleburne," was detailed to occupy a skirt of woods opposite the extreme left of the Union line preliminary to a Confederate attack on that flank. "Sharp work soon took place," reported Col. Benjamin Hill, the commander of Cleburne's Second Brigade, between Palmer's company and the Federals until Cleburne's division moved forward against the Federal left and Brig. Gen. Thomas J. Churchill's division, having approached the battlefield by way of a ravine, fell upon the Union right. The Federal line, now commanded by General Nelson, was caught in a double envelopment and "began a confused retreat," and all attempts to rally it were routed. Nelson lost 206 killed, 844 wounded, and 4,303 captured or missing. Smith's casualties amounted to only 78 killed, 372 wounded, and one man missing.[36]

The Confederate victory at Richmond opened the way for Smith to occupy Lexington and the capital at Frankfort and opened the route to Cincinnati. Bragg, in the meantime, departed from Chattanooga on 27 August, moving to Smith's support.

[Maj. Gen. Don Carolos] Buell moved north out of Florence, Kentucky, to intercept the Confederates, and on 8 October, the armies met unexpectedly at Perryville. Bragg ordered an attack on the Federal army's left flank, forcing it back about a mile, but Union reinforcements arrived to stabilize the line.

Smith pleaded with Bragg to follow up on his success: "For God's sake, General, let us fight Buell here." Bragg replied, "I will do it, sir," but then, displaying what Polk's son and biographer, William Mecklenburg Polk, called "a perplexity and vacillation which had now become simply appalling to Smith, to Hardee, and to Polk," he ordered his army to retreat to Murfreesboro, Tennessee. Bragg's senior officers charged that he had failed in his campaign, abandoning the fruits of their victory, and demanded that he be replaced in command of the army. Jefferson Davis declined to remove Bragg, but his relationship with his subordinates was severely damaged.[37]

> Knoxville, Tenn.
> Oct. 23rd, 1862

Dear Sister,

Tonight, for the first time in months, I can enjoy the sweet, delightful pleasure of writing to you, my dearly beloved sister. Not since a long while before I left Tupelo have I had an opportunity to send a letter home until now. Oh, how happy it is once more to be able to communicate with the dear ones at home, and how glad I am to be able to inform you that I am well and came out of two bloody, fierce battles without a single scratch. Yes, Sister, I am unharmed, and I thank Him "who is the giver of every good gift" that I am still among the living. Many changing scenes have I gone through since I last wrote to you and many are the hardships I have undergone, but, I am happy to say, I am in fine health and spirits.

I have not heard from you by letter since 14th June, but have seen several from Lauderdale Co., who give me some news from home. I heard for the first time the 12th inst. that our good, kind, affectionate Grandfather was dead. Oh, how it wrung my heart with anguish to hear of the death of my good guardian, for a guardian of my wandering, erring footsteps he has been from my earliest boyhood days, beginning back when I went astray and guiding and supporting with his fatherly council and sound advice. Greatly, oh, how greatly will we miss him. But the good Christian has gone to a better, happier world than this where his happiness will not be disturbed by the trump of hostile armies and the clashing of arms, and we should not murmur at the decree that calls him from this to a better world than this. Oh, how I wish that I could be with you and my dear Grandmother to cheer you up in your hours of loneliness and attempt in some degree to fill the place of the lamented dead in supplying your every want and doing, thinking, of nothing but adding to your comfort. How happy I should be with those who are dearer to me than all the world besides.

But sister mine, you know this cannot, must not, be. My country calls for men, and every man must and will stand by her in her hour of darkness and trouble. She calls upon me to assist in hurling back from her soil the base hirelings who come to plunder our homes, devastate our land, and insult our loved ones. Can I . . . can any man of feeling, even one spark of patriotism still lingering in his breast . . . resist the call and fold his arms and see his country ruined? No. I must remain until the bitter end and pray and work for her welfare. I trust that the war will soon be brought to a successful termination and then on the wings of love will fly to greet you, my adored sister, and what happy, happy times we will then have.

In the meantime, I beg of you, that you will be cheerful, hopeful, confident, never despairing, but driving off all gloomy thoughts by a determined will which allows nothing to disturb your peace of mind.

It would be well, I suppose, to give you a short account of my wanderings since last I wrote you. I went from Tupelo to Chattanooga, horseback, by the way of Aberdeen, Tuscaloosa, and c. Had quite a pleasant time from Chattanooga. Our brigade (Cleburne's) was ordered to Knoxville. From K[noxville] we marched to Clinton. From Clinton to Barnardsville, from B. to Cumberland Ford, then back to B. From there to London, Ky., from L. to Richmond, where, with 3,000 men, we whipped 10,000 of the enemy. Killed and wounded about 3,000. Captured and paroled over 6,000 and captured an immense amount of army stores of every description. Our loss was very slight. It was a hard fight, but we whipped them at all points. This fight was on the 30th Aug.

From Richmond we marched on to Lexington, from there to Paris, thence to Cynthiana, thence to Williamstown, thence to Crittenden, thence to Florence[, Kentucky,] and from F. to within sight of the enemy's fortification at Covington, Kentucky. Our regiment on the 12th Sept. was out as skirmishers, as we thought, to bring on the attack upon Covington, Kentucky. We could see the men at work on the fortifications, hear the car whistle in Cincinnati, and the troops shouting as each train would come in, but instead of attacking, we fell back that night to Florence, thence to Crittenden, and c. to Georgetown, from G. to Frankfort, from there to Shelbyville, 28 miles from Louisville. Were at that delightful place a week and enjoyed the time finely with the most pleasant ladies.

From Shelbyville we fell back to Frankfort and from there we marched to Harrodsburg where we made a junction with Bragg's Army on Sunday before the fight at Perryville. While there, Tom came over to see me and we spent two or three hours in pleasant talk of our loved ones at home. He was looking much better than when I saw him at Tupelo and seemed to be in fine spirits. He said he had not heard from you for some time but had written to you a few days before. I also saw Bob[?] Holcombe—he is surgeon of [Brig. Gen. Daniel P.] Donelson's Brigade—is looking finely.[38] I saw Dr. Bostwick.[39] He is surgeon of the 154th Tennessee.

On Tuesday the 7th inst. we marched out to Perryville. Remained in line of battle all day, calmly listening to the occasional firing of cannon and firing of skirmishers. Wednesday morning, we was up at daybreak. Soon heavy skirmishing was heard, which grew warmer and warmer until about 10 o'clock when our entire line was ordered forward and we soon came upon the enemy in strong force and in strong position, and he met our attack with steadiness and coolness. The fight raged with unparalleled fury from then until dark, we driving the enemy from every position for a distance of at least 2 miles with immense slaughter. Our loss was heavy, but not near so great as the enemy's.

I had a gun and have the satisfaction of knowing that I repaid the wounds they gave me at Shiloh. I escaped unhurt but had my 1st Lieut. [George N. Davie] killed upon the field and four men out of sixteen wounded. That night we camped on the battlefield with the dead and dying all around us. Next morning about 8 o'clock our forces began falling back to Harrodsburg. It was said that the enemy was heavily reinforced and we were not in condition to fight them.

From H[arrodsburg] we came to Camp Dick Robinson where we remained some three days.[40] From there we came to Crab Orchard, thence to London, thence to Barbourville, thence to Cumberland Gap, which is one of the strongest places in the world. From there we came to Danville, and from there we came to Knoxville, the point from which we started.

Take your map. Look at those places and you will see what a long, long march we have made. I had my horse or I never would have made the trip. My leg is not as strong as it was before I was shot, however it doesn't pain me but very little except when I walk a great deal. Then for a day or two it pains me a good deal. We had a great many men to give out from exhaustion and are now in the lines of the enemy.

We are here now but will not tarry long. We must soon be again on the tramp and quit ourselves us like valiant men if we would drive the invader from our country. I am of the opinion that most of the army will go immediately by rail to Murfreesboro, Tennessee, and make an attack upon Nashville and, if successful there, establish our lines on the Cumberland River and rest quiet during the winter. I hope this will be the plan and that we will accomplish this and more. Then I can get to come home and spend a few happy days with you all and recount to you my various adventures since last I saw you.

I send you my horse by Logan.[41] The horse looks very badly now. He's worn out almost entirely, but if you let him rest and have him well rubbed and fed, he will soon recruit and be a fine horse again. I make you a present of him and hope he will do you a great deal of good. He is perfectly gentle, and you can ride him anywhere. I bought me a fine horse today.

Gen. Wood has offered me the position of adjutant general, and I shall accept.[42] I will be assigned to duty to him tomorrow. He has not yet recovered from his wound but will be well in ten days. The position he offers me is a very nice one and I will be much more comfortable than I have been heretofore. I shall get along finely with him.

Tom W[inston] was slightly wounded in the shoulder at Perryville. I did not see him, but in hunting around the hospital at Harrodsburg the day after the fight to see who of my friends were there, I found Sylve Perry (of Tom's company) slightly wounded in the leg.[43] He told me that Tom was wounded in the shoulder, that he cut a horse loose from a battery that we had captured and rode back to Harrodsburg. I looked around for him but could not find him. I suppose he came on with the train of wounded. He could not have been hurt much or he could not of rode ten miles horseback, then been walking about town. Some of his company told me they saw him walking just before I got there, so you need not be uneasy, for he is not hurt much and will soon recover and probably come home until he gets entirely well and you will get to see him, and I know you will be happy.[44]

Send my Marion or George, which ever you think will suit me best, by the very first chance. Logan or Willie [Kennedy] can find out when someone will be coming. Let which ever you send have good warm clothing and bedding.[45]

Tell Willie he must stay with you all and attend to things around home.

If you have them, I would like to have some good socks.

Well, sister dear, I have written enough for once. I will write by the very next opportunity. Give my love to all the young Ladies. To Grandma give my best love and wishes. Write to me by every opportunity and let me know how you are getting along and what you think of your horse.

Goodbye, dear one, and trust we soon shall meet,
Your Devoted Brother,
Orlando

Estell Springs, Tenn.
Nov. 19th, 1862

Dear Sister,

Tonight, whilst everything is quiet and nothing is heard save the sighing by the winter winds through the dense forest and the gentle murmur of the babbling brook, I am thinking of thee, of my dear native home, the happy, happy hours I spent with you, and of the future—that awful future which has in store such varied fortunes for us all. I am thinking of my boyhood innocence—joyful days when you and I knew not what it was to be parted from each other, but were ever together in sunshine and tempest to share each other's joys and soothe each other's sorrow! I am thinking of college days and of the many pleasant acquaintances I made there, but, oh!, where are they now? Some are the tenant of the tomb; some are in the army, toiling like heroes for their country and good; whilst others, alas, have forgotten the teachings of our good President and gone the way of the world, to vice, folly, and shame.

It does one good occasionally to recall the past and the many scenes which have made so deep, so lasting, an impression, and draw encouragement and inspiration from its changing picture.

I have now gone regularly to work. The General returned yesterday and has assumed command of his brigade. He has entirely recovered from his wound and is in excellent health, looking very well. If I had known he was not coming back earlier, I could have remained at home three days longer and nothing would have given me greater satisfaction. But a soldier cannot risk these things. He must be punctual to the hour or direful may be the consequences.

I received my commission today as assistant adjutant general in the Confederate States Army, so there is no doubt now but that I shall remain with Gen. Wood. I am getting along very finely with him and am just getting into the routine of the office business. I have two excellent young men with me as clerks who are quite intelligent and very intimately acquainted with the business of the office. This renders it much easier for me than it would otherwise be. I am pleased with my position. I can learn all about the expected movements of the army and have a better opportunity to become intimately acquainted with military science than I could have in the army.

When I arrived here the General had not returned, and I called on Gen. Preston to ascertain if he knew anything of the whereabouts and probable movements of Gen. Wood. His assistant adjutant general had just left him, and he asked me to assume duty on his staff until the return of Gen. Wood. Wishing to become intimately acquainted with so distinguished a statesman, I cheerfully accepted his offer and went on duty on his staff and found him to be one of the most agreeably entertaining, intelligent, and fine men I have ever yet had the good fortune to meet with. He is so excessively clever that he you soon become easy in his company and are drawn to him by such a charm that you cannot resist it, even if you denied it. His conversational powers are unsurpassed, mixed with the finest portions of history, poetry, romance, anecdotes, and politics, all so finely and perfectly proportioned as to blend with one harmonizing whole, which attracts, amuses, and captivates. I shall never forget the few days I spent with him.[46]

I have made the acquaintance of several other of our Generals and c. and find the most of them to be excellent gentlemen.

We have no news from the enemy except that they have thrown a heavy column into Nashville, which is now garrisoned and defended by about forty thousand men, rendering the place entirely too strong for us to take, unless we sacrifice more men than adequate to the good to be derived therefrom. What we will attempt I do not know for certain, nor ought to say if I did, for we know not where this letter might go to on errant.

We can not place reliance on the mails. There is no certainty in them. I trust, however, that we should do for the best and that the country will yet have good reason to be proud of us.

I hope that the Feds will not again get into north Alabama and again disturb the quiet of my dear loved ones at home, for I think they have already been sufficiently disturbed by the destruction of our peace and happiness. But I am fearful some untoward event will again give them access to the good old home.

Not that I have any good grounds upon which to base an opinion that they will, yet my great concern for those at home is father to the unpleasant thought. I suffer more uneasiness about you than anything else. I do not want you ever again to be within the enemy's lines if it can be possibly avoided. I intend to send you some money by the first opportunity so that you will have something to go on if you desire to leave north Alabama.

I saw Frank F[oster, Jr.,] the other day and gave him a letter. He told me he had heard from Tom, that he was still at Harrodsburg and was doing well. He will soon be well and, I hope, will come down to see you. Frank is quite well, and c.

George and Marion are both very well and getting along finely. George's eye is doing very well.

Have you heard anything of your horse?

Do not forget to send your ambrotype by Oliver and tell Oliver I expect him to bring me those of two certain young ladies. He knows who.

I received a letter from Elias the other day. He is still at Marietta and doing finely.

Give my love to all the dear ones at home and all the young ladies.

Tell Uncle Jesse that I will be under lasting obligation to him if he will look after our matters while I am absent.

Write very soon and often.

Address
Capt. O. S. Palmer
Asst. Adjt. Gen.
Wood's Brig., Buckner's Div.
Tullahoma, Tenn.
Your Devoted Brother,
O. S. Palmer

Shelbyville, Tenn.
Nov. 27th, 1862

Dear Sister,

Some person is coming from Florence here almost every day—Frank Foster today. I expected a letter from some of you by some of you by some of them, but I am always turned off with the reply, "nothing for you." Yes, nothing for me. Not a word of news from home, not a word of comfort and encouragement from those I cherish. Why it is you all, or at least some of you, do not write I cannot comprehend. I was told by Mr. Leftwich . . . also by F[rank] Foster . . . that they saw Oliver. Why he could not manage to send letters for you and himself, I am at a loss to know. I have written several times and can get no response from home. Perhaps I may get some news soon. I trust so.[47]

I have not been very well for the last week. I was taken with a severe cold which threw me into a chill. I was quite sick for two days, but then I was at the residence of one of the first citizens of the town who had a daughter fair and charming. I was never treated more cleverly by anyone. Miss Maggie, the young lady in question, was by far the most agreeable, charming, and attentive [of] young ladies I have ever had the good fortune to become acquainted with. She was constantly knocking at my door, and in the softest, sweetest tones saying, "Captain, how are you doing? Is there anything I can do for you? Do not hesitate to call on me, for I am anxious to render you comforts and c."

I would very frequently tell her she could do something for me. She could come in and cheer me with her bright, sweet smile and charm me away from all thoughts of my condition with her excellent conversation. She would come in, take the chair by my side, and, oh, how good I would feel.[48]

Of course, I soon recovered under such kind, gentle treatment. I am now as well as ever before unless I am suffering from a wound in the heart, which I, of course, would not confess. I wish you could see her. When I left, she held me by the hand and looking me in the face with a winning smile told me if I got sick any more whilst near Shelbyville, I must not fail to come to her house and let her nurse me. I, of course, promised, and if I should unfortunately get sick again, I will not be slow to fulfil the promise.

We have no news here . . . nothing of interest stirring. Gen. Bragg has his line of defense drawn.[49] It is this place, Murfreesboro, and Manchester. At these points we are to contest the advance from getting any further South. I think we shall succeed, for we have a fine army and fine Generals. General Joseph E. Johnston is here or expected soon, and he comes with a splendid reputation which we all firmly believe he will sustain and add fresh laurels to his already glorious name. The army has unbounded confidence in him, and he will soon do something to confirm their confidence.[50]

I hope we will be able to hold Tennessee and thus keep northern Alabama free from the tread of the dastard Hessians. I fear there is more danger of north Alabama being disturbed by the force from Corinth than from the enemy at Nashville.

If they should approach from either quarter, there is a prospect of their getting possession of Lauderdale County. I desire most anxiously that you should leave there and go wherever you prefer, so you are outside the Yankee lines. In order that you may do this more effectually, I will send you some money. I do not know how much now, but will send you all I can spare, and I desire you to save it for a flight from the Yankees and then use it as your own.

I understand you have gotten your horse. Is it true? If so, how do you like him?

Tell Oliver that Gen. Wood says he will come up here and report himself to the General. Advise him not to come, however, until he has recovered his health. If he comes, tell him to bring me a good hairbrush and coarse comb as mine were lost while I was gone. Do not forget this, for I cannot get them any[where] here.

I am doing finely. Have employment to occupy my time and prevent my mind from dwelling on the many fruitless objects of contemplation which idleness will produce. I have not written to Miss Ada, but I will when I shall ascertain that there is a mail line to Lawrenceburg. If you find out anything about her whereabouts, you must let me know.

Nov. 28th. There was a pretty heavy skirmish in front of Murfreesboro yesterday, which, however, resulted in nothing of any consequence.

I have hired George to Frank Foster for $20 per month and will send you the proceeds.

You must write to me by the very first opportunity, for I am anxious to hear from you. Tell Oliver and Delia to do the same.

I have not heard anything of Tom since I wrote you before. He was doing very well when I heard from him. He will return soon, I think.

I send you one hundred and fifty dollars which you can use as you think proper. I make you a present of it to fly from the Yanks if necessary.

My love to all.
Address
O. S. Palmer
Asst. Adjt. Gen.
Wood's Brig.
Shelbyville, Tenn.
Your devoted Brother,
O. S. Palmer

Shelbyville, Tenn.
Dec. 3rd, 1862

Dear Sister,

I have written to you repeatedly since leaving home, but not a line have I yet received from you or any one at home. But nothing daunted, I write again hoping that I shall yet have the good fortune to hear from you sometime.

I am quite well and doing finely. I am head and ears in love with the young lady I wrote to you about taking such good care of me while I was sick. I see her every day and like her better, if possible, every time I meet her. She is the "Belle" of the place and one of the most charming creatures I ever saw. However, I shall not attempt to make her your sister until after this horrid war winds itself to a glorious close.

We are having a gay time here. We have a party every other night almost. There is to be one tomorrow night to which I am invited. I don't know whether I shall go or not. I think, however, I shall. If we can stay here this winter, I will enjoy it hugely.

We have no military news here of importance. There has been some skirmishing in front of Murfreesboro, which, however, resulted in nothing of importance. Everything is quiet, but I fear it is only the calm that precedes the storm. I think in less than four weeks we will have a battle here or near here. It may not come off, but I think it will.

We may fall back to Bridgeport and there fight them, but I think Gen. Bragg intends to contest every inch of the soil and hold this country if possible. I do not know, nor can I imagine what will be the final result of the matter at this point.

Tell Oliver that Gen. Wood says he must, as soon as he is able, go to Jackson or Chattanooga or come to this place and use every exertion to effect his exchange.

I have no time to write more.

Give my love to all and write soon.

Your brother,

O. S. Palmer

Write to me at this place.

Triune, Tenn.
Dec. 9th, 1862

Dear Sister,

I have written time and again since leaving home and not the scratch of a pen have I received from any of you. It seems that everybody can hear from home but poor unfortunate me. No sweet missive from home comes freighted with good news to cheer my hours of gloom and despondency. Strange, passing strange it is that none of you write to me, or if you do that your letters do not reach me. There is constantly someone passing from Lauderdale to this part of the army, and they bring a great many letters, but none can I get. This very singular silence renders me uneasy, and a thousand fears constantly haunt me like grim specters with their hideous forms. I know that out in the country, where you are, there is very little opportunity for you to see anyone passing to the army, but what is there to prevent you from sending your letters to Florence and have them forwarded from that point? I hope soon to receive a whole bundle of letters to make up for this long and unexplained silence.

We moved from Shelbyville to this place some four or five days since. We are on outpost duty in advance of the entire corps, but not in the immediate presence of the enemy.

Gen. Wharton with a brigade of cavalry is some ten miles in our front and within ten miles of Nashville.[51] He is guarding our front in a most gallant style. We know that while the brave Texan with his chivalrous command confronts the enemy and protects us, we are secure from all harm and cannot be surprised.

He has some skirmishing with the enemy every day, but nothing of importance has yet transpired on our immediate front. The army is gradually moving up and closing in on Nashville, thus shutting the enemy up in their chosen position. Whether we will advance and attempt to drive them from their stronghold, or they will advance on us in order to secure freedom to their movements is a question now of importance and doubt. No one knows which party will assume the aggressive. We are now on the stand-still; so are they. Each party is standing quietly, looking fearfully and doubtingly at the antagonist. The wary combatants are intently watching the movements of each other in order to take advantage of some unguarded point and thus, by seizing the opportune moment, hurl his opponent to the ground and come victor in the great impending struggle.

We have news of a most brilliant exploit of the indomitable Morgan. He went across Cumberland River a few days since and attacked the enemy at Hartsville, defeated them, captured 800 men with all their arms and accoutrements, a large amount of supplies and wagons, and recrossed the river pursued by 8000 of the enemy. He brought off everything he captured and only lost in the engagement 50 men while the enemy's loss in killed and wounded was much heavier than this. This was one of the most dashing adventures of the war and will add new laurels to his already glorious name.[52]

There is something strange about this mans' success. He has never met with a reverse but always comes off with triumph, victor in every battle. Destiny has surely pointed him out as the great partisan warrior of the Revolution. If all our generals were as successful as him, we would soon drive the vandals from our soil and peace would spread her bright banner and, oh, what a thrill of joy would vibrate through the heart of this great country.

Gen. Joseph E. Johnston is at Murfreesboro and a more confident tone pervades the army than before, although I was well satisfied with Gen. Bragg. I am not disposed to join in the clamor against him. I think he is all right and will prove it.

My love to Delia, Georgia, Burton, Grandma, and everybody.[53]

Write soon and often.

Where is Oliver?
Your devoted Brother,
O. S. Palmer

Received of Orlando S. and Artimisia Palmer, twenty three hundred dollars for two Slaves, viz: Jesse—aged 16 years—and Belle—aged 6 years—in exchange of lots [*word illegible*] division of slaves—which titles I warrant to be good. In testimony whereof I have this day—11th December 1862—hereunto set my name and seal.
 E. R. Kennedy *Seal*

Triune, Tenn.
Dec. 11th, 1862

Dear Sister,

Lieut. Andrews goes to Florence this evening. I drop you a note to inform you that I am still in the land of the living and have not heard a word from you since I left home.[54]

We are doing finely, having some little excitement and fun with the Yankees. Gen. Wharton, who is in our front, occasionally giving them a little thunder in the way of shot and shell.

We are on outpost and have so much to do that we have no time to do anything save to visit the women. There are a great many pretty ones around here and we have a glorious time with them. I am ordered out by the General to see them all and invite them to Review this evening. I am in love with several dozen of them and am having a huge time generally. We are going to have a Ball at our headquarters soon. Come up and join us in the amusements of this section in camp life.[55]

I wrote to you all the news yesterday by Mr. Hooks.[56] I sent you a hundred and fifty dollars by Dan Coleman.[57] Did you get it? Have you got your horse?

I have not heard anything from Tom. I think he will return in a few days, and I will send him to you for instructions.

Lieut. Andrews will return in a few days. You must write to me soon and often, giving me all the news.

My love to Delia, Georgia, Burton, Jennie F., and Jennie E., and all the good people at home.

I am interrupted and cannot write more now.

Goodbye and may God bless you.

Your Brother,

O. S. Palmer

Triune, Tenn.
Dec. 13th, 1862

Dear Sister,

Capt. Bailey starts home in a few minutes and I write to inform you that I am well.[58] I have not heard one word from you or any one at home since I left there. Why do you not write? I am very uneasy. I do not know what to think.

No news except that President Davis is at Murfreesboro reviewing the troops in the Department. I have not seen him. I think he will be here tomorrow.[59]

Joe Johnston is here also. There must be something of importance to be done here as so many great men have turned their attention to this point.

I think we will have a great battle somewhere near here soon. I think we will whip them and soon be in Nashville, before Christmas any way. There is a skirmish in front every day. Our cavalry engages them almost every day. We had several killed yesterday.

All right.
My love to all.
Write soon.
Goodbye and may God bless you.
Your Brother,
Orlando

[Oliver S. Kennedy to Georgia Foster]
Chattanooga, Tennessee
Dec. 18th, 1862

My Dear Georgie,

I wrote you from Huntsville by Father but thought I would write again as your father is going directly to Florence. I saw him soon as I arrived at the hotel. He informed me he was going to carry your trunk for you—that he had had found it. So that prevents me having that pleasure. I had intended sending to Mr. Lawrence Watkins in care of Maj. Jones and request them to forward it to Florence, but none of this would have been the safest as there is great uncertainty about transportation of baggage on the R. Roads now. I am glad you will be certain to get it now.

I met your uncle, Gen'l R. C. Foster, at the hotel.[60] Was introduced to him by your father. I have seen him several times in Nashville but had not been introduced. I like him very much. He is going to Florence to spend the Christmas.

I wish so much I could be with you all Christmas. You will enjoy it, I know. Do you intend spending any of Christmas with old Col. Goode? If so, you will have a nice time as he always has mirth and gaiety around him when the youthful throng round his board.

From all I can learn here, it will be some time before there will be an exchange of prisoners, and I know not what to do. Col. Wood ordered me here to be exchanged, but I see nothing to be gained by remaining in camps here two or three months. So, under the circumstances I do not know what to do. I dislike the idea of staying in camps with strangers in the cold and rain and c. of winter when nothing is to be gained. Gen'l Wood has given me the privilege of coming here, going to Jackson, or coming to the Brigade. So, I shall look around here today and if I can do nothing else, I will report to Gen'l Wood and ask permission to go to Grand Ma's until exchanged. The impression here is that there will not be an exchange before spring. It would be so much better to spend the winter with those I love at home than being in camp here with strangers. If it is possible, I am going to come down and spend the winter. If I do not, it will not be my fault, for I am anxious to come and shall use every endeavor. I will report for duty, however, if there is any chance to be exchanged, I shall effect it and report to my Regiment for duty.

Evening: I have been to report to Lt. McIntosh and find there are no exchanges going on here. So, if I am exchanged, I will have to go to Vicksburg or Va., I suppose.

If I can get the proper authority here, I am coming back and will be there by Christmas. I do not know what to do. I am almost tempted to go to Va.

Your father will give you all the news.

Give my kindest regards to Jennie and be certain to tell her I regretted very much not seeing her before leaving.

My respects to Judge Foster's family.

In haste, but much love. I remain

Yours,

O. S. Kennedy

Triune, Tenn.
Dec. 21st, 1862

Dear Sister,

I have written home so often and can get no response that I am discouraged to so great an extent that I do not feel much like writing. I cannot imagine why I have not heard from you. I know you have written, for I cannot believe that you would allow so long a time to elapse without letting me hear from you. I am uneasy—very. I fear that all is not as I could wish at home.

I am in excellent health and doing as well as heart could wish. We are on outpost duty and have just enough excitement to prevent time from hanging heavily on my hands. Brig. Gen. Wharton, the gallant Texan, is in our front and at all times, ready—yes, eager—to give the enemy such a reception as he deserves. He occasionally has a skirmish. He had one today. His pickets were attacked by a vastly superior force and driven some 2½ miles with the loss of some 2 killed, 4 wounded, and 3 or 4 captured.[61]

I was sent out to the front to gather information of the enemy's movements and probable strength. I mounted "Mark," my gallant steed, and sped on the wings of the wind to the front. After dashing along in a sweeping lope for seven miles I found Gen. Wharton.

He told me that the enemy had retired and that he had sent a gallant band of one thousand men in pursuit of him. He expected to overtake them and revenge the death of his brave comrades. I was anxious to go with him and witness a cavalry fight, but I was compelled to come back and report the state of affairs to the General. I have no doubt but he will have a fight tonight and he will punish them severely, for he was very mad when I saw him. The loss of his two men seemed to hurt him very much. He is a gallant man. I have taken a great fancy to him.

We see men or women, one, from Nashville every day who inform us that the city is very strongly fortified, and that the enemy are about forty thousand strong, making every preparation for a desperate resistance. They do not think we will attack them, nor do I. They will not attack us for some time yet. They would do so now, but they cannot. It is absolutely impossible for them to advance. You will see from the following statement. All their provisions have to be brought by the N[ashville] & L[ouisville] R.R., and in so large an army as they have at Nashville, between there and Louisville they consume the supplies almost as fast as they can arrive. They have not more than six days' rations on hand, and as long as this is the case, they cannot advance.

When the [Tennessee] River becomes navigable, then they can advance, but how far Gen. Bragg will permit them to come is another question. He may throw some obstacles in the way, which they cannot overcome. Their movement may and will be somewhat retarded by a band of as brave hearts as the world ever knew. We have a fine army, eager to encounter the enemy and revenge our wrongs.

Maj. Gen. Buckner has been assigned to the command of the Department of the Gulf and Maj. Gen. Cleburne commands his Division. I was in hope that Gen. Wood would go to the coast with Gen. Buckner, for I have become very much attached to Buckner and I have more confidence in him than any of them. I had rather fight under him than any other General in the service.[62]

I wrote you about my falling in love at Shelbyville. I have forgotten the old love (two weeks standing) and falling desperately in love with a red-haired girl from Nashville. I am desperately smitten with her charming manners, her intellectual attainments, her mild eye beaming with truth and love and sweet pouting lips. She had banished the image of Miss Maggie Whitesides from my heart and hers is there instead. She lives about four hundred yards from our headquarters, and I can slip off and spend a few short moments in her charming company at any time.

Half of the 16th Alabama is in love with her, but I flatter myself that I am ahead of any of them—that I stand higher in her estimation than any other man.[63] It may be that they all think the same, so you see, Sister, I am not without a sweetheart, no matter where I am.

I have not heard one word from anybody since I left home. I cannot learn anything in reference to Tom. I am of the opinion, however, that he is well by this time and probably at home. I would go over to his regiment and see if I could not learn something from him, but it is so far off that I cannot get there.

Bill has arrived here. He tells me you have got your horse. I am glad of it. How is he doing and how do you like him?

I bought me a fine horse the other day. Gave three hundred dollars for him. He is the best saddle horse I ever saw. I loped him seven miles today and it did not hurt him in the least, so, you see, the Yanks cannot catch me.

How and where is Uncle Spinks and Jesse, Aunts Mary and Olive, Delia, Misses Georgia, Burton, Jennie, and c., and c., and c.? When you do write, give me all the news, for I have not heard from any of you since I left home.

Tell Delia to write.
My love to all.
Your devoted Brother,
Orlando S. Palmer
George and Marion are well and send love to their mothers.
Address
O. S. Palmer

Adjt. Gen., Wood's Brigade
Cleburne's Division
Murfreesboro, Tenn.

[Oliver Sylvester Kennedy to Artimisia Palmer
Undated]

Miss Missie,

Excuse this folly of my wandering muse. I mean by addressing Miss Missie instead of Cousin Missie, for I have just arrived at home once more after my long absence of 3 months and, oh!, ye lovers, listen to what I have to say. On arriving at home, I found that my hopes were departed forever, for another gent of Ripley [i.e., Thomas B. Winston] had stepped in before me and was going to make the confession that he had her "ugly" [ambro] type in his possession, and, moreover, that he carried it with him wherever he went. So, he must be taking on considerably! Don't you think so? If you don't, I know who does. Kennedy does.

But, after all, I really don't believe my heart will break with woe.

For if she's a mind to love that chap, why, just let her rip.[64]

I like to have made a rhyme, didn't I?

Panthea [Narcissa Kennedy] is coming up there the first opportunity, she says.[65] She wants to go back with us all, but there is no way for her to go.

I have not yet seen your sweetheart yet. I will see him Christmas, I suspect. Answer this, and when I see him I will answer your letter.

My love to all.

As ever, your true cousin,

O[liver] S[ylvester] K[ennedy]

Triune, Tenn.
Dec. 23rd, 1862

Dear Sister,

I was for the first time greeted with a long letter from you, which gave me great pleasure and relief. I was sorry to learn that Delia was sick, but glad to know that she was improving so fast and trust when I hear from you again that she will be entirely well.

I am to infer from your letter that you are well, but you say nothing about the state of your health. I am confident if you were unwell your candor would not allow you to conceal. I am glad that you have your horse back but am surprised that you have never rode him. I sent him to you for you to ride him every day for your health and pleasure and to revive your drooping spirits. There is nothing so exciting and so well calculated to drive away care and sorrow as a rapid ride on horseback. Then it is the most healthy exercise in the world. I insist that you take time to ride some every day. It will do you good and it is my earnest desire that you try it.

As to your exchange of lots in negroes, I am perfectly satisfied. I think you have done very well. I am not disposed to demur from any of your actions. I do think, however, that Uncle Enoch ought to have had more respect and feeling for you than to attempt to force you into an exchange by his violent manner. Nothing could justify him in so doing and I am sorry he did so.[66]

As for the property, I care nothing for that as far as I am individually concerned. I can carve my fortune out of the rough world and will do it, but I am determined as long as I live to see that you, my sweet, lonely sister, have your every right. I am satisfied that Uncle Spinks, Wesley, and Jesse advise you for the best and that you were right in following this advice.

As to the money I sent you by Capt. Coleman, I can tell you where it is.[67] He gave it to Lt. Andrews who left it at Mrs. Dr. [Mary] Crittenden's. I have no doubt that the money is there for you now, and if you have not got it yet, send down there at once and see why they have not sent it to you. I trust you will get it, for I want you to use it in the manner I specified if no necessity should arise.

I know that you are very lonesome at home, and I do not know what you will do when Delia goes home. You and her ought to stay together, and, if possible, I desire that you do so. You are very much attached to each other and I would dislike to see you and she separated.

You look upon the future as gloomy and with no happiness in store for you as it is for all of us, but then, you should not look upon the future as gloomy and with no happiness in store for you. Sister mine, I know this is a dark hour for you as it is for all of us, but then you should not look upon the future as containing nothing of happiness for you. I hope . . . I believe, yes, I know there is a happy future for you.

Cheer up, dear Sister. Yield not to the dark thoughts which continually present themselves. I believe that your fear as to Tom are without foundation. I have no doubt but that he is very nearly well by this time and will soon land amongst us safe and sound. I have not heard a word from him since what I wrote about Frank hearing from him. He saw Col. Hunt who told him that he had heard from Tom and that he was doing well. Also, that he, Col. Hunt, was going to have Tom made major of his regt.[68] I have not seen Frank since that occasion, nor do I know where he is or anything about him. I am sorry he has not written to D[elia]. I do not know why he has not. Probably he does not have an opportunity to send a letter. He may be where he cannot find anyone passing to Florence.

I have forgotten my Shelbyville sweetheart and have fallen in love with a Miss S[allie] Davis who lives in about four hundred yards of our headquarters. She is a charming creature, and what is more, she is very intelligent and thinks your Brother is one of the greatest fellows in the world. She writes better than any girl of her age I ever met with. She is really a lady of genius. I showed her your letter and this was her reply. "Your sister's letter is so sweet and melancholy. Dear Missie! I know she is very lonely." She told me to give you her love and tell you she was anxious to see you and sympathized with you in your troubles. She truly loves you from what I have told her of you. I wish you were here to see and love her. I know you would like each other.

We have most glorious news. Seward and Burnside, say Northern papers, have resigned and say they are willing to recognize us.[69] At the battle of Sharpsburg they acknowledge they were terribly whipped with the loss of nearly twenty thousand men.[70] It is also stated that Forrest whipped the enemy at Corinth, all of which is good news for us—very good.[71]

I have not heard one word from Uncle Enoch lately. He is at Marietta, Ga., however, and was well when I heard from him last. I am still doing very well and am doing finely. Give my love to all and write soon.

Marion and George are well and anxious to see Jesse. Send him along by Capt. J. J. Bailey or anyone passing.[72]

Write soon and let me know that you have thrown off the gloomy thought which seem to have settled down upon your mind.

Goodbye and God bless you.
Your devoted Brother,
O. S. Palmer

* * *

Following his wounding at Perryville, Thomas B. Winston applied for a certificate "on which to ground an application for a leave of absence." The board of examining surgeons meeting at Jackson, Mississippi, found that he was "unfit for duty" and on 26 December 1862 granted him a convalescent leave of sixty days, "at the expiration of which time he will report to his regiment or be considered a DESERTER." On 23 January 1863, however, the post surgeon at Selma, Alabama, extended his furlough for a further fifty days.[73]

On 24 October, Maj. Gen. William Starke Rosecrans relieved Don Carlos Buell as commander of the Army of the Ohio, which Rosecrans renamed as the Army of the Cumberland. Rosecrans slowly followed the retreat of the Army of Tennessee after Braxton Bragg's barren victory at Perryville.

Early in November he moved south out of Nashville toward Murfreesboro, Tennessee, to which Bragg had retreated, arriving on 29 December, but before he could attack the formidable Rebel defenses, Bragg launched his own attack on 31 December. In a letter to his mother, Lt. Alfred M. Moore, the adjutant of the Thirty-Third Alabama Infantry, Wood's brigade, told how "we drove the Yankees a long ways, and slept that night on the battlefield. Where we slept, the Yankees were lying dead all around and a good many wounded ones, but most of the wounded had been carried to the hospital. Our men found a great many things the Yankees left on the field. A great many knapsacks were left by them piled up before going into the battle, and our men took all of these. . . . They are nicely fixed up, and have everything you can imagine." Although successful in driving back the right wing of the Union army, the Rebel assault failed to break Rosecrans's line, nor did it interdict the Union supply line to Nashville, as Bragg had hoped.[74]

On 2 January 1863, Bragg renewed his offensive, launching an unsuccessful attack against the well-defended Union left flank. Rosecrans received reinforcements, and, realizing that the tide of battle had turned against him, and with the concurrence of corps commanders Hardee and Polk, Bragg withdrew his army from the field to Tullahoma, Tennessee. "On the night of the third, about 12 o'clock," wrote Lieutenant Moore, "our brigade was withdrawn from the front and we commenced to move from Murfreesboro." Once again, as at Perryville, Bragg had turned a tactical victory into a strategic defeat.[75]

Albert Sidney Johnston

Braxton Bragg

Sterling Alexander Martin Wood and Staff. Orlando Palmer is seated on the left.

Patrick Cleburne

*Flag of the 1st/15th Arkansas Infantry.
Courtesy of the Old State House Museum, Little Rock, Arkansas.*

Joseph Johnston

John Bell Hood

Mark Lowery

William Hardee

Thomas Brown Winston

Thomas Brown Winston, c. 1900

Oliver Sylvester Kennedy

The Battle of Mill Springs

The Battle of Nashville

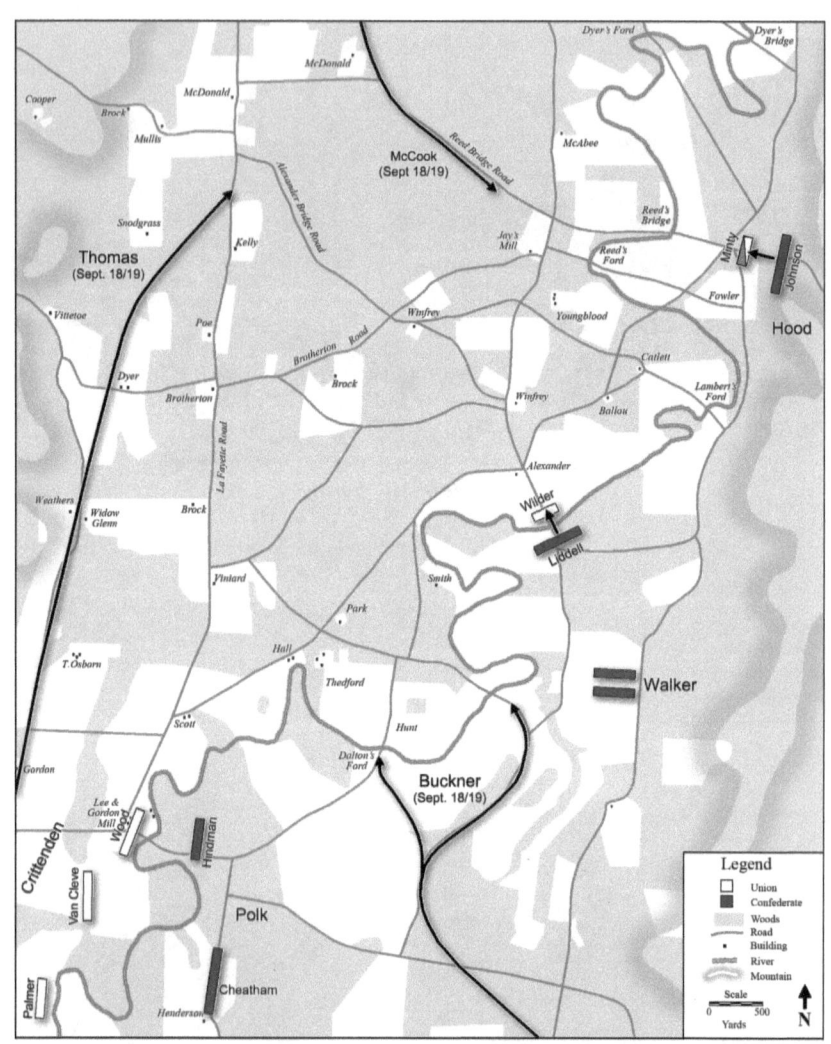

*Overall troop positions at the outset of the Battle of Chickamauga.
Map by David Friedrichs.*

Chapter 4
1863

"This Dark and Troublesome Time"

Tullahoma, Tenn.
Feb. 3rd, 1863

Dear Sister,

As Capt. Simpson is going directly home, I will again write you, although I have written so very often and not one word had been received in response to any one of the several letters. Why I have not heard from you I cannot imagine. Others are getting sweet missives laden with good news from dear ones at home, every day, and their hearts are made happy and gay by their reception, whilst I in vain enquire of everyone arriving from North Alabama and send to the P.O. every evening and am always disappointed with a sad heart full of grief and chagrin at my great disappointment.

I turn me again to my work with a resolute purpose to drive away care and sorrow with constant close attention to my duties. How anxiously I have expected to hear from you, no one can tell who has not been in the army and experienced its loneliness, its utter desolation of everything like home comforts and joys, can tell. It is the reception of delightful script missives from those we hold dearest and in whom our whole interest is concentrated that brings around the heart the warm comforts and social pleasures of home, and when we are denied them, the heart, cold and icy, contracts into itself and thoughts, bitter and cheerless, falls back upon its own dark recesses and dwells with an anguish upon the cruel and disagreeable realities of the dull, joyless camp life.

If I could but hear from you regularly, I would be contented and happy. You are the only being in whom my heart's purest, warmest, and entire feeling is all concentrated. I have no fair lady love with whom my affection for you is divided. No; I have no sweetheart, no fair creature of whom to dream and to whom to dedicate my whole thoughts and affections, as most young men have. In this I may be more unfortunate than they, but nevertheless, it is true, but I think I am fortunate in not being classed with those who are constantly harassed with doubts as to the truth and constancy of their Dulcineas.[1] I can repose with constancy and without fear upon your love, your affection, and your sympathy.

But away with all this. It is tiresome to you, and I will change the theme, but to what? That's the question. Ah. I have it. I know. I will get your attention now. I received a letter from Tom yesterday. It was the second I had gotten from him. He was still at Dr. Rivers.' Was very well but could not leave [Sylvanus William "Doc"] Perry who was still quite sick. He expected to come up in a short time, and, I have no doubt, is with you by this time, and how happy you then must be, and I, for sooth, must be happy too since you are.

I wrote to you several times about having heard from Oliver, but as you have not answered any of my letters, I fear you have not gotten them. His arm is still weak and in no condition to again go back into the ranks. I think he ought to get some position in the Quarter Master's Department or somewhere where he can take good care of himself. He could get in with Uncle Elias, who is at Chattanooga, and, I think, should do so. Tell him when he starts back to the army to come by and see Elias and ask him if he has any place he can give him. In the meantime, I will write to Elias and see what he can do for him.

I hope I will be able to get him some place where he will be pleasantly situated and where he will have an easier time than he has had heretofore. I will write to him soon and tell what I can have ascertained. But if he does not hear from me, he must come by to see Elias anyway.

We have been looking for Oliver for several days. He has been written to frequently to return and I cannot tell why he has not done so, but I suppose he is so taken with his young, charming, sweet wife that he cannot leave her, and he has forgotten the stern and strict rules of the military law. He ought to return immediately if he does not wish to get into trouble.[2]

He married and did not even send me a note informing me that he was to marry and invite me to attend. It is true, he knew that I could not come, but still, he might have paid me the empty compliment of inviting me. This would not have troubled him much. Nevertheless, I wish him and his fair bride all the happiness this troublesome, stormy world contains. May soft joys decked in gay and gaudy flowers dance attendance to their footsteps and the joyous sunshine of happiness ever be with them.

I wish that I could have been there at the time. I might have found some charming creature and fallen in love with her and perhaps formed an attachment for her which might soon have had the same happy consummation as Oliver.

But, alas! Imperative duty holds me closely to my post and I must not let go, even to secure that which might prove my greatest blessing here below. However, I will not repine at the stark duties which detain me here. I feel that I am doing all in my power to prevent the vile invaders from again disturbing the peace and happiness of those who are nearest and dearest to me. I feel that I am doing my whole duty to my country and the great interest involved in the mighty struggle. Hence my conscience is easy and I care not.

Then, too, Miss B.[erta?] has failed to answer the letter I wrote to have her dream come true. I did not wish her to be disappointed in her expectations, hence I wrote without even expecting a reply. I knew she cared nothing for me and that she did not desire to hear from me. But why she should send me such a message when she did not intend to reply, I have not yet been able to tell. Perhaps your woman's heart and ingenuity can solve this mystery for me, and I trust you will inform me of the secret of the matter when next you write. Although she has treated me with so great discourtesy, please to present her my compliments when next you see her and tell her I shall not cease to think kindly, friendly, of her, and that she cannot expect any warmer feeling after such unkind treatment of the unfortunate missives I, in an ill-advised moment, sent her.

Has Miss J[ennie] E. married the gentleman from Tippah, or has she reconsidered the matter and concluded to wait for the soldier who has used his utmost—and endeavors to prevent the enemy from despoiling her happy home?

How is Miss Polk? As happy, as joyous and pretty as ever, I trust. Give her my best respects and tell her I often think of her. Remember me, also, to Miss Mollie, Bettie, and c., and c.[3]

I send you files of the latest Southern papers, so it is useless for me to say anything of the general news. Gen. Johnston is here. I have seen him several times. He is quite a military looking little man, and I think under his and Bragg's care this army will be all right and will yet convince the enemy that we are able to whip him anywhere and will do so.[4] Since Gen. J. arrived here, we have commenced to fortify. This is proof sufficient that we are not going to leave here without one more effort to hold Tennessee. Rosecrans, on his part, evinces no disposition to move forward. Everything at Murfreesboro is as quiet as we could wish. We can hear of no preparation on the part of the enemy to advance, whilst we are making every arrangement to give him a warm reception when he does come. The signs of the times, however, indicate important movements and mighty battles. Soon we expect to hear of another terrible conflict at Vicksburg and to hear the welcome shout of victory.

Another important battle must soon be fought in Virginia, and we do not fear but that Lee will again hurl them back. In N. Carolina and South Carolina, the shock of the contending hosts will be felt, and the clash of arms be heard and the glorious sounds of triumph again float upon the joyous air of Dixie.

If we are successful at all these points, and there is every prospect that we will be, almost all are agreed that we will then have peace, but if we are not victorious at all these places, the war may draw itself out for several years yet to come.

God grant that we may be victorious at all points and that peace may soon smile upon our distracted land and render our now desolate land happy, free, and prosperous!

In speaking of peace, I cannot but think of Miss S. D[avis]. I have not heard from her for some time now. The Yankees have cut all communications with Triune off. I am denied the pleasure of her soul-cheering letters. She writes better letters than any I have ever received except from Miss Ada. I hope I will soon hear from her again and have my heart cheered by her magic pen.

If you have not sent me the quilts written for some time ago, please do so at the earliest opportunity. I wish that you would knit me some cotton socks for summer and send them to me by the last of April or as soon as you can have them completed.

How is your horse doing and how do you like him? I trust you find him a good riding horse and perfectly gentle.

Send Jessie to me the first opportunity. I can hire him to a good man at any time for much more than you can get from him there. George and Marion are both well and send their love to their mothers.

My love to Grandma, Uncle Jesse, and Aunt Olive, and tell Delia that she must consider this letter as much to her as you, and write to me. Frank is very well. Capt. Simpson will return in ten or twelve days and has promised to call at Uncle Jesse's for letters and c. for me. Please write me a long letter by him.

With much love,
Your affectionate Brother,
Orlando S. Palmer

Huntsville, Ala.
Feb. 8th, 1863

Dear Sister,

The General and staff and 500 men arrived here yesterday. The General is assigned to duty here to defend the Tennessee Valley. You may expect to hear from us soon. We will send off cavalry in pursuit of the marauders and hope to be able to punish them severely for their impudence and insolence.

We do not know how long we may remain here . . . probably some time, however.

The red-haired girl is well. I have heard from her twice. I am afraid she is a flirt—at least I hope so.

Give my love to all and write soon.
Your Brother,
O. S. Palmer

Hd. Qtrs, Wood's Brigade
Tullahoma, Tennessee
Feb. 8th, 1863

Dear Sister,

Last night for the first time since the opening of the year I was kindly greeted with two very welcome letters from you and a note from Delia! I need not say how happy I was to receive them and how my soul was rejoiced and gladdened at their reception. The cloud of sorrow which for some time had hung like an incubus on my soul was cleared away and the bright, joyous sunshine of love and pleasures entered and repaid me for all the suffering I had endured. I thank you from the bottom of my heart.

I thank you for the sweet words of affection and encouragement and endeavor to show my gratitude by replying on the instant. I was rejoiced to learn that you were well and had had such a calm, quiet, happy time at Mr. [William Lytle or Benjamin Franklin] Foster's and was so highly pleased with that elegant and accomplished family. More particularly, with a certain fair maiden whose lovely image, quiet, unassuming, polished manners and great attainments often occupy a very large portion of my thoughts. I trust that your connection with them will be a source of great pleasure to you.[5]

I am sorry to learn that Oliver is still sick and hope that the kind attention and devoted love of his fair young bride will soon restore him to health and send him, doubly strong, to do battle for his great country in this, her hour of greatest peril.

I never received his dispatch inviting me to attend and officiate as one of his attendants with his charming cousin, but it would have been impossible for me to have come. No leaves of absence for matters of this sort are granted by Gen. Bragg. It would have been a great satisfaction to have been there and enjoyed for even a few fleeting hours the society of the elegant young ladies who were there in all their pride of beauty and loveliness. But a higher duty than that of seeking the pleasure of soft enjoyments of this world called me. My country, in this, her hour of gloom and imminent peril, appeals to every principle of manhood and with outstretched, bleeding hands implores every one of her sons to fly to her assistance. Can I, should I, for one hour desert my post?

You speak of committing matrimony when a certain gentleman very dear to you arrives. I can only say such a course would meet with my hearty and cordial approval in every particular. Consult your own heart and good sense, then act accordingly. I am sure you will act for the best.

You desire to know if Gen. Wood would permit me to come if you were to marry. In reply, I say after consulting him, that it will be impossible for me to come without a permit from General Bragg. No one can leave the army without the authority of the Commanding General. I do not know whether he would give me the authority or not. Gen. Wood will approve and recommend, but then, whether the other Generals will or not is a very doubtful question.

It seems that there are only two pleas on which a man can get away from here. One on Surgeon's Certificate and the other to go off and marry. If you can arrange all the preliminaries, have the day set, and c., with the lovely girl you would like to call sister, I can then ground my application on that with some prospects of having it approved by Gen. Bragg. Now what say you? Can you arrange this match satisfactorily to all parties? I am now willing for you to intervene in the affair and am anxious to know what success you will meet with.[6]

It would certainly be a great pleasure to you, as well as to myself, for me to be present at your marriage, but then, if it is not possible you need not permit my absence to prevent the consummation of that which you so devoutly desire. Do not hesitate on account of my inability to come. You know that although I may be absent, you will have my best wishes for your perfect happiness and will have my warmest blessing. However, do not fail to dispatch to me when it will come off. I will use every effort to come, and it may be possible at that time for me to get off.

You ask me if I don't wish I had a nice wife. Candidly, I answer "yes" and would consider myself the happiest of mortals did I possess the pure, warm, trusting heart of some fair creature whose only effort it would be to promote my happiness and on whose sympathizing heart could, with confidence, repose in hours of grief and storm. I am not disposed to be a bachelor any longer ... too long even now have I been without that greatest treasure of earth, a wife, and rest assured, I shall avail myself of the first good opportunity to get me one.

You and Miss B___ think I am a "great flirt," and she arrives at that conclusion from letters you have shown her from me. I am sorry my communications were so wrongfully, unjustly interpreted by you and her. I was only playing with my pen on that subject for want of another, to amuse and entertain, not for a moment thinking that anyone would consider me in earnest.

I regret that you, too, in particular, should form such a cruel opinion of my character. She must, indeed, consider me a terrible monster, without heart or one manly, honest impulse or principle, and under the inspiration of this new light I understand why she has refused to answer my letter. Please convince her that I am not such a horrible monster as she thinks and reinstate me in her good opinion. I like and miss her very much and would be pleased to correspond with her. Tell her that if she could not answer my letter as a friend, I expect her to do so now, as I am her Cousin. Surely, she will not fear her unworthy cousin and can condescend to occasionally render him happy by writing him an interesting, friendly letter. Remember me kindly to her.

We have no news here. The same ominous quiet prevails. The storm is silently, slowly gathering its fury and the battle cloud may soon burst with terrible fierceness over our devoted heads. We are preparing for it by throwing up fortifications very rapidly. I will keep you informed of what is going on here.

Marion and George want to know how their mothers are, to whom they are hired, and how getting along.

Tell Oliver and Georgie I am particularly waiting for them to answer my letter and would be happy to hear from them.

Delia's letter was promptly delivered. I will write to her soon.

My love to Grandma, Oliver, Georgia, Delia, Aunt Olive, and c., and c.
Write soon and often to
your devoted Brother,
O. S. Palmer

Huntsville, Ala.
April 11th, 1863

Dear Brother and Sister,[7]

As I have an opportunity of sending you a note, I write, although there is nothing of importance or interest to communicate. It is true, there has been a terrible bombardment at Charleston, but there was no one hurt on our side. Beauregard sunk one of their boats and drove them off in handsome style. This is of no consequence except that it gives the enemy some idea of our readiness to meet them at that point and give them a warm, proper reception whenever they choose to visit the Charlestonians.[8]

Everything in army circles seems to be remarkably quiet. No movement on either side of any consequence. We now have the lull before the terrible storm which is fast approaching and must burst in all its fury soon. The crisis of the Confederacy is now near at hand, and we must meet it like men who are determined to be free, or we will sink beneath the fierce fury of the storm which now calashes the waves roughly against our battlements.

I have no fears as to the noble commander of the Army of Tennessee. He will be able to breast the fury of the storm as "the rock in mid-ocean that braves the rush of whirlwinds and crash of waves." He is ready for them and will hurl them back.

I know nothing as to the condition of affairs elsewhere. I trust we are ready and prepared at all points to give the enemy such a thrashing as their many evil deeds entitle them to.

Uncle Elias is at Courtland . . . left here the day before we got here. He is well and hard at work trying to get the corn out of the valley. I do not know whether he has heard from the communication in reference to the detail or not. I will write him about it this evening.

I do not know when I shall see dear old Lauderdale again. I am anxious that we should come back to that section where we have spent so many happy hours. But duty alone must now be listened to. Farewell for a while to pleasure.

Write me soon and often. I want to hear from you regularly and desire you to let no opportunity pass without writing.

My love to Grandma and all the rest.

Your affectionate Brother,

O. S. Palmer

I go to see Miss Sue M. this evening, and I think I will propose. What think you of her character and the match's prospects?

Tullahoma, Tenn.
April 17th, 1863

Dear Brother and Sister,

I have but a moment in which to write. I wrote you just before leaving Huntsville and gave you what news we then had. Since that, nothing of very great importance except the capture of a train of cars between Murfreesboro and Nashville by [Maj. Gen. Joseph] Wheeler, taking several prisoners, amongst whom were several of Rosecrans' staff.

Van Dorn had another fight at Franklin in which he and Forrest were slightly worsted, but they sustained the high character of the cavalry for daring and impetuosity. It was quite a severe and gallant fight for cavalry to make, and such as we seldom hear of.[9]

Everything is quiet here, work on the fortifications still going on. This place is now strongly fortified and will soon be much more so. They are being strengthened and enlarged every day. If we fight here, it will be greatly to our advantage and with anything like half the force of the enemy we can whip them readily and easily.

I do not know that we will fight here. Some think we shall, others that we will not. I fear that Rosecrans will attack from some other quarter and not march on this place.

I saw Miss Maggie W[hitesides] yesterday evening. She is here and will remain for a few days. Is as charming as ever.

Who else do you suppose is here? Miss Sallie D[avis] is here. I have seen her often and like her better than ever. She is one of the most intelligent girls I have ever met. I hope you will like her from what you have heard me say of her. She speaks of you often and wishes you much happiness. She thinks you do not like her. She leaves here tomorrow. Is going to Mississippi to visit her grandmother.

I have been very busy. We have a heap of work to do getting things straight again.

How are you getting along? How is Grandma, Aunt Olive, and all the relations?

Marion, George, and Jesse are all well.

My love to all.

Write soon and every opportunity. I am anxious to hear the news from home. I want to know what is going on in Lauderdale. Write long letters full of news of all characters.

Your affectionate brother,
Orlando

Tullahoma, Tenn.
April 18th/63

Dear Brother and Sister,

I wrote you yesterday by Allington, but as he was going on to Florence it may be some time before you receive my letter.[10] There is nothing new or interesting transpiring at this time. No movements being made by either of the armies of which I am informed. (Fortifications are being thrown up here and everything being made ready to receive the enemy in proper style when he pays us the visit so long expected and promised. He seems, however, to be very loath to leave Murfreesboro and advance on this point. Something, I know not what, deters him. He probably thinks the place will be a little more difficult to take than Murfreesboro was and hesitates to venture on so strong an army so well prepared for him.

Miss Maggie Whitesides has been here several days. Is as charming as ever, or at least attracts as many visitors. I have met her several times as also one other you least expect me to see, to visit Miss Sallie D[avis]. She came here on Tuesday, and I have been to see her often since that time. She is looking well and enjoying herself finely. She often speaks of you and sends her kindest wishes for your perfect happiness. She will leave in a few days for Mississippi.

We will have a sham battle here next week. What day I do not now know. It will be quite a brilliant affair and a novel, interesting scene to all. I wish you were here to witness it. You would be pleased and amused and see something similar to what we witness so often on the field of carnage.

I send you four (4) yards of Cadet cloth out of which I wish you to have made a coat and pair of pants for myself. Have it made by Hannay or Grobin in Florence.[11] The cloth is very valuable and I do not wish it spoilt in the making. Have it made regulation by whichever tailor you think will make it best. Get Oliver to go down to town [and have] his measure taken and let my coat and pants be made by his measure. I think they will fit me. The trimming the tailor will have to furnish. Get the best trimming, staff buttons, and c. you can. Do not have the buff put on the sleeves or collar nor gold lace placed on the sleeves of the coat. All this has been abolished by the department. Have the captain's bars on the collar of gold lace of the proper width and the edges of the coat (around collar) and the front trimmed with a buff binding.[12]

Have them made as early and handsomely as you can and send them to me by some responsible person who will bring them safely and without injury.

I have not time to write more now. Write to me soon and often. I will send you some papers if they come this evening.

My love to all.

Your affectionate brother,

O. S. Palmer

Have the pants trimmed according to former regulations from Congress. The tailor will know.

[Sylvanus William "Doc" Perry to Thomas B. Winston]
Summerfield, Ala.
Apr. 18th/63

Dear Tom,

I was truly glad to hear from you and your lovely wife. You thought I ought to write to you, but I would like to know how I could write. You ought to be more thoughtful. You have forgotten that I am not married, but [*word illegible*] me all my time to court Miss ___ ___ and then I am about to lose her and then I did not know that you would get a letter if I wrote it. The mails and Yankees are so irregular.

Well, I shall leave for the Army Saturday, and, oh, how I hate to leave this dear place. I had such a nice time and have met so many nice acquaintances. But, alas, I must.

Mrs. Rivers has been in such bad health ever since you left, but is getting better now as the spring is coming on. I hope she will get well soon. She and the Dr. sends their best love to you and lady, and Miss Rivers says she will answer your letter soon. Misses Laura, Kate, and Lucie send their best respect to you and wishes you much happiness. All the young ladies were very glad to hear from you.

I send my best love to you and Missie and hope you both will live long and be very happy and at last get home to Heaven.

Your true friend and Bro,

Dock

H^d Q^{trs}, Wood's Brigade
Wartrace, May 2nd, 1863

Dear Brother and Sister,

I have written several times since leaving home and as yet not one line in reply. I have been patiently, anxiously waiting and wishing to hear from you, but it seems that I am doomed to disappointment. I cannot hear one word from anyone in North Alabama—not even from Uncle Silas, who promised to write often and give me all the news both of a private and public character. I do not know what to think of the strange unaccountable silence. Something must have occurred from the usual current and deterred you from writing. I am daily in hopes of hearing from you and trust soon to have my curiosity and anxiety gratified and learn that all is well.

We have strange, startling news from Tuscumbia, Courtland, and c. The enemy, it seems, had driven Col. Roddey from Tuscumbia, pursued him to Courtland where Gen. Forrest met him day before yesterday and repulsed him with heavy loss and he is now in full retreat to his base of operations. This news of the fight Forrest had with them comes by telegraph and we trust that it may be true.[13]

From previous information from various sources which were deemed reliable, we were made to believe that Gen. [Grenville M.] Dodge had about twelve thousand men and was laying waste to the whole country.[14] Under the impression we had no expectation of hearing of their defeat by the inferior forces of Forrest, hence my reluctance to credit the dispatches in today's papers. However, I shall yield my incredulity and hope soon to hear that the enemy has retired beyond Bear Creek and our gallant cavalry pressing him home to his fortifications at Corinth and hemming him up in so that he cannot by any possibility commit any more of his thieving, ruinous raids through the country.

I have been trying by every means in my power to get some reliable information on the injuries inflicted by the marauders in their excursion but cannot get anything that I consider reliable. A thousand flying rumors shake the wings of my tent door and ask for admittance and credence, but I invariably command them to take their forms from out my sight and not disturb me with tales of sorrow and crime which have no foundation in truth and wish that some kind friend would give me a true statement of that concerning which I feel so deep an interest.

Everything is remarkably quiet in this region. Nothing stirring of any interest or importance that I am aware of. A week ago, it was expected that we would have some exciting times and active work. The little "War Child" Wheeler had gotten into a very dangerous and precarious situation, and we were going to get him out, but with his usual skill and address and great ability he gave the enemy the slip and came out safely, saving us the trouble of cutting his way out for him, for which we are very grateful.[15]

Wartrace is sixteen miles nearer Murfreesboro than Tullahoma. We moved up here for what particular object or design I know not, nor have I inquired. We have a much healthier, pleasanter, and better camp in every respect than the one we left. The army is now in excellent condition, the men in fine spirits, health, and discipline, ready for the enemy at any moment and anxious for him to advance.

I saw Doc Perry a few days since. He was returning to his Regiment, not looking very well, but said he could not stand it to remain away any longer. He was anxious again to be in the army. Some gal must have kicked him and rendered him desperate. He asked many questions of you both and sent many kind messages.

I am well and doing finely.

Give my love to Grandma, Delia, Aunt Olive and c., Oliver and Georgia, and Cousin Annie.

Did you get the cloth I sent you to have made into a uniform for me? Don't under any circumstances permit the Yankees to get hold of it.

Write soon and often.

Your affectionate Brother,
Orlando S. Palmer

Wartrace, Tennessee
May 5th, 1863

Dear Brother and Sister,

I have written repeatedly and cannot hear from you. It seems that you have forgotten how to write since I left you . . . not one word. Not even a scratch of your pen to satisfy me that all were well and you were in good spirits and enjoying yourself.

Your pen is now well rested if you treated all your other correspondents as silently as you have me, and you can give it considerable exercise for its health and training, giving me a summary of all the news, local and general.

We have any amount of news here, all of an interesting and cheering character. Forrest has captured the sixteen hundred men who were advancing on Rome, Georgia. The Yankees, with more dash than they were ever known to exhibit before, struck boldly out for the heart and centre of the Confederacy. But the gallant, immortal Forrest with his band of noble heroes pursued them with rigor and overtook them, fought them desperately, and captured the whole force, entering Rome in in glorious triumph, dragging the conquered foe at his chariot wheels. One thousand ladies, the fairest that Georgia contained, assembled to crown with honor their gallant deliverer. And his entry was the most splendid of the war. North Alabama, too, ought to weave a chaplet to bind the brow of the chieftain who has rid the country of such a band of marauders, thieves, and house burners. All honor to whom honor is due. His name is now immortal and future generations will hold in their memory his name as that of one who fought gallantly and successfully in this great Revolution.

The news of another terrible battle and glorious victory in Virginia comes upon the wings of the lightning to cheer and encourage and herald the breaking of the glorious dawn of peace and our Independence. The enemy crossed the Rappahannock on the 2nd inst. On the 3rd, the glorious, immortal Stonewall was in their rear and attacked them while Longstreet, with two divisions, engaged them in front. The result was the enemy was driven with heavy loss out of the "Wilderness" where the battle was fought and compelled to fall back to Chancellorsville. Here the enemy massed his forces for the great struggle and Lee led forward his gallant army of patriots and formed them in battle. The contest raged long and fiercely, but the invincible valor of our troops gained for us a great victory. The enemy was driven from every position. His dead and wounded cumbered the ground and the prisoners taken were numerous. The enemy is now in full retreat.[16]

All the fords of the river in possession of the forces of "Stonewall" and the victorious army of Lee is pursuing eagerly on the shattered, demoralized columns of the foe. No particulars of this great battle are given except that the brave, staunch old soldier whose name has been rendered immortal on so many hard-fought battlefields and whose presence ever was the beacon to victory is severely wounded.

Yes, Stonewall Jackson, honor and reverence to his name, was severely wounded. How dangerous the wound is, the dispatch does not state. It is hoped by all that his wound will not prove fatal, for when he falls, one of the strongest and firmest pillars of our government is gone.

Some think that tomorrow we will hear of the total route of the army of Fighting Joe Hooker and the capture of the largest portion of his forces.[17]

There is nothing of interest or worthy of note stirring here. Everything in Army circles is remarkably, ominously, quiet. I can hear of no movement of forces on either side or any demonstration of any character.

The fury of the storms is gathering, and the fierceness of its fury will, before many weeks can pass by, burst in terrific grandeur. We must fight here. We must fight, and all the chances are in favor of our gaining a brilliant victory, equal to the one in Virginia.

When the collision will occur is vain to conjecture. No one knows. We are only waiting the attack and preparing to repel it. The sooner it comes, the better.[18]

Miss Sallie Davis was here several days, and I had the pleasure of seeing her often and find her as interesting and intelligent as ever before. She has many admirers, and many lances are shivered on her account. I am an impartial (?) spectator.

We have a delightful encampment, and our soldiers are in fine health and c. George has a slight attack of bilious fever but is better now. Marion is well and sends his love to his mother and c.

I heard from Uncle Elias the other day. He was well but had been hard at work.

Write to me soon and give me all the news. Did you get the cloth I sent to have a uniform made out of? If so, what have you done with it?

Write to me soon.

My love to Delia, Aunt Olive, Oliver, Georgia, and c.

Affectionately,

Your Brother,

O. S. Palmer

Wartrace, Tennessee
May 9th, 1863

Dear Brother and Sister,

I have written to you so often since leaving home that I am about ashamed to write again, I not having heard a word from you since leaving home. I fear you have not received my letters and hence every opportunity I send you a few lines to relieve your mind of any uneasiness as to my condition.

I am well—getting along finely and spending the time as pleasantly as could be expected. We have a delightful encampment, good water, fine peach groves, and waving fields of most promising grain to gladden and refresh the eye.

There is no news here except of the great victory in Virginia, the repulse and signal discomfiture of Fighting Joe Hooker and his mighty host. Five thousand prisoners were captured, one general, any amount of arms and c., and the enemy's dead were thicker than ever seen before. Our loss was very heavy, but theirs greater.

I heard from Elias the other day. He had received a detail for Tom to report to him.

Write soon.

Have you had my uniform made? What did it cost?

My love to all.

Affectionately,

Your Brother,
O. S. Palmer

Wartrace, Tennessee
May 16th, 1863

Dear Brother and Sister,

Yours of the 30th ult., the first line from you since leaving home, was received day before yesterday, and as Mr. Lowery returns this evening, I have but a moment to devote to the pleasant duty of writing to you.

I was quite happy to hear from you but sorry to learn that Tom's arm was not improving. It seems that it recovers but slowly and it may be some time before it gets much better.

I heard from Uncle Elias the other day. He has gotten a detail for you, Tom, to report to him as his assistant, but had not then had an opportunity of sending it down. I am glad you have received the detail, for it will render you much more pleasantly situated than you could otherwise have been.

Miss Jennie [Kendrick] blushed when you asked her about my socks, but you did not say what reply she made to your remark. I am looking for the socks and will raise a terrible row if she does not come up to her promise to knit and send them to me. Remind her of it and urge her to send them. What could have caused her to blush so? I cannot comprehend the why and wherefore.

You say nothing of my charming cousin Annie when you knew at the same time I was pining away because I could not hear from her. None of my correspondents except Delia will say anything about some of the those whom I am ever happy to hear from.

Miss Sallie D[avis] is at Winchester. We have quarreled a little and are not now on the most friendly terms. The amicable relations have been slightly disturbed by the bellicose. Whither the straw drifteth I know not. Time will show where the current is strongest, deepest. Then you will be fully and thoroughly informed.

I wrote to you sometime since that I saw Doc Perry here. He was on the way to his regiment. Not looking very well, but better than I expected. He inquired very particularly about both of you and sends much word, which at this time I cannot remember.

There is nothing strange or unusual here. Everything is quiet at this place. No movement, demonstrations, or preparations since my last that I am aware of.

All eyes are turned, and all interest is concentrated on the movements and operations in Mississippi. Affairs down about Jackson assume a gloomy, a discouraging, aspect. I send you papers from which you will gather all the information afloat as to army movements. Reinforcements are pouring into Mississippi by thousands. The great Captains of this age, Beauregard and Johnston, are there and we may be able to redeem all we have lost and more, too, crush the insolent, daring Grant. It is rumored that the enemy have Jackson. Confirmation not yet received.

You will see by the papers that we have gained a glorious victory in Virginia, but that great hero, the immortal Jackson, is no more.

Are you having my uniform made? Hannay would make it better than any other.

Come to see me, Tom, and bring it with you. First get your detail from Elias. Then you can come and go at pleasure.

Can you not buy us some butter and send it by Mr. Lowery when he comes? Any amount would help us very much. We cannot get anything of the sort here.

Your affectionate Brother,
O. S. Palmer

Wartrace, Tennessee
May 27th, 1863

Dear Brother and Sister,

As Mr. Hopkins is going home tomorrow, I again write you, though I am not in the humor for doing anything tonight. I have been constantly on the move ever since Sunday and am nearly worn out. On Sunday I left here for Decatur with Marion, and after a tiresome journey reached there Monday at 9 A.M. Got Marion a good place at Dr. Daney's . . . had every arrangement made for his proper care and treatment. Left George to wait on him until his mother arrived.

He stood the trip finely and was better when I left him than when we started from here. I think there is no doubt but that he will recover soon, but he will not be able to return to camp for six weeks or two months. I told him to go home when he got able and remain there until he entirely recovered.

Miss Sue [M.] was very well and as pleasant and agreeable as ever.

I returned to Huntsville the same day and to this place on Tuesday. On arriving here, I learned that our Division had marched out to Hoover's Gap, some twelve miles from here, the evening before for the purpose of intercepting and capturing, if possible, some six thousand of the enemy who were attempting to make a raid on McMinnville.

I started immediately for the scene of action and arrived there a little after dark and found that the enemy had retreated and all was quiet. We returned to camp this morning, so, you see, I have had no rest for four days and am worn out nearly.

There is no news here from any quarter except Vicksburg upon which formidable place Grant has made 13 successive desperate assaults and been repulsed with immense slaughter each time.

In the meantime, Gen. Johnston is collecting a mighty army in rear of the daring Grant and, it is hoped—believed by some—that the whole of the enemy force will be captured. Troops are pouring into Jackson from all quarters and a large army will soon be assembled there. What the result of all this may be, I know not. That we shall gain a signal victory is the hope of all.[19]

Miss Sallie D[avis] sends her love to you. She is now at Winchester. Have not seen her since I wrote you last.

Write soon and often.

My love to all.

Your affectionate Brother,

O. S. Palmer

Vallandigham, the great orator of the North West, has been banished from the United States and sent to our lines. He arrived at Shelbyville day before yesterday and is going to Richmond soon. What he will do or what position he will now assume, no one can tell.[20]

O. S. P.

* * *

As a component of Maj. Gen. Grenville M. Dodge's expedition into northern Alabama, 15 April-8 May 1863, a force of 1,380 troopers of the Tenth Missouri Cavalry under the command of Col. Florence M. Cornyn, a Jesuit-educated medical doctor, left Corinth, Mississippi, on a raid into Lauderdale County. On 28 April, one of the dozens of times that Florence changed hands during the war, Cornyn's regiment burned the foundries, mills, and tanyards along Cypress Creek, including those of the Kennedy family, destroyed food supplies, captured horses, mules, and cattle, and liberated slaves, as well as sacking and burning Palmer's alma mater, Wesleyan University (now the University of North Alabama) and its library of 4,000 volumes. Brig. Gen. Philip Dale Roddey's brigade met the Federals near Cox Creek but were forced from the field. Having completed his mission, Cornyn ordered a block of Florence homes and other buildings burned to cover his withdrawal.[21]

Shortly after his return to Corinth, Cornyn was tried by court martial for his excesses at Florence. On 10 August 1863, during a break in the proceedings, he and his regiment's lieutenant colonel, William D. Bowen, who had brought the charges against him, confronted one another. Harsh words led to blows, and Bowen drew his revolver and shot Cornyn, mortally wounding him. Bowen was dismissed from the service and the regiment's command devolved upon its major, Frederick Benteen, who would go on to achieve a sort of fame as one of Lt. Col. George Armstrong Custer's battalion commanders at the battle of the Little Bighorn.[22]

Wartrace, Tennessee
June 14th, 1863

Dear Brother and Sister,

My uniform and the butter you sent were duly received and highly appreciated. The butter was a real treat. We can get nothing to eat here except what is issued to us by the commissary, and you can readily imagine how great a treat anything nice from home is.

My coat does not fit very well, being too large for me, but it will do very well until I can get it changed. I will send you the money by the first safe person passing. If there is enough of the cloth left, I would be glad if you would have me a vest made of it. I have none, and I sometimes need one.

I have received several letters from you, but do not now remember whether or not they have all been answered. There has been no one passing since Mr. Hopkins went down. I will send this by mail, but do not think there is much chance of you getting it.

We have heard from various sources of the disastrous raid of the enemy into Lauderdale and of the failure of our forces to capture the enemy or make any great effort to punish the insolent marauders. Everyone seems to concur in the censure of the commanding officers. Some throw all the blame on Col. Hanson, whilst others are willing for the indominable Roddey to shoulder a portion thereof.[23]

The deed has been done. The enemy have laid waste the country and committed irreparable damage, and the only interest we can take in ascertaining who is to blame is to find the guilty party, remove him, and place someone in command who has the inclination and capacity to defend the country.

Everything here at this time is quiet. A few days ago, everything was in motion and a general engagement with the enemy momentarily expected. Now all is quiet. No prospect that I am aware of a battle coming off soon.

The fate of Vicksburg is still undecided and uncertain. The grand result draws near, and we expect the most glorious or the most disappointing news. The army in Virginia is again in motion. What the intention is at this time I cannot conjecture.[24]

Remember me kindly to all.
Write soon and often to
Your affectionate Brother,
O. S. Palmer

Wartrace, Tennessee
June 21st, 1863

Dear Sister,

Your very kind letter giving me an account of your trouble and trials was handed me by Uncle Elias yesterday evening. I was and am very much grieved to hear how unhappy you are in the old homestead where the most pleasant and joyous hours of our life was spent and around which so many fond memories cluster. The scenes of our childhood, sportive, innocent, happy hours when all passed peacefully, quietly by and the hopes and aspirations which made us look hopefully and exultingly to the glorious future full of honor and happiness to us in our youthful imagination, that spot shall ever be dear to me. I cannot forget the home of my youth, the only house I have had for years.

I regret that the troubles my Grand Mother has suffered has imbittered her nature and rendered it unpleasant for you to be with her. I hoped that you would be perfectly happy there where you would be treated with the greatest kindness and cherished as your goodness of heart and disposition deserve and entitle you to. But it seems that they cannot, will not, be. No one can regret it more than I. I suffer almost as much as you can and most sincerely sympathize with you.

As to going to board with Cousin Joe, you can and must exercise your own judgement.[25] You and Tom can decide what is best for you, and whatever you do I shall be entirely satisfied, only hoping that you may secure your happiness in every respect. I shall always do everything in my power to smooth your pathway through life and contribute in every way I can to render your life as bright and joyous as you desire.

I heartily join with you in the wish that the war may soon close and we may all be near each other in a home of our own where all the happiness the world can afford may be ours. No one is more anxious for this unnatural war to end than I am. The best years of my life are being passed in the Army where all the opportunities of cultivating and improving my mind are denied and the highest station to which I have aspired in civil life thus probably forever denied my ambition.

I have the opportunity of marrying one of the most charming and elegant of women and, if the war would end, I have as fine a prospect for happiness as heart could wish, and with will, energy, and luck my most ardent expectations might be more than realized. These reasons all conspire to render me as anxious as anyone can be for this war to terminate.

I regret one thing very much. I am really grieved at it. Sadly, you do not entertain a favorable opinion of her who is more dear to me than any other in the world, excepting you. You think that I am going to marry a lady unworthy of me . . . am throwing myself away. If you could only see her, your opinion would change. You would love her dearly and applaud my choice. She has a sweet, amiable, intelligent face and a heart full of kindness and love, a frank, open countenance expressive of kindness and presenting a fine index of the generous, noble mind.

She knows you do not have any particular love for her. She understands how someone has misrepresented her to and placed her character before you in a false light and regrets it as much as I do. Nevertheless, she says "I know I shall love Missie when I see her!" She has good sense enough to understand how it is that you judge her so harshly . . . why you have not that love and esteem for her that is so much to be desired, and she is not in the least offended at you.

I know not from whom you imbibed your prejudice. I would like exceedingly well to find the man who knows her and would speak one word disrespectful of her . . . to mention her name in disparagement. I hope you will be kind enough as to inform me as to who it was that gave you such an account of her as to cause you to dislike her and to think her unworthy of me. If there is any unworthiness in the matter, I am unworthy of her. No one who knows her well can speak any other way than complimentary of her unless they do falsely, knowingly, and maliciously!

Is there not a photograph of mine at home that I brought to you from Lebanon when I returned from the Law School? If so, please send it to me. I want a picture of mine of some sort to give to my Sallie [Davis]. She will give me hers in return. Do not disappoint me in this. I am anxious to have it.

She has gone home to Sparta, Tennessee. Is going to return to school in September. Says she will be the most accomplished woman in Tennessee.

I wrote you several days since about my uniform. The coat does not fit at all.

I will send you some sugar the first chance. We are going to send an ambulance down this week. Please send me as much butter as you can. Also, some onions, Irish potatoes, chickens if they are to be found. If you cannot get these things otherwise, buy them. We are willing to pay any price.

The ambulance will go to Mr. Simpson's. You can find out from there when it will come back. It will go by Aunt Olive's. Will leave word there when it will return. Send me whatever you can to eat.[26]

Cheer up, Sister, and do not think no one loves you. All must love you who know you well. Do not be uneasy about me. I am well and doing finely. There is no prospect for a fight here soon.

Write to me soon and often.

Remember me kindly to all.

Your affectionate Brother,

Orlando

Wartrace, Tenn.
June 22nd, 1863

Dear Sister,

I wrote to you yesterday, but, as I am sending George home with an ambulance, I will drop you a line. There is nothing new or strange. Uncle Elias came up day before yesterday and will return tomorrow. I send by him sixty-five (65) dollars to replace the amount you paid out for me. I sent by George some thirty lbs. of sugar for you. It was all I could get at this time. I will be able to get some more sometime soon and will send it to you.

George will come back with the ambulance and, if Marion is well enough, I wish him to return. George will know when the ambulance will start back and can tell you by what time to have anything that you may wish to send me at Aunt Olive's.

Send me as much butter as you can get. Also, potatoes and onions if they can be procured. If you cannot get enough of these things at home, buy them in the neighborhood and I will replace the money.

We can get nothing to eat here except what is issued by the Commissary, so anything you can send us from home will be very acceptable.

I wrote you yesterday how very sorry I was you did not like a certain young lady I wrote about. You have formed an unfavorable opinion of her. I regret it very much. She is in every respect worthy of your confidence and love, and you will someday love her as well as I do. She has good sense enough to understand how it is that someone has spoken unkindly of her to you and that you have been deceived in reference to her. She says she knows she will like you when she sees you and convince you that she is a pure, high-minded, noble woman. Send me a photograph of mine that is at home. I gave you one when I returned from Lebanon. Send it to me. She wants it.

Send me some beets, also.

I think we will go to Tullahoma to relieve Gen. Polk's brigade and allow him to go off and marry.[27] Continue to write me as usual at this place for the present.

Cheer up, Sister, and do not despond. Do not be uneasy about me. I am doing finely. No prospect for a fight here.

My love to Grandma, Aunt Olive, and Delia. I will write to them soon.

Your affectionate Brother,

O. S. Palmer

Tullahoma, Tenn.
June 28th, 1863

Dear Sister,

Once again, I essay to write, but the truth is, I have written so repeatedly here of late and received no response that I have exhausted each and every subject and twice repeated everything I could think. I fain would send you something to interest, cheer, and amuse you, but in turning over the small stock of thoughts I have on hand, I do not find one worthy of consideration. If I were to speak of the bitter cold, unpleasant weather we now have, it would fill your sympathetic heart with anxious thoughts as to the hardship and suffering of the soldiers. This, of course, would afford me neither pleasure nor amusement, and I would have to quote Don Quixote to remove the impression from your mind and say that "arms are our ornament, warfare our repose."

But that you may not be uneasy or suffer one unhappy moment as to my comfort and well being, I will say that I am in a good, warm tent, well floored with a good chimney, which renders me as comfortable as if I were at home could I but surround myself with the same pleasant thoughts and comfortable fancies. But, alas! This cannot be. The kind association of persons and ideas which alone can render one happy and free from care whilst at home with the kind loved ones who cannot accompany us whilst engaged in martial pursuits.

Do not infer from this that I am unhappy or dissatisfied, for I am as pleasantly and agreeably situated as one can possibly be when in the army. The General treats me with great kindness and consideration, never speaking or treating me harshly, but trusting and confiding everything to me as one friend would to another intimate and esteemed friend and companion.

His enemies have done him great injustice, which time will demonstrate to the world, cover them with shame and disgrace, and place him in his true character as a gentleman and a brave, energetic, and skillful officer, giving his whole time and talent to, and facing danger in, its many thousands of shapes for the safety of his country and the achievement of its independence.[28]

Capt. William Simpson is my boon companion and trusted friend with whom it is a pleasure to have associated.[29] Then I am constantly meeting with gentlemen of great social worth whose friendship it is worth having.

Camp life is not dull. At least it is not to an adjutant general who has constant employment to occupy his mind from frowning and growing sad over that which is inevitable. I have enough to keep me busy most of the time, and when that is not the case, I get hold of some good book and pass the hours pleasantly in friendly communication with master spirits who are gone and who devoted their time and their talent to afford amusement and instruction to those who came after them. A blessing to their memory. How many hours that would otherwise been sad have they rendered pleasant and happy. Books are a never-failing source of pleasure to me, and I long for the war to bring itself to an end so that I can seek some fair companion as fond of books as I could have here to be of my [sic] and hunt some lonely, secluded spot full of romance and beauty and there enjoy the happiness of literary pursuits.

I trust that day is not far distant when the war will terminate, but where to find the intelligent companion with whom to link my destiny is a question I have often asked myself and never yet answered. There is the trouble of the matter, which I trust to your sisterly interest in me to assist me in solving. I am not so fortunate as lucky Cousin Oliver who, I understand, was married last night. I wish him all happiness and joy. May life be to him and his fair, sweet bride one of happiness unalloyed and joy uninterrupted by the rude shocks and clashes of this rough world.

I am glad to know that they have married immediately after getting home from Kentucky, had I been him and enjoyed the society of my bride all this time. As it is, he married and has to return to the army immediately. We are looking for him here every day, and he had better return for if he remains away much longer it may get him into serious difficulties.

My love and a kiss to Cousin Georgia, and tell her my best wishes will ever attend her and c.

I have never received any invitation to the wedding, but I could not have gone anyway. I went to Shelbyville day before yesterday and saw the charming girl who treated me so kindly when I was sick. She is well and as sweet as ever.

Do you ever hear anything from Ripley? I can hear nothing from there or, in fact, from anywhere. I have not heard from you since the letter brought by Frank [Foster], whilst others are getting letters daily, by mail and hand from Florence. None come freighted with good news and cheer for me. Why is this, Sister?

I have written to you two or three times about Tom, but, for fear that you have not gotten the letters, I will again state that I received a letter from him. He was well. Was at Summerfield, Alabama, and was coming to see you as soon as [Sylvanus William] Perry got well. He is probably with you by this time. If so, you are happy and so am I.

Write to me and send me the quilts I wrote for by Oliver or someone else if he has left.

Very affectionately,
Your Brother,
O. S. Palmer

* * *

Captain Palmer's correspondence was interrupted for nearly a four-month period from July until the third week in October, in all likelihood on account of what he referred to as the "derangement and uncertainties" of the Confederate postal service. "I have written to you twice since the battle of Chickamauga," he wrote to his sister, but have never heard a word from you. It may be that my letters never reached you." During this period, in September 1863, the Fifteenth Arkansas was consolidated with the Second Arkansas Infantry, and in December the Twenty-Fourth Arkansas was also melded into its depleted ranks. At that time, the consolidated regiment totaled 295 men.

Of greater importance, on 4 July 1863, Vicksburg fell to U. S. Grant, and Robert E. Lee's then-to-fore seemingly invincible Army of Northern Virginia suffered a decisive defeat at Gettysburg, Pennsylvania. These two Confederate disasters were in part offset by a smashing victory over William S. Rosecrans' Army of the Cumberland at Chickamauga, Georgia. The largely demoralized and disorganized Federals retreated into Chattanooga and Braxton Bragg's Army of Tennessee laid siege to the city, threatening to starve the garrison into surrender. Heavy rains in late September washed away mountain roads, and on 2 October, Maj. Gen. Joseph Wheeler's cavalry intercepted and burned more than 700 Union supply wagons at Anderson's Cross Roads, Tennessee. By the end of the month the Federal soldier's ration had been reduced to "four cakes of hard bread and a quarter pound of pork" every three days.

> Hd. Qtrs., Lowrey's Brigade
> Near Chattanooga, Tenn.
> October 19th, 1863

Dear Sister,

I have another opportunity of sending a letter to Lauderdale County and will make an effort to get a letter to you. I have written so often and have never been able to hear if any of them ever reached you, but I am discouraged not knowing whether any having reached you. Yet, [word illegible] not knowing whether any line I write will ever be received by you. Still, it is a pleasant and happy duty to write to you and nothing shall deprive me of it when an opportunity arises.

I have written to you twice since the battle of Chickamauga but have never heard a word from you. It may be that my letters never reached you. If they did not, your anxiety may be very great to learn what was the fate of your brother on the bloody battle field. I thank God, who protected me all through the dread battle unharmed. I am and have been in perfectly good health and am blessed with just enough business to transact to prevent me from ennui and having my mind filled with idle regrets and pining for things which, in the nature of things, it is impossible for me to enjoy. My position as a soldier in this great Revolution demands that I should be happy and contented, and I am willing to suffer on until the great day of victory and rejoicing shall arrive.

It is useless for me to attempt to describe the great battle of Chickamauga. My pen is not equal to the task. Suffice to say that we fought for the greater part of two days during which time the battle raged with great fury, greater than any battle I have ever been in, Victory sometimes inclining to our standards, then deserting to perch in dread defiance on the banners of the enemy. But about sundown Sunday evening, the 20th of September, we drove them from every position. We routed them and they ran with a wild [word illegible] from every portion of the battle ground. We gained a complete victory, whipped the enemy at every point, and were once masters of the battlefield.

We lost severely but not so heavy as the enemy. We captured over seven thousand prisoners and fifty pieces of artillery and twenty thousand stand of small arms, but, alas!, many a gallant spirit poured out its dearest blood on our country's altar. Doc Perry was killed, a good, brave, accomplished young man. No more we will we see his smiling face. I had many friends that I esteemed very highly who were killed and wounded. They have fought their last fight and some of them rest on the blood-stained field they fought so gallantly to win.[30]

We are now, and have been ever since the battle, entrenched directly in front of Chattanooga, the two armies being less than two miles of each other and both being strongly fortified. Neither party demonstrates[?] any desire[?] to attack. Both are sternly, calmly looking at each other, anxious for the other to assault. But the two Generals are too discreet to do anything so foolish as to advance upon an enemy strongly entrenched and in great force. So, you see, there is no prospect for another engagement. I do not think we will have another fight soon. No one thinks so. There can be no other battle until one party makes a flank movement and thus forces a battle in defense of communications. When this plan will be attempted by either army is hard to say. There are many difficulties in the way of such an attempt which it will be very difficult to overcome. I hardly think it possible for such a plan to be carried into execution until next spring. Insurmountable difficulties will intervene all the winter. I may be mistaken, but I do not think I can be.

The President was here last week. Issued a very fine address to the army, complimenting the soldiers on their late, great achievements and encouraging the men to continue in our exertion to drive back the insolent foe and gain our independence. He seemed hopeful . . . confident . . . of success, and some think he supposes peace not to be very distant.[31]

We have just received information of another great victory gained by Lee on the immortal field of Manassas. How great a success it is for him we have not yet learned.[32]

General Wheeler just returned, having accomplished a very successful raid on the enemy's line of communications, destroying large quantities of commissary stores, wagons, and other public property, burning several important bridges. This will render the enemy quite uncomfortably situated and cut their supplies very short. It is thought that by frequently cutting the Rail Road and destroying the supplies in their rear we can force them to abandon Chattanooga and retire to Murfreesboro. I do not think it possible. The Yankees can accomplish almost anything that requires exertion or physical energy apart from courage. They may have some difficulty in getting their supplies during the winter, but they are prepared to encounter difficulties of this character and they can well overcome them.

Gen. Wood has resigned. Why he did so I will explain at some future time. Col. Lowrey has been made brigadier general and commands our brigade. I am still adjutant of the brigade. The removal of Gen. Wood had no effect on my position or standing in any way.[33]

Write to me, sister, and give me all the news. I have not heard from you for a long, long while. Be cheerful and hopeful. Drive gloom and sorrow away from your heart. I saw Tom yesterday. He and Uncle E. are well. I send you a letter from Tom.

My love to Grandma, Aunt Olive, Cousin Joe, etc.

Affectionately,

Your Brother,

O. S. Palmer

Marion and Jesse are with me and very well. Where is George?

[*first page of letter missing*]

I am happy in hearing that you had so many good things at home and trust you may continue to have plenty to eat and never suffer for anything you need or desire.

I may get off long enough to come and enjoy the good apples you have with you sometime this winter. I will pay you a visit if it is possible. I shall make application for leave if there is any prospect of getting it. What time I may come, I cannot now say. Everything is uncertain, unsettled now and may be for some time. The two opposing armies are so close to each other that some strategic movements will certainly be made before we can go regularly into winter quarters. The contending hosts will have to be farther apart than they now are before anything can be settled. We still occupy Missionary Ridge, three (3) miles from Chattanooga. The enemy are in that stronghold. Our pickets are in two hundred yards of the enemy. I can see a Yankee at that distance any time by going down to our picket line. The pickets do not fire upon each other. On the other hand, the Yankee pickets are disposed to be very friendly, anxious to converse with our men and exchange coffee for other articles from our men. But our orders are very strict and no communication with the enemy is permitted under any circumstances. The severest punishment is inflicted upon anyone who violates the order.

We are camped on the side of the ridge. The rain is now descending in torrents and our poor soldiers, who have but scanty protection from the descending torrent, suffer very much. Many of them are already sick and many more will necessarily succumb to the slow inroads of disease brought on by exposure and bad weather. [*page missing*]

If you have any chance, send George to Tom or I. We can take care of him. If neither of us get to come home, hire out the negroes the best you can. You can get Uncle Enoch to assist you.

On 17 October, the Lincoln administration gave Maj. Gen. Ulysses S. Grant command all Union forces in the theater and replaced the hapless Rosecrans with Maj. Gen. George Henry Thomas. It also reinforced the army in Chattanooga with 15,000 men under Maj. Gen. Joseph Hooker from the Army of the Potomac.

On 27 October, Thomas opened his line of supply by linking his Army of the Cumberland with Hooker's relief column, thus allowing supplies and reinforcements to flow into Chattanooga over the so-called "Cracker Line," and by mid-November an additional 20,000 men had arrived from Vicksburg under Maj. Gen. William T. Sherman.

Grant planned to break the siege of Chattanooga with a flanking attack on Bragg's line, with Sherman to attack Tunnel Hill at the northern end of Missionary Ridge on 23 November. At the same time, Hooker's corps was to move against the Confederate left on Lookout Mountain.

Maj. Gen. John C. Breckinridge, commanding the center of Bragg's line, ordered his men to fortify the crest of Missionary Ridge, but his works, as historian James L. McDonough has pointed out, he "placed along the physical crest rather than what is termed the 'military' crest"—that is, the top of the ridge line rather the highest line from which the enemy could be seen and fired upon—a placement that "severely handicapped the defenders." In addition, Breckinridge left half of his men in the rifle pits along the base.

Thomas, in what Grant expected to be a supporting role, was to move out of Chattanooga and advance halfway to Missionary Ridge in a feint to occupy the Rebels' attention.

The main focus of Grant's attack, however, was to be the right flank of Bragg's line, defended by Lt. Gen. William J. Hardee and some 9,000 Confederates from Cleburne's and William H. T. Walker's divisions. Sherman's Army of the Tennessee—16,600 men in the three divisions—crossed the Tennessee, threatening the north end of Missionary Ridge. At dawn on 25 November, the scheduled time of his attack, Sherman faced only three small brigades under Cleburne—about 4,000 men—but Sherman unaccountably delayed his attack until about 9:00 a.m. and then sent forward only two brigades.

This inadequate force launched a series of assaults against Cleburne's position but was repulsed. Cleburne then ordered a general counterattack. Charging down the hill at 4:00 p.m., the Confederates routed

Sherman's men, capturing a large number of prisoners. Sherman had committed only a fraction of his available force in a direct assault on a strong position, costing him almost 2,000 casualties.

Thomas, in the meantime, deployed 23,000 men in four divisions to attack the 9,000 Confederates holding the rifle pits at the base of Missionary Ridge and the 20,000 men defending its crest. The Federals quickly overran the rifle pits and then, without orders, began an inexorable advance against the Rebel center. As Bragg had not provided a tactical reserve, his defenses on the ridge were only a thin crust that cracked with astonishing speed. Realizing that their line was untenable, the defenders began to melt away down the ridge's counter slope in a headlong retreat. Only Cleburne's division was not in disarray. It was the last unit to withdraw and formed the rear guard of Bragg's army.

During the night, Bragg ordered the demoralized and largely disorganized Army of Tennessee to withdraw toward Chickamauga Station and the following day toward Dalton, Georgia. Grant's pursuit was effectively thwarted by Cleburne's rearguard action at Ringgold Gap. The fighting on Missionary Ridge had cost the Federals 5,824 casualties of about 56,000 engaged and the Confederates lost 6,667 of about 44,000.

After his failed campaign in Kentucky, his inexplicable retreat from Murfreesboro, and his disastrous rout at Chattanooga, Jefferson Davis relieved Braxton Bragg of command—belatedly most historians believe—recalling him to Richmond to serve as his chief military advisor.[34]

> Hd. Qtrs., Lowrey's Brigade
> Tunnel Hill, Georgia
> Dec. 12th, 1863

Dear Sister,

Learning that there will probably be an opportunity to send you a letter tomorrow, I eagerly avail myself of it to relieve you of any uneasiness that you might suffer on my account, hearing, as you doubtless have long since that time, that there has been another battle fought by this army, and not having since that heard anything from me, I know you have been and still are very anxious to learn something of the fate of your brother.

I am happy to inform you that I am perfectly well and came out safe. Our Brigade, although occupying a position where a great deal of the fighting could be seen, and where we were constantly expecting an assault, the heavy columns of the enemy was not heavily engaged. On the 2nd ult., the day the great disaster befell us on Missionary Ridge, we skirmished some with the enemy, but our Brigade was so fortunate as not be assaulted on that disastrous day.

I am not prepared to give you a general description of the battle, not being sufficiently informed to do so with any satisfaction. The battle was fought on Missionary Ridge, so imagine a long ridge some five miles long and much higher and steeper than the old "Sliding Hill" at home and you will have some idea of the ground on which the dread shock of war occurred. Our troops were drawn up on the ridge. The enemy, with an army vastly superior to ours in number assaulted us with desperation and dogged determination. The right wing of the army under the command of the immortal Cleburne stood firm as the rock in midocean, and the mighty hosts of the enemy were thrown against it but to be broken and driven away in great confusion, their dead and dying literally covering the ground.[35]

But the left wing and center of our army did not stand so firmly, and late in the evening the enemy broke through, took possession of the hill occupied by the left center of our army, taking several pieces of artillery and some few prisoners. This necessitated the retreat of our army. That night we withdrew to Chickamauga.

Next morning early the retreat commenced. The enemy followed closely. Our division (Cleburne's) brought up the rear. At Ringgold, the enemy pressed us so closely we were forced to turn on them to prevent the capture of our wagon train.[36]

The Division was placed in position on Taylor's Ridge, just this side of Ringgold, early on the morning of the 27th. Soon the pursuing force of the enemy came in sight and engaged our skirmishers. Their lines were promptly formed and they moved steadily and boldly to the attack. But they were met by the invincible Division of the Army and right royally did we repulse them time and again. Every time we would repulse them, they would bring up new lines, but all to no purpose. To come up that hill was certain defeat and death to them. As to their great loss and cost [*illegible*] they can't [*illegible*] ascertained. We held our own against vastly superior numbers until our wagon train had all reached a place of safety, and then we slowly and sullenly retired from the field where the division had rendered itself immortal. The enemy were badly whipped. They dared not follow us any farther.[37]

The next day they burned the bridge and the town and retreated to Chattanooga. We afterward ascertained that the enemy buried over five hundred of their men who were killed in this sharp engagement. Our loss was very slight.[38]

We have been at this place ever since, quietly resting and preparing winter quarters.

I trust that strategy will soon do its work and we may be so situated that we can build winter quarters that render ourselves comfortable. I do not think the two armies will thus silently confront each other much longer. Movements will be made, but I do not think we will have another general engagement soon. Strategy will now decide the winter campaign.

Rosecrans has now been relieved from duty and Thomas is the immediate commander of the army, Grant commanding the Department. We are rejoicing over the removal of Rosecrans, looking upon him as we do as the greatest General in their army. I think we can deal with Grant more successfully than with Rosy, and Gen W[ood] has resigned, you were rightly informed.

You asked me why he resigned. I ought not to write the facts fully and cannot, for reasons that will be apparent to you, do so in this letter. I will at some future time. Suffice it to say that General Cleburne was dissatisfied with the manner in which Gen. W handled his Brigade in the battle of Chickamauga. He said that Gen. W was too timid for the battlefield. In consequence of this, Gen. W tendered his resignation. Col. Lowrey has been promoted and now commands Wood's old Brigade.

I retain my position. The resigning of Gen. W did not, does not, nor can it affect me in any shape, form, or fashion. Maj. Gen. Cleburne in his report on the battle of Chickamauga paid me a high compliment, saying "Capt. O. S. Palmer, A.A.G., was distinguished for coolness and bravery," and c. This is a great compliment from a man of such distinguished courage and ability as Gen. Cleburne. He is one of the bravest officers in the Army and a General of the very first character. His reputation is equal to that of any general in the Army.[39]

On the other hand, Lt. Gens. Polk and D. H. Hill have been relieved from duty with the Army, as also Maj. Gen. Hindman, on account of some difficulties, the nature of which I will not now attempt to explain. These are important changes, whether for the better I cannot say. Time alone can settle this matter.[40]

Our Army is in tolerable fine condition, ready to meet the enemy at any moment. When next we have an engagement with the foe, I trust we shall completely ruin them.

In order that you may know how we live in the Army, I will tell you what I had for dinner. I had fine, thick soup with any amount of Irish potatoes in it and fine beef and good corn bread. The soup was as good as any I ever saw. We have it every day, but do not always have potatoes in it.

We live much better than you imagine and are not suffering so greatly as many suppose. But nevertheless, I would much prefer being at home and eating some of Grandma's and Aunt Olive's good country dinners.

I wear undershirts in winter and would be obliged to you if you would send me a couple. I am also in need of socks. I hope to get those you are knitting.

As for Sallie [Davis], I have not heard from her since I left her in Tennessee. I understand she's at Sparta. I cannot well answer your questions for I do not know what the state of her feelings are as I cannot hear from her. I do not love her less. Could I but see her, then I could answer your question.

I am not one of those who think that absence conquers love's time nor separation can conquer the little blind God. He rises superior to all difficulties and troubles. I do not know whether I love her as well as I did or not. I only know that I am very anxious to hear from her, to see her, and then I can answer your questions satisfactorily to myself and you.

I can say, I will say, if she remains true to me, my heart shall never sever from its loyalty, my plighted faith shall not be disregarded. Sister, she is superior to most girls of her age. Her intellect is stronger, purer, and better cultivated than any girl I ever saw, and I should be proud to call her wife. You know that I have always been an admirer of intellectuality in woman, hence my great warmth of feeling for Sallie.

I send you by Lieut. Smith a letter from Tom. He desired me to send you some money also. I will send some if I think it advisable when Lieut. Smith starts.

It seems a large body of the enemy are moving up by way of the Tuscumbia, and if this be true it may be that Smith will be captured. I will think on it, and if I deem it prudent will send you some money—seventy-five or one hundred dollars.

Sister, you must write to me every opportunity and let me know how you are getting along and whether you need or want anything. I desire to know exactly how you are doing. With only you and one other to love, it is naturally that I should desire to know [*illegible*].

[*Illegible*] suffered many unhappy moments since the disastrous news reached us that a large portion of Sherman's command passed through Florence and that some of them passed up the Military Road. Although I cannot hear anything from you, I am satisfied the enemy must have annoyed you all very much. I am much distressed because I cannot hear from you to know certainly how they treated you all and in what you suffered. I am very anxious to hear a full statement of all their doings and am constantly hoping to hear from you. I have not heard from you for some time and hence know nothing as to what is going on at home.

I know that the good and loyal people of Lauderdale must have suffered heavily from the presence of the hated foe in such large numbers for so long a time in their midst. They have now felt the dread realities of war and I sincerely hope they may henceforward be far from the inroads of the enemy, although I do not see how they are to escape, for the enemy can come there whenever they think proper or desire.[41]

I am very sorry you are still in a country so subject to raids from the enemy and regret that you did not go south sometime since. I am very anxious for you to go to Tuscaloosa or Summerfield. So is Tom.

I have written to Uncle Spinks to know what chance there would be to secure a hack at Tuscaloosa to send after you if anything can be obtained. Tom and I will try to get someone to go after you. One of us might possibly get off long enough to come after you, but I think it very uncertain. It is next to an impossibility to get away from the Army now under any pretense whatsoever. I would be very glad were it in my power to do so to come to see you and spend a few pleasant days with those so near and dear to me, but I fear this pleasure cannot be mine.

In this hour of our country's need, everyone is required to remain at his post.

Tom is at Dalton, Uncle Silas at Kingston. I heard from Tom yesterday. He said that all were well.

Write to me every opportunity.

My love to all.

Your affectionate Brother,

O. S. Palmer

[*Page missing*] our [*illegible*] Army is near this place in fine condition and ready for the enemy whenever he sees proper to come out and give us battle.

Gen. Bragg was relieved from the command of the Army. Lt. Gen. Hardee is now in command. Whether he is to remain in command or not I am not informed.

I got my valise from Ripley with some socks, [*illegible*], shirts, and drawers, [*illegible*], and c. All were doing tolerably well. Georgie had a fine daughter.[42] She and it were doing as well as could be expected under the circumstances. The Yankees had just been down in Coosa[?] County, carrying destruction and desolation with them, killing all of Grandpa's hogs and c. and c. Uncle John is still in bad health. Oliver is not improving much but is very convinced that he will be well enough to rejoin the Army next Spring. I am glad he is [illegible] he can not, but I fear he will never entirely recover his health to withstand the hardships, privations, and toils of [illegible] camp. I fear his constitution is so badly shattered that he will be an invalid for many years if he is not cut off in the prime of his manhood to fill an early and lamented grave. Delia writes me that she is in fine health. She spoke of you and wishes she were with you. She has [illegible] discard Frank, an act deferred much longer [illegible] than I could have [illegible].

    I heard from Tom yesterday. He said all were well.

    Write to me every opportunity.

    My love to all.

    Your affectionate brother,

    O. S. Palmer

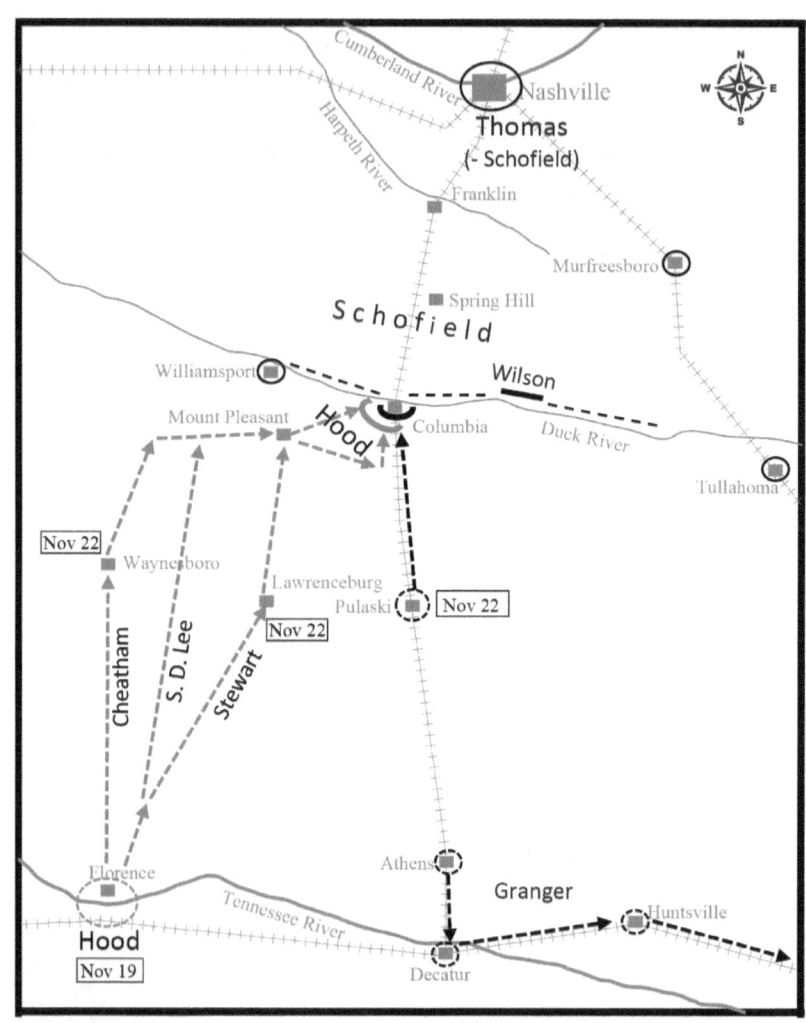

Hood's invasion of Tennessee that would lead to the battles of Spring Mills, Franklin, and Nashville. Map by Matt Spruill.

Chapter 5

1864

Bone and Muscle Could Not Endure

> Hd. Qtrs., Lowrey's Brigade
> Tunnel Hill, Georgia
> Jan. 1st, 1864

Dear Sister,

As Capt. Carson[1] starts for Florence tomorrow, I take great pleasure in availing myself of this opportunity to write my first letter for the year of 1864 to you, my cherished, my loved Sister. To you my first, no, my greatest duty is due, and my greatest pleasure ever had been to think of fondly and kindly the sweet sister who has ever been loving and affectionate to her wayward brother. I would that I could be with you, comfortably seated around the old family hearthstone, talking over the events and trials of the memorable year which has just closed. To pour out every thought and emotion of my heart to you and have your affectionate sympathy and confidence would be a pleasure almost sufficient to wipe away the remembrance of the troublesome, dangerous times through which I have passed.

But then, dear Sister, this cannot be. The stern dictates of duty, the perils which beset our country, and the imperative necessity of every man remaining steadily and contentedly at his post retain me here. We should not murmur at the decrees of fate. It is our duty cheerfully and patiently to submit to every inconvenience, hardship, privation, and suffering which follow in the pursuit of and obedience of moral obligation. To murmur, fret, and be impatient but adds to our unhappiness and takes away what remains of our joy and pleasure. Patience under suffering and trial are the highest attributes of a refined and enlightened Christian civilization, and we cannot too assiduously and energetically cultivate this most commendable of virtues. By the observance of this great attribute of the deity in man we can gain something of pleasure in any situation of life and the sunshine of joy will ever break beautifully, refreshingly through the darkest, most threatening cloud.

Hence it is that I so calmly and submissively endure all the privations incident to a soldier's life. I murmur not and patiently endure all things and hopefully look forward to a bright, a happy future with the loved ones around whom my heart strings are so closely twined that no earthy power can tear them away.

Do you ever become impatient and murmur against the decrees of fate? I trust not. I hope your better judgement, your gentle disposition teaches you to calmly endure all in anticipation of the glorious, happy future which cannot, let us trust, be very far distant. Think of the happy days we will have when peace shall have been declared and we shall once more be firmly reunited, never to be severed on our pathway through life.

If you have not been patient under trial and separation during the past year, now with the new year enter upon new resolutions and carry them strictly out.

My greatest wish is for your happiness, your pleasure, your welfare. Let me but be assured that you are as happy and comfortable as my heart wishes you and I can quietly and with comparative happiness endure any fate, however hard, however sundered from every worldly joy.

With no other to love as warmly, devotedly, and entirely as I do you, and no one to care for me so much as you, it is natural that my first, greatest wish should be for your comfort and worldly happiness.

It is true, I have many devoted and loving relatives. My dear, good Grand Mother, my kind, affectionate Aunts and fatherly Uncles, and dearly do I love them all, but none of them can, in the nature of things, be so close to my heart as you, my only sister. The purest and most devoted love of my heart, ever there to thee, my own dear sister, as the one nearest and dearest on this earth.

I am sometimes very uneasy about you. I have not heard from you for a long, long time, but I cannot think any misfortune has befallen you, for evil news always travels fast.

I know nothing of what is going on at home. I cannot learn anything of the treatment you received from the enemy when they passed through Lauderdale and so near to you all. They must have annoyed you a great deal and injured everybody, more or less. To what extent they injured those in whom I am more particularly interested, I cannot learn from any source, so I am left to conjecture how you all were treated and what you suffered. But being of a hopeful disposition, I am glad to believe they did not trouble you much. I am induced to believe this since I have heard nothing to the contrary.[2]

I have written to you every chance and have been anxiously expecting to hear from you, but as yet not one word, not one line has reached me. I know you have but very few chances of sending letters and cannot go out to find persons coming to the army. From this fact I am not much at a loss to know why I cannot hear from you. But Capt. Bailey will return in a few days, and I know that I will hear all the news from you by him as he promised to deliver or send you my letter and bring me one from you. You cannot imagine how anxiously I am awaiting his return. Then I shall learn all that my heart is so anxious to know.

This is one of the coldest nights I ever felt. Everything is hard frozen, but I am very comfortably situated by a large, warm log fire and do not suffer any. We have a front room, floored, planked up on the side and covered with a tent fly with a large kitchen-like chimney and a good thick tent for a sleeping compartment. I have a good soft mattress, plenty of thick army blankets, and sleep almost as comfortably as if in a house. The troops all have substantial cabins, are tolerably well clothed and fed, and are doing finely.

To show that we are not starving, I will give you a bill of our fare for our dinner today. First, fine beef soup with Irish potatoes in it. Second, a fine turkey and sweet potatoes and some splendid roast beef . . . a very substantial dinner, that, for a soldier. I have two fine sweet potatoes in the fire roasting now and must stop to eat them.

I have finished eating the potatoes. They were excellent. I thought of you and Grandma all the time, picturing to myself what you were doing and flattered myself with the thought that you were thinking and probably talking of me. At the same time, I was so deeply in reverie and looking into the old familiar room in my fancy. Oh! would that the fancy were a reality and the happiness were mine to be with you a few short, pleasant hours.

But we must be patient a while longer. I cannot get off long enough to visit you now, but will as soon as possible. There is a system of furloughing the army. It applies only to soldiers and officers of the line, and I do not come under the provisions of the order. As soon as I can get a leave long enough, I shall certainly come to see you.

Tom and Uncle Elias are at Dalton. Both are well and getting on finely. They would write but I did not know until today of a chance to send letters and hence could not inform them in time. I am going down to see them sometime soon and will get them to write letters and send to me so as to have them ready for the next one passing.

I have not heard anything more from Tippah since I wrote you last, nor have I heard from Uncle Spinks and family recently.

I will write every opportunity. I hope to hear from you often.

My love to Grandma and all the relatives and such friends as may inquire of me.

Gen. Johnston is in command of the army, and we are all hopeful of good results in the next campaign.³

May God bless you, my sister,

Your affectionate Brother,

O. S. Palmer

Hd. Qtrs., Lowrey's Brigade
Dalton, Georgia
March 6th, 1864

Dear Sister,

I was very happy to receive your letter and to know that you were in as good health as could be anticipated. I cannot too deeply regret or lament the unhappy, wretched state of affairs in Lauderdale County. With the bands of tories, dark hearted marauders roaming at will through the country and laying their sacrilegious hands on everything that should be holy and sacred from the touch of war. I know the sad state of affairs. I lament the depredations they have made on you and Grandma.⁴

I did hope that they would not trouble you, but it seems they will not shun you. But, then, these things cannot, will not, last always. There is a better day coming. The bright sunlight of liberty, peace, and happiness will soon break through the gloom that now surrounds us and fill every heart with joy and pleasure. We must in the meantime be patient and calmly submit to the evil we cannot avoid.

To grieve over present troubles and have our minds entirely filled with the gloomy contemplation of unavoidable sorrows is heaping unnecessary trouble on our heads and doubling our sorrow. What cannot be cured must be philosophically endured. If you will look to the happy future, Sister, and refuse to dwell upon the gloomy present, you will find much more happiness and save yourself many hours of grief and sorrow.

I know how you are situated. I know the many good causes you have for sorrow, and my heart sometimes overflows at the thought of your isolated, unhappy situation. Gladly, oh, how gladly would I fly to your assistance were it in my power. But this cannot be. Other duties retain me here. Besides, you must not leave home now to go anywhere you might desire.

I received a long letter from Aunt Mary yesterday. All were well . . . doing finely. She regrets very much that you are not with her and sympathizes very deeply and sincerely with you all. She says she is very anxious for you to come to her house where she can render you every act of kindness in her power and expresses her hope that you may come whenever you are able and says she will render every effort to get you out of Lauderdale and bring you to her house.[5]

I think you were mistaken when you thought she did not want you with her. She would be happy for you to come stay with her and would do everything in her power to render you comfortable and contented. She has a kind heart, and you occupy a prominent place in it. She gives Elias, Tom, and myself a very pressing invitation to come to see her. I wish I could go, but I cannot. I must remain here.

I received a long letter from Oliver not long since giving me a minute history of every one of the family. He was still in bad health . . . did not know when he would be able to come to the army. Georgia was doing well. The baby (Sue Agnes) was improving some, but was a puny little thing.[6]

The remaining members of the family were doing tolerably well. Delia was in tolerable good health and improving. The most unpleasant part of the letter was an account of the killing of Uncle Roe Griffin by Uncle John P[almer]. He did not tell me what was the cause of the difficulty, merely said it was of a private nature and I could not know what it was until I saw some member of the family. It seems that Uncle Roe had determined for some reason to kill Uncle J. He made threats loudly and openly, and the day of the unfortunate occurrence he loaded his gun or pistol, ordered Aunt Sallie to pack up his clothing, went to Uncle J's home to kill him, did not find him at home, went on to Grandpa's and visited many threats.[7] Grandpa attempted to get him to go back home and cool down. "No, he would kill him that day," and started on to Uncle Roe's. On the way he met Uncle John and Aunt Cynthia and told him he had come to kill him and commenced getting out his pistol. Then Uncle John shot him down. He died almost instantly.[8]

Now this is all I know of it except that Aunt Sallie gave Uncle John notice that Uncle R was going to kill him that day. Aunt Sallie's and Uncle John's families still visit and are on the close terms of intimacy they have ever been. I am completely in the dark. I cannot imagine out of what the difficulty grew. I have written to Uncle Spinks to know something about it, and I suppose he will tell me.

It was a very unfortunate occurrence and very much to be regretted, no matter what the circumstances were. Uncle John was tried in the magistrate's court and acquitted almost without a hearing. I am very anxious to have an explanation of the matter and shall use every exertion to get one. I will inform you as soon as possible of the whole affair. You know as much of the particular state of feeling pervading the whole family as I do and come as near unraveling this mystery as I can, so we will drop the subject for the present.

We have had some stirring times here. The bold and rapid advance of Sherman in Mississippi, it seems, had given some alarm to the powers that be, and reinforcements were being hurried from the army of Gen. [Leonidas] Polk as rapidly as possible. Cheatham's Division of Tennesseans was being hurried forward and all of Cleburne's Division except this brigade was on the way. Our brigade did not get off, but I did. I obtained permission to go in advance of the brigade and join it at LaGrange. I went on down to see the young lady I wrote you about sometime since. I spent three days with her very pleasantly, and hearing startling news of fighting and preparations for the battle at Dallas, I hastened back.[9]

Cleburne's Division was all returning with the greatest speed, and everything indicated a general engagement when I reached here.

I got here late in the evening and in hunting for my command I passed along a great portion of the line, and all along the sharp, quick rattle of small arms and the occasional deep-toned thunder of the artillery gave token of an approaching battle. It seemed to me that every arrangement of position by the two armies would be completed that night and the rising sun of the next day would look down upon the two mighty armed hosts reeling in the mad fury of the dreadful conflict.

That night all was quiet. The opposing forces (I thought) were calmly resting, gathering strength for the death struggle of the morrow. But the morrow's sun rose on a far different scene from what I anticipated. The enemy had quietly withdrawn during the night and were in rapid retreat for Chattanooga. What the movement was intended to accomplish, I cannot imagine. Some think that they thought our army so weakened by sending off forces to Mississippi that we would not dare to oppose their advance, and they came out to drive us away, but when they felt our position, they found we were ready for them at all points and they did not feel disposed to hazard an engagement. There was but little fighting. Several sharp assaults were made by the enemy and each time repulsed in gallant style by our forces.[10]

Our army was never in finer fighting condition and humor and would have fought with great spirit and determination. Everyone has the greatest confidence in Gen. Johnston. We can safely trust our cause in his hands. He will act wisely and gallantly under all circumstances and, I think, will lead us to triumph over the vandal horde.

This summer campaign is one of great importance to us. If we hold our own, and all think we will, the war will end. Our independence will be established and happy hearts will fly home to loved ones. I think this year will end the war. Our success cannot be doubted. We will certainly whip the enemy. If we but do our duty, independence is ours, and it seems we will do our entire duty. Every attempt at an advance this year by the enemy has failed. We have thrown back every movement and we have only to be true to ourselves to do the same through the entire campaign.

I am getting on very well and have the best of spirits because I have the greatest confidence in the success or our cause. I see no cause for despondency. The faint streaks of the bright and glorious day of Independence are now distinctly to be seen and it cheers my heart to think this cruel war will soon be over and I can hasten home to greet loved ones from whom I have so long been separated. Let me urge you to gather comfort from hopes.

I saw Uncle Jesse and Cousin Ed the other day. They are both very well and doing finely. Roddey's command is now picketing our front and I expect to see Uncle Jesse often.

I am head over heels in love again. Do not censure me, for I cannot avoid loving a pretty woman. Love is the weakness of my nature.

Give my warmest love to Grandma and c. Tom is very well. So is Uncle Elias. Write to me every opportunity and give me all the news. I will write by everyone I can find passing.

George and Lige arrived safely. George is with Tom. Marion is very well and sends love to his mother.

Your affectionate Brother,
O. S. Palmer

> Hd. Qtrs., Lowrey's Brigade
> Dalton, Georgia
> March 31st, 1864

Dear Sister,

I have just seen Uncle Jesse and as he starts for home tomorrow morning, I take the opportunity to write you again.

I have not heard from you in a long while and I am very anxious to know how you are all getting along. If I could but know you were well and comparatively happy, a great burden would be removed from my heart, and I would be as merry and lighthearted a soldier as we have in our army.

I am doing very well. Am in excellent health and spirits and hopeful as to the results of our cause.

But the uneasiness I suffer on your account sometimes renders me sad, very sad, and disqualifies me from the prompt and efficient discharge of my duties as a soldier. To know that you were enjoying yourself in any way would relieve me of many unhappy moments and make me a much better soldier.

However, it is our duty to bear all without a murmur.

The army is in fine condition, hopeful, strong, and brave, ready to do battle heroically when the hour of trial and trouble comes.

All seem to think that this year will see the end of the war, that our independence will be firmly established, and we will return joyously to our homes to enjoy the blessings for which we have suffered so much to secure. God speed the glorious day.

However, Uncle Jesse can tell you much more about the army and our prospects than I can write.

I have not heard from Ripley for some time. I know nothing of them all.

I hope soon to hear from you and learn that you are doing finely.

My love to all.

Write every chance.

I have not time to write more now as it is night and I have to carry this up town to Uncle J[esse] tonight as he leaves by daylight tomorrow.

May God bless you and protect you is the constant wish of

Your affectionate Brother,

O. S. Palmer

> Hd. Qtrs., Lowrey's Brigade
> Dalton, Georgia
> April 20th, 1864

Dear Sister,

Capt. Simpson will leave for Florence tomorrow, and I avail myself of this opportunity with pleasure to write to you and the charming little nephew I am so anxious to see. I received Delia's letter a few days since and was happy to know that you were doing so well and that the boy was so stout and healthy.[11] It made my heart leap for joy to hear once again from those so dear to me. And the little stranger . . . what can I say of him that will come up to the desires and expectations of a fond and proud mother? I feel that I can say nothing worthy of the occasion or that would express the deep emotion that fills my bosom. If to wish him to be strong and healthy and vigorous in his babyhood and boyhood and sprightly, intellectual, and distinguished in his manhood as a doting mother could desire were anything like appropriate, know that you cannot entertain a hope for him that does not find an echo in my breast. May he be all that our continued hopes would desire him to be.

I know that you are very proud of him and think there never was such a boy before since he is so much like Tom. I can appreciate your feelings and trust that he may live to be your support and stay in your declining years to bless you with his love and attention and render you proud of his high standing among his fellow men.

Tom has been thinking as to what name to give him. I do not know whether he has yet decided on that important question or not. I suppose he has. No matter what name he has, he shall ever be near my heart, and if fate should decide that I am to be a jolly old bachelor, I shall take him under my particular care and endeavor to acquit myself of the trust as to render his mother still more fond of him.

Kiss him for me and give him very warmest love. Tell him I even now hear him in my fancy calling me Uncle, and I involuntarily search for gray hairs that should make him reverence and respect me, and not only look for, but I find some of them, and if this war should continue many years longer, he will be able to find my head thickly sprinkled with frost.

I am more anxious now than ever to visit home. Oh, how pleasant it would be for me to be with you all for a short time and how gladly would I fly to that haven of rest and home of happiness were it in my power. But you all advise me not to come and I cannot get off now anyway. The season for active operations has now arrived and every man should be at his post, for now more than at any previous time in the history of the war does our bleeding, suffering country require the services of every true and faithful son. The enemy are preparing and will soon be ready to make a last, desperate, mad effort to overthrow our Government and trample our liberties under their unhallowed feet. The final struggle of the war is to be made this year, and if our armies still hold their own and our banners still and proudly flaunt in triumph in face of a defeated and whipped foe, our independence will be established beyond doubt, and we can return to the arms of the loved ones at home. I entertain no doubt as to the result. Our cause is just, and a just God will deliver us from the hands of our enemies. How soon, no one save He can tell. We must hopefully and trustingly await His good time and pray for His blessing.

I received another long and affectionate letter from Aunt Mary a few days since. All were in good health. Uncle Spinks had just been home, and they had had a happy time of it. She gives me a pressing invitation to pay them a visit and, as I understand, offers me a sweetheart whose charms are irresistible. This is a very great temptation, and I am very anxious to go.

She gave me the first information that I had of the little stranger at home. She is very anxious to have you come and stay with her and says she will do everything she can to get you down there. She says she needs a pet and must claim your boy and is very anxious to have you and him with her.

I am glad Delia is with you and Grandma. She will be a great deal of company to you.

I am sorry to learn that the tories have treated you all so badly and robbed you so thoroughly. I wish it were in my power to render you some assistance, and I may be sometime this summer.

The army is quiet and in fine fighting trim. I do not know what the prospects are for an early engagement.

My love to Grandma and the boy.

Write to me every chance.

With many wishes for the health [and] happiness of yourself and the boy.

I remain, your affectionate Brother,

O. S. Palmer

[*in margin*]

I will send a long letter to Delia by Capt. Simpson on Monday.

Hd. Qtrs., Lowrey's Brigade
In the field, June 29th, 1864[12]

Dear Tom,

I have not written you for some time but have kept Uncle Elias as well posted as to my condition and asked him to inform you. I am quite well now but was a little unwell ten days since when we first reached our present position. But the kindness of Uncle E___ in sending me some very necessary articles revived me and I am now prepared to endure more hardships.

Since we have been here, we have had some severe skirmishing and once on the 27th the enemy charged us with seven lines of battle. We have whipped them all the time in the several skirmishes and repulsed them with great slaughter on the 27th.[13]

At 9 a.m. on the 27th the enemy opened a severe artillery fire on the left of our brigade which lasted for ½ hour. Then the enemy massed two brigades in column of regiments, one close behind the other in a thick wood and slight ravine in front of our left (32nd Miss.) Regt. With fixed bayonets and loaded guns, the huge mass surged forward. In the meantime, with grape and cannister and minnie balls we were making fearful gaps in their ranks.

On they came to within forty yards of our works. Then the front of the column staggered and fell, and the second brigade charged over the first and came within less than 30 yards of the section of artillery on our left. But bone and muscle could not endure the terrible leaden hail poured into their faces. They halted, lay down, and finally fled back in wild disarray to their works.

Some came up to surrender, not caring to run back under so galling a fire. It is estimated that the loss of the enemy in front of our line and Polk's where they charged could not be less than 1500 killed and wounded. They removed their dead under flag of truce last night and the colonel in charge of this party states that their loss was not less than 1500. We had only one regiment and part of another engaged and lost but four or five men. We were well protected by breastworks and have lost but few men.

At the same time, similar assaults were made on Cheatham, Walker, Loring, and Stevenson, and everywhere they were repulsed with terrible slaughter. A general engagement was anticipated yesterday, but nothing more than the usual skirmishing occurred as far as I can ascertain.

The Atlanta people can yet rest easy. Sherman will not eat his dinner there on the 4th of July.

A Lady friend near LaGrange, Ga., has promised to send me a box of vegetables addressed to your care at Atlanta. If the said box comes at all, it will be there in a few days, and I would be glad if you would send it up to Uncle E___ at once and get him to inform me.

Please get me a pipe and send it up the first opportunity.

Affectionately yours and c.,

O. S. Palmer

[William Lytle Foster to Oliver S. Kennedy][14]
Selma, Alabama
Wednesday, August 17th[, 1864]

Dear Oliver,

Your letter of the 5th reached me at this place. I wrote to Georgia twice, also a long letter to you, before leaving Talladega. After recovering from the [illegible] I had at Alexander[?]White's, I became so [illegible] with the place that I determined to "change my base" to this place and found when too late that I have "jumped from the frying pan into the fire." I am having a very lonely and disagreeable time, being forced to keep [to] my room more than half the time and, when up, meeting but few of my former friends and associates. I shall not remain here longer that I can hear from Robert, when I think I shall join him in Griffen, [Georgia,] or perhaps endeavor to make my way to North Alabama. If I determine upon the latter step, I will write to either Georgie or yourself before starting.[15]

Enclosed you will find my last letter from Robert. It contains some information that might prove interesting to Georgie. Uncle Frank [Benjamin Franklin Foster, Sr.] passed here yesterday on his way back to Florence. He had his negroes with him and intended (I think, very foolishly,) to take them home. He reported all well in Florence. The only one of his servants who went with the Yankees was Jenny[?] who died very soon after going off. The others were all still at home. All of Uncle Washington's [i.e., George Washington Foster's] that were north of the river except the girl Louisiana left. He still has some twenty or thirty in his Courtland farm.[16] Uncle Tom [Thomas Jefferson Foster] is at present on his plantation and has lost no negroes during the last year.[17] Mr. [James Hood?] Simpon lost nearly everything, so, with the permission of Corndice[?] G., James visited Nashville for the purpose of seeing how he would like Yankee freedom, and after an absence of some four or five weeks returned, fully determined to remain in his present condition. He reports that old Delia and all her children together with every other one of [*page torn. two words illegible*] family negroes were disgusted with the Yankees and had all returned to their former homes.

I can give you but little army news that you will not get in the public prints. Everyone from Atlanta is confident that our army will hold the place. The Yankee cavalry has been completely demolished as most of it, if not all, was sent out on different raids and in every instance except at Okmulgee have been defeated and most of them captured.[18]

On Monday last, Wheeler, with his whole command, were ordered to the rear of Sherman's army, and it is reported (I know not upon what authority) that he succeeded in getting to the Atlanta and Chattanooga R.R. If such is the fact and he can cut off the Yankee supplies, Sherman will be forced to retreat or hazard everything on an attack on our fortifications. In either event, I cannot doubt the result and feel confident that our boys will prove the victors and [*three words illegible*] their forces.[19] As regards Mobile, the general opinion is that we will [must?] leave[?] to [*illegible*] the city. I doubt it. I [*illegible*] you to [*illegible*] when I was in the city. I do not know whether or not [*illegible*] them. I have not heard from or of him lately. The board of [*illegible*] there are without doubt the [*illegible*] I have [*illegible*] met. Write me and [*illegible*] to any [*illegible*] I may [*illegible*] to go. To your father's family, one and all, present my kindest regards. To my dear Georgie and her sweet child, God bless you all.

Sincerely and truly yours,

Will L.

* * *

In May 1864, the Fifteenth Arkansas was consolidated with Lieut. Col. William H. Martin's (formerly Fagan's) First Arkansas Infantry and placed under the command of Col. John W. Colquitt. From May through July the consolidated regiment took part in the battles of Kennesaw Mountain, Dalton, Resaca, New Hope Church, and Atlanta, during which it suffered 15 killed, 67 wounded, and 3 missing. On 23 July—the day following the battle of Atlanta—the brigade's commander, Daniel Chevilette Govan, reported the total strength of the First/Fifteenth Arkansas at only 114 men.[20]

In his report of the 1 September 1864 battle of Jonesboro, Col. John Weir who was temporarily commanding Lowrey's brigade, reported that Palmer and aide-de-camp T. J. Williams had "rendered me efficient service, and were conspicuous for their gallantry and courage."[21] In that battle, however, the First/Fifteenth Arkansas and its colors were captured, along with Colonel Govan and much of the rest of his brigade. The regiment was quickly exchanged, however, and returned to the army one month later, in time to participate in John Bell Hood's disastrous Tennessee campaign.[22]

On 19 November 1862, Palmer had written that Nashville was "entirely too strong for us to take, unless we sacrifice more men than adequate to the good to be derived therefrom." Even so, with Jefferson Davis's blessing, John Bell Hood—"all lion, none of the fox," in Stephen Vincent Benét's evaluation—led the remains of the once mighty Army of Tennessee back toward Nashville in a foolish and futile attempt to draw Sherman out of the Confederate heartland.

Following his loss of Atlanta in September 1864, Hood had hoped to disrupt Maj. Gen. William T. Sherman's line of communication with Chattanooga, thereby forcing him to give up his prize. Sherman, however, opted to abandon his line of supply and "live off the land" in Georgia's rich farm country.

With Sherman marching for the coast, Hood and the 39,000 men remaining in the Army of Tennessee moved north into Tennessee, hoping to recapture Nashville and continue north into Kentucky. The Federal commander, however, taking advantage of his vast numerical superiority, divided his command in two, leading one half toward Savannah while entrusting Maj. Gen. George H. Thomas's 60,000-man Army of the Cumberland with the defense of Tennessee. Rather than being dismayed by the presence of a Rebel army on his rear, Sherman declared that this was exactly what he wanted and that if Hood "continues to march North, all the way to Ohio, I will supply him with rations."[23]

After spending the first three weeks of November in the area of Florence, Alabama, Hood marched north, attempting to drive between the two widely separated halves of the Union army, planning to destroy each in detail. But Maj. Gen. John McAllister Schofield retreated rapidly from Pulaski to Columbia on the Duck River where he erected fortifications before the Confederate arrival on 24 November. As the short story writer, journalist, and poet Ambrose Bierce, then a first lieutenant in the Ninth Indiana Infantry and the topographical officer on the staff of Col. Philip Sidney Post and therefore "naturally favored with a good view of the performance," wrote of his experiences of the campaign, "For several days, in snow and rain, General Schofield's little army had crouched in its hastily constructed defenses at Columbia, Tennessee. It had retreated in hot haste from Pulaski, thirty miles to the south, arriving just in time to foil Hood, who, marching from Florence, Alabama, by another road with a force of more than double our strength, had hoped to intercept us. Had he succeeded, he would indubitably have bagged the whole bunch of us."

At Columbia, Schofield delayed Hood's advance until the twenty-ninth when he received orders from Thomas to withdraw toward Franklin. Then, wrote Bierce, "we pulled up stakes and crossed to the north bank [of Duck River] to continue our retreat to Nashville, where Thomas and safety lay—such safety as is known in war."

On the morning of 29 November, Hood sent the corps of Maj. Gen, Benjamin F. Cheatham and Lt. Gen. Alexander P. Stewart across the Duck River to flank Schofield out of his position. With his army in danger, Schofield retreated ten miles north to Spring Hill where Hood failed to capitalize on the opportunity to intercept and destroy the Federal command, which slipped away, marching twelve miles into Franklin on the morning of the thirtieth.

His back to the Harpeth River, Schofield, without pontoon bridges with which to withdraw, determined to defend Franklin and so began preparing a formidable semicircular line of fortifications with both flanks anchored on the Harpeth. If the Confederates had not arrived by the evening of the thirtieth, Schofield had planned to abandon Franklin and pull back across the river, but Hood appeared at 1:00 p.m. and immediately ordered a mad frontal assault on the entrenched Union forces.

Cheatham protested that he did not "like the looks of this fight; the enemy has an excellent position and is well fortified." Forrest proposed that his cavalry be supplemented with a division of infantry with which, he was sure, he could flank Schofield out of his position "within an hour." Hood, however, maintained that he would rather fight an entrenched enemy at Franklin than at Nashville where "they have been strengthening themselves for three years."[24]

He was determined that "before the enemy would be able to reach his stronghold at Nashville, to make that same afternoon another and final effort to overtake and rout him, and drive him in the Big Harpeth river at Franklin."[25]

As Sgt. William E. Bevens of the consolidated First/Fifteenth Arkansas recollected, however, "the Yankees had been reinforced and had entrenched at Franklin, behind the works they had built some months before. In front of their works was an open field with not a tree or ravine for a mile and a half. Just before the breastworks was an open ditch six feet wide and three feet deep. At the end of the ditch next to the breastworks, were placed poles sharpened spear-shape. Their main works were six feet at the base. The cannon-breast portion was cut down so that the guns, resting on oak logs, were on a level with our bodies."[26]

With Cheatham's corps on the left and Stewart's on the right, the Confederates began moving forward at 4:00 p.m. Lt. Gen. Stephen D. Lee's corps, and almost all of the army's artillery, had yet to arrive from Columbia. Hood's attacking force, between 19,000 and 20,000 men, crossed two miles of open ground with only two batteries of artillery in support.

Cleburne's was the only division in the Confederate Army allowed to carry colors other than the Confederate national flag, fighting, instead, under its Hardee-pattern flag, a blue field with white border enclosing a full moon image and surrounded by the names of the battles in which the regiment had played a significant and honorable role. The flag of the Fifteenth Arkansas bore battle honors from Shiloh, Perryville, Richmond, Murfreesboro, Farmington, Bridge Creek, Tuscumbia Creek, Tunnel Hill, Liberty Gap, Ringgold Gap, and, most prominently, Chickamauga.[27]

"Friends and foes soon learned to watch the course of the blue flag that marked where Cleburne was in the battle," wrote William J. Hardee. "Where this division defended, no odds broke its lines; where it attacked, no numbers resisted its onslaught; save only once—there is the grave of Cleburne and his heroic division."[28]

Cleburne, in common with almost every other senior officer of the army, objected to the attack on Franklin, but obeyed. "Boys, we are ordered to charge the works. I don't think we can take them, but we can try. Forward!"[29]

Hood's was an unconscionable tactical blunder. The Confederate assault, sometimes called the "Pickett's Charge of the West," resulted in a devastating loss to the Army of Tennessee in men and leadership, with fourteen generals and fifty-five regimental commanders killed, wounded, or captured. Among them was the redoubtable Patrick Cleburne whose "inspiring voice," wrote his adjutant, was "hushed by death" at the head of his division. The Fifteenth Arkansas and the numerous other regiments with which it had by then been consolidated sustained a sixty-six percent casualty rate in the slaughter at Franklin, including Capt. Orlando S. Palmer, "the gallant adjutant of Lowery's brigade," who was mortally wounded, dying of his wounds on 19 January 1865 in Columbia, Tennessee. A monument marks his burial place in the Kennedy-Stutts Cemetery near his family home at Green Hill, Alabama.[30]

Afterword

> Florence has had so many of her brave and gallant young gentlemen killed in this dreadful, dreadful war.
>
> —Sallie Independence Foster diary, September 30, 1864, Sallie Independence Foster Collection, Collier Library, University of North Alabama Archives and Special Collections.

Historian Wiley Sword has characterized the disastrous battle of Franklin and Hood's equally ruinous assault on Nashville as "the Confederacy's last hurrah."[1] If, as Sam Watkins of the First Tennessee Infantry wrote, Franklin was "the finishing stroke to the independence of the Southern Confederacy," then Nashville was its Armageddon.[2]

During the night of 30 November, John M. Schofield withdrew from Franklin, occupying the defenses of Nashville on 1 December. There he came under the direct command of Maj. Gen. George H. Thomas, whose combined force then approximated 55,000 men and occupied a seven-mile-long semicircular line, studded with forts, with both flanks anchored on the Cumberland River.[3]

The Army of Tennessee arrived before Nashville on 2 December, but, because he realized that he lacked adequate force to assault the Union lines, the aggressive Hood assumed a defensive posture, anticipating that Thomas would attack him. Hoping to lure the Federals out of their works, on 2 December, Hood detached a division from Cheatham's corps to demonstrate against the Nashville and Chattanooga Railroad and the city of Murfreesboro, on Thomas's rear. Three days later, he reinforced this diversionary force with two additional brigades of infantry and two divisions of cavalry, all under Bedford Forrest's command. Although Forrest cut the railroad in several places, he was unable to overcome the garrison at Murfreesboro, and Thomas maintained his lines at Nashville.

But simply holding his line was not enough. Lt. Gen. U. S. Grant, now the general-in-chief of the United States armies, and the Lincoln administration strongly urged Thomas to take the offensive and destroy Hood's army or at least to drive it from Tennessee. "If I had been in Hood's place," Grant later asserted, "I would have gone to Louisville and on north until I came to Chicago," and Lincoln complained that Thomas's apparent inactivity was a reprise of "the McClellan and Rosecrans strategy of do nothing and let the rebels raid the country." Under such pressure Thomas, known somewhat derisively by his fellow officers as "Old Slow Trot," was equally avid to assume the offensive, but he prepared cautiously.[4]

When, by 13 December, Thomas had not yet moved, Grant ordered Maj. Gen. John A. Logan to Nashville to assume command. Moreover, Grant himself departed Petersburg on 14 December, intent upon taking personal command if, before his arrival, Thomas had not moved. On 15 December, however, before Logan or Grant had arrived, Thomas moved out of his trenches and attacked Hood's lines.

Thomas opened the battle with a diversionary attack on the Confederate right, designed to cause Hood to divert troops from his left where the main Union attack was to fall. The diversion was repulsed however, sustaining heavy casualties, and failed to cause the Confederates to shift any troops from their present locations.

Despite this check, Thomas ordered a wheeling movement to strike the Confederate left. The onslaught fell on A. P. Stewart's corps at about 2:30 P.M., capturing much of Hood's defenses and sending the defenders scrambling to the rear. Only determined rearguard actions kept the retreat from becoming a rout.

The shattered remnant of Hood's army formed a new line, much more compact than the one that it had occupied at dawn, a mile or two to the south, this one anchored on the east on Peach Orchard Hill and following a line of hills leading south from Compton's Hill, and a series of dry stack stone walls. But although the Confederate defenses atop Compton's Hill appeared to be strong, the hill's crest was exposed to Union artillery fire, its fortifications were only slight, and, as had been the case at Chattanooga, the trenches were constructed on the geographical crest of the hill rather than on the military crest commanding the slopes.

Thomas renewed his attack on 16 December, and although fire from the entrenched Confederates broke up a diversion against their right, Schofield's corps delivered the main assault against the Rebel left, overrunning Compton's Hill, disintegrating and rolling up the Confederate left flank from west to east, and sending the demoralized remnant streaming south through Franklin and, on 19 December, across the Duck River at Columbia. Only a masterful rearguard action conducted by N. B. Forrest saved the once mighty Army of Tennessee from annihilation.

Thomas reported 387 killed, 2,562 wounded, and 112 missing in the two days' fighting, while, at best estimate, Hood lost 12,500 killed and wounded in addition to 4,561 captured. On 20 January, Hood reported the effective strength of the Army of Tennessee, that had begun the campaign with approximately 38,000 men, at 18,742 infantry and artillery.

In the words of Sam Watkins, "The once proud Army of Tennessee had degenerated to a mob. We were pinched by hunger and cold. The rains, and sleet, and snow never ceased falling from the winter sky, while the winds pierced the old, ragged, gray-back Rebel soldier to his very marrow. . . . Our country is gone, our cause is lost. *Actum est de Republica*."[5]

Hood retreated to Tupelo, Mississippi, resigned on 13 January 1865, and was never again tendered a command. In the sardonic words of a song, sung to the tune of "The Yellow Rose of Texas" by the retreating Rebels, "the gallant Hood of Texas played Hell in Tennessee."

In the meantime, William T. Sherman redeemed his pledge to "make Georgia howl." In the face of virtually no resistance, his army group advanced from Atlanta to Savannah in a sixty-mile-wide front, destroying infrastructure and supplies and, to a large degree, the South's will to continue the war.

The remnant of Govan's Brigade that survived the Tennessee Campaign remained with the Army of Tennessee through its final engagements in the 1865 Carolinas campaign. In the reorganization of the Army of Tennessee at Smithfield, North Carolina, on 9 April 1865, the Fifteenth Arkansas was consolidated with nine other depleted Arkansas regiments, the First, Second, Fifth, Eighth, Thirteenth, Nineteenth (Dawson's), Twenty-Fourth, and the Third Confederate Infantry, in which the survivors of the Fifteenth Arkansas were consolidated into a single understrength company, "Company H," of the new First Arkansas Consolidated Infantry, which surrendered with the Army of Tennessee at Greensboro, North Carolina, on 26 April 1865.

On 17 February 1877, Oliver and Georgia Kennedy moved to Fort Worth, Texas, where he studied law under his former regimental commander, Judge William Basil Wood, with whom he entered into practice.

There, too, Kennedy became a real estate developer, purchasing the portion of Tarrant County on which the city of Kennedale, Texas, was built. Kennedy platted the city and donated every other lot to the Southern Pacific Railroad. He also owned the land upon which the historic Castle of Heron Bay now stands. Oliver S. Kennedy died of pneumonia on 26 February 1909 and he and his wife are buried in the city's Oakwood Cemetery.[6]

After the war, Thomas Brown Winston returned to college in Florence, ultimately earning a master's degree and becoming an educator.[7] By 1880 he and his wife had returned to Tippah County, Mississippi, where they established a school. "If you want to send your boy to a school of healthy and moral surroundings," said an item in a local newspaper, "we can consciencely recommend Blue Mountain Academy." The tuition and fees, the notice continued, "are exceedingly moderate," and "Prof. T. B. Winston is a thorough gentleman and an accomplished and successful teacher." Winston later served as the superintendent of public education in Searcy, Arkansas. He then opened a school in Hope, Arkansas, but by 1900 the couple and their family had moved to the rapidly growing railroad town of Texarkana on the border of northeast Texas and southwest Arkansas, where Winston established Winston's School at Eighth and Walnut. He died there on 25 September 1907, and Missie—who had suffered a spinal injury in a stairway fall in her home and lived, according to her obituary, "for many years an invalid"—died on 18 May 1922. Both are buried in Woodlawn Cemetery, Texarkana, Arkansas.[8]

But Missie had brought with her, her brother's letters, and after her death they remained, unknown and unclaimed, in the attic of her home at 203 Wood Street. Not until 2016 were they discovered and donated to the Wilbur Smith Research Archive, Museum of Regional History, Texarkana, Texas, where they are now housed.

Notes

Introduction

1. Orlando Sylvester Palmer (his middle name is sometimes seen as Stutts) was born at Green Hill in 1839. His younger sister, Artimisia Palmer, was born in Tippah County, Mississippi, in 1841, but with the death of her father in 1844 she moved with her family to the home of her maternal grandparents in Green Hill and as a young woman attended the Female Seminary in Florence.

    Little is known of the life of Paschal Palmer. He was born on 15 November 1815, the son of Randolph Eubanks Palmer and Sarah Walker. On June 26, 1837, was commissioned a captain in the Second Brigade, First Division, of the Alabama state militia, presumably for service in the Second Seminole War. By 1840 he and his family had moved to Ripley, Mississippi, to become farmers. There he was the owner of three enslaved men, presumably the George, Marion, and Jessie mentioned in these letters.

    Orlando Palmer had a great many paternal aunts, uncles, and cousins, but he seldom mentions them. In fact, as he wrote to his sister, one of his young cousins would never know "there was ever such a chap in existence as myself except it knows me but to curse and scorn and loathe me, for it is to be expected it will be trained up in the way in which its parents think it should go."

    Martha Person "Patsy" (Kennedy) Palmer was born on March 8, 1821, the daughter of Hiram and Mary Spinks Kennedy. She died in Green Hill, Alabama, on July 28, 1851, and is buried in the Kennedy-Stutts Cemetery. "Family Register," Kennedy Family Bible, copy in Palmer papers, Wilbur Smith Research Archive, Museum of Regional History, Texarkana, Texas; Iola Edwards Field, "Miss Vernon Winston: Childhood through College," typescript, 1949, Wilbur Smith Research Archive, Museum of Regional History, Texarkana, Texas, 1–3.

2. John Alexander Kennedy to North Carolina congressman Archibald McBryde. January 1812, Archives of the War Department, Washington, D.C. See also Blackwell P. Robinson, *The History of Moore County—1747–1847* (Southern Pines, N.C.: Moore County Historical Association, 1956); Bill Case, "Rifles of Bear Creek: A Look at the Colonial Kennedy Long Rifle

Factory," *The* [Pinehurst, North Carolina] *Pilot*, 26 March 2018; K. S. Melvin, "David Kennedy" in William S. Powell, ed., *Dictionary of North Carolina Biography* (Chapel Hill: University of North Carolina Press, 1988), 3:350.

3. Blackwell P. Robinson, *The History of Moore County—1747–1847* (Southern Pines, N.C.: Moore County Historical Association, 1956).
4. Green Hill was founded in the 1830s at the site of Sweetgum Flat Primitive Baptist Church. Green Hill was called Cornish in 1830, Cherry Grove in 1841, and finally Green Hill in 1850 to honor Green Berry Hill, a captain in the Mexican War. Green Hill extends from the Tennessee state line southward for about nine miles, bordered by Shoal Creek and Blue Water Creek. Earliest settlers came from Moore and Cumberland Counties in North Carolina and were in the area by 1810. Travel to the area was expedited when Andrew Jackson's Military Road was completed around 1820, bringing stagecoach stops and inns to the community. *The Heritage of Lauderdale County, Alabama* (Lauderdale County Heritage Book Committee, 1999).
5. Florence's Wesleyan University—until 1855 known as LaGrange College—was sacked by Union troops on April 28, 1863. All of its buildings, including its 4,000-volume library, were burned. Rebuilt after the war, it is now known as the University of North Alabama.
6. On the envelope to one of his letters from Bowling Green to his sister, Palmer scratched out "Sgt. Major" in the return address and wrote above it "1st Lieut." The postmark gives the date only as January. *List of Staff Officers of the Confederate States Army, 1861–1865* (Washington, D.C.: Government Printing Office, 1891), 124; Joseph H. Crute, Jr., (Powhatan, Va.: Derwent Books, 1982), 127, 216.

    Palmer served as Wood's adjutant from October 9, 1862 until January 1, 1863 and as Lowery's from October 1863 until November 30, 1864.
7. For an excellent analysis of the importance of irregular operations, see Daniel E. Sutherland, *A Savage Conflict: The Decisive Role of Guerrillas in the American Civil War* (Chapel Hill: University of North Carolina Press, 2009).
8. Walt Whitman to Horace Traubel, December 15, 1889. Jeanne Chapman and Robert Macisaac, eds., *With Walt Whitman in Camden* (Carbondale: Southern Illinois University Press, 1982), 6:194.
9. Orlando S. Kennedy, "United Confederate Veterans Descriptive List," Southwest Collection, Special Collections Library at Texas Tech University, Lubbock, Texas.
10. The Oliver S. Kennedy papers are housed in the University of Teas at Arlington's special collections library. James Edmonds Saunders, *Early Settlers of Alabama* (New Orleans, La.: L. Graham and Son, 1899); Willis Brewer, comp., *Brief Historical Sketches of Military Organizations Raised in Alabama*

during the Civil War, reproduced from *Alabama, Her History, Resources, War Record, and Public Men, from 1540 to 1872* (Montgomery: Alabama State Department of Archives and History, 1966), 616; *History of Texas, together with a Biographical History of Tarrant and Parker Counties* (Chicago, Ill.: Lewis Publishing Company, 1895), 315–16.

Chapter 1

1. The Cumberland School of Law, the oldest in Tennessee and the first west of the Appalachian Mountains, was established in 1847 by Judge Abraham Caruthers, an innovator in legal education. In a time when legal study was conducted by apprenticeship or through lectures, the Cumberland School pioneered an instructional method based on intensive trial practice.
   The school's buildings were burned by Federal troops in 1865, but it continued its programs. In 1961, the law school moved to the campus of Howard College, now Samford University, in Birmingham, Alabama.
2. The best guides to the secession movement in Arkansas remain Michael B. Dougan, *Confederate Arkansas: The People and Politics of a Frontier State* (Tuscaloosa: University of Alabama Press, 1976), James M. Woods, *Rebellion and Realignment: Arkansas's Road to Secession* (Fayetteville: University of Arkansas Press, 1987), and Mark. K. Christ, ed., *The Die is Cast: Arkansas Goes to War, 1861* (Little Rock: Butler Center Books, 2010).
3. This would seem to be Anna Simonton of Lawrenceburg, Giles County, Tennessee, twenty-three miles north of Florence, Alabama. On 11 April 1872 she married Benjamin Franklin Reed, also of Giles County, who served as a private in Company K, Ninth Tennessee Cavalry.
4. Solon E. Rose, a Pulaski attorney, was born in Tennessee in or about 1819.
5. Levi Marion Rodgers was born on 5 March 1840 in Warren County, Tennessee. He died on 19 April 1926 in Stanford, Greene County, Arkansas, and is buried in the Mount Zion Cemetery, Walcott, Arkansas.
6. William Lowndes Yancey was born on 10 August 1814 in Warren County, Georgia, but was raised in Troy, New York, by "a fiercely abolitionist stepfather and an emotionally unstable mother" leading him to the belief that Abolitionists were "cruel, meddling, and hypocritical." Yancey attended Williams College from 1830 to 1833 but left without graduating and then studied law in Greenville, South Carolina, and was admitted to the bar in 1834.
   By the time he moved to Alabama in 1836—ultimately locating in Wetumpka where he operated a plantation and edited two newspapers—Yancey was firmly committed to the institution of chattel slavery. In 1841 he was elected to the Alabama legislature, became a state senator in 1843,

and in 1844 was elected to the U.S. Congress. He resigned in 1846, however, to lead the resistance to the growing Abolition movement in the North. As a response to the 1848 Wilmot Proviso, Yancey drafted the so-called "Alabama Platform," in which he insisted that Congress lacked the Constitutional authority to bar slaveholders from moving their property into Federal territory.

Although the "Alabama Platform" was rejected by the 1848 Democratic National Convention, it garnered substantial support throughout the South and at the Democratic National Convention in Charleston in 1860, it won qualified acceptance, prompting the Southern delegates to withdraw and nominate a rival ticket.

Yancey supported John C. Breckenridge and the "Constitutional Democrats" in the election of 1860, and when Abraham Lincoln was elected he drafted Alabama's secession ordinance. In 1862 he was elected to the Confederate Senate, where he served until his death in Montgomery, Alabama, on 27 July 1863.

Shortly after his death, Lt. Alfred Moore, serving in the Thirty-Third Alabama Infantry, wrote to his brother that in Yancey's death the state "has lost one of her greatest statesmen, a great loss at this time. Oh, that [he] could have lived to see the final result of this war and see the South a free nation." Eric H. Walther, *William Lowndes Yancey and the Coming of the Civil War* (Chapel Hill: University of North Carolina Press, 2006); Alfred Moore to brother, 2 August 1863, Harrison, Tennessee, Alfred Moore letters, Alabama Department of Archives and History, Montgomery, Alabama.

7. Thomas Porter Weakley, a schoolteacher, was born on 14 July 1839 in Triune, Tennessee, but by 1860 was a resident of Nashville. On 1 May 1861 he enlisted in Company C, Second Tennessee Infantry, and was elected as his company's sergeant. On 1 July 1863 he was promoted to regimental major. He died on 26 July 1910 and is buried in Nashville's Mount Olivet Cemetery.
8. The grave of Andrew Jackson, which is adjacent to that of James K. Polk on the Tennessee capitol grounds, is now adorned by Clark Mills's famed equestrian statue.
9. Joseph Bridges Anderson, a Lebanon attorney, was born on 12 December 1844 in Wilson County, Tennessee. During the war, he served as a corporal in Company G of Col. William S. McLemore's Fourth Tennessee Cavalry. He died on 18 June 1892 in Gordonsville, Tennessee.
10. On 9 May 1860 the national convention of the Constitutional Union Party, consisting largely of former Whigs from the South who opposed secession, nominated former Senator John Bell of Tennessee for president and former Secretary of State Edward Everett of Massachusetts for vice president. In

the presidential election that November, Bell and Everett finished third in the electoral vote and fourth in the popular vote. Michael F. Holt, *The Election of 1860: A Campaign Fraught with Consequences* (Topeka: University Press of Kansas, 2017; Joseph Parks, *John Bell of Tennessee* (Baton Rouge: Louisiana State University Press, 1950).

11. David Lewis Kennedy, a Methodist minister, was a son of Mary and Hiram Kennedy. He was born in Lauderdale County, Alabama, on 2 March 1826 and died in Madison County, Florida, in 1863. He is buried in the Kennedy-Stutts Cemetery at Green Hill, Alabama.

12. Delia was Adelia Parthenia Kennedy, born on 28 July 1844 in Tippah County, Mississippi, the daughter of William Wesley and Cynthia Walker Palmer Kennedy and the younger sister of Oliver S. Kennedy. She died on 17 May 1921 in Little Rock, Arkansas.

13. Aunt Olive was Martha Palmer's sister, Olive Elizabeth "Ollie" Kennedy, born on 9 August 1836 at Green Hill, Alabama, only three years before her nephew Orlando. On 23 November 1857 she married John Jesse Westmorland Brooks. She died on 3 July 1896 at Kemp, Texas, and is buried in Florence, Alabama.

14. This child seems to have not survived infancy.

15. Here Palmer slightly misquotes John Milton's description of Eve in *Paradise Lost*. (1667) book 4, l, line 10.

16. Joseph Milner was born in 1824 in Leeds, Yorkshire, but was living in Lauderdale County, Alabama, no later than 1860 when he married Missie's sometime friend, Margaret A. Woodell. He died in Florence, Alabama, on 28 January 1894.

    Elias was Orlando Palmer's uncle, Elias Windsor Kennedy.

17. Sir Walter Scott's Waverley Novels is a series of more than two dozen medieval romances published between 1814 and 1832. Among the most notable works in the series are *Waverley* (1814), *Guy Mannering* (1815), *Rob Roy* (1817), *The Heart of Midlothian* (1818), *Ivanhoe* (1819), *Kenilworth* (1821), and *Quentin Durward* (1823).

    The series deals with Scottish history, establishing Scott as the founder of the historical novel genre.

    These intensely romantic novels often privilege the heroic traditions of the past over practical visions of the future, inspiring Mark Twain to write *A Connecticut Yankee in King Arthur's Court* in rebuttal. Twain, in *Life on the Mississippi*, claims that "the South has not yet recovered from the debilitating influence" of Scott's books and refers to the South's continuing Lost Cause mentality as "the Walter Scott disease." According to Twain, the Waverley novels set "the world in love with dreams and phantoms; with decayed and swinish forms of religion; with decayed and degraded systems of government; with the sillinesses and emptiness, sham grandeurs, sham gauds, and sham chivalries of a brainless and worthless long-vanished society." Such literature would, of course, appeal to Palmer's hyper-romantic sensibilities.

18. Washington Irving, an American short-story writer, essayist, and historian, was born in Manhattan, New York, on 3 April 1783. He is best known for his stories "Rip Van Winkle" and "The Legend of Sleepy Hollow," both of which appeared in his collection *The Sketch Book of Geoffrey Crayon, Gent*. He also served as the United States' ambassador to Spain in the 1840s. Irving died on 28 November 1859 in Tarrytown, New York.

19. The presidential election of 1860 pitted John Bell of Tennessee and Edward Everett of Massachusetts, the moderate Constitutional Union candidates, against John C. Breckenridge of Kentucky and Joseph Lane of Oregon, the pro-slavery Southern Democratic contenders. Palmer fails to mention Stephen A. Douglas of Illinois, the regular Democratic candidate, and the election's ultimate victor, Abraham Lincoln, who was profoundly unpopular in the South and who, in fact, was not listed on ballots in the Southern states.

20. Alfred Osborn Pope Nicholson was born on 31 August 1808 near Franklin, Tennessee. He graduated from the University of North Carolina in 1827, studied law, and was admitted to the bar in 1831. While practicing law in Columbia, Tennessee he also edited the *Western Mercury*. He served in the Tennessee House of Representatives from 1833 to 1839, and in 1840 was appointed to fill the United States Senate seat vacated by the death of Senator Felix Grundy, serving from 25 December 1840 until 7 February 1842. In 1843 he moved to Nashville where he served in the Tennessee State Senate, edited the *Nashville Union*, and served as president of the Bank of Tennessee. In 1853 he declined appointment to President Franklin Pierce's cabinet.

In 1859, Nicholson was elected to the United States Senate, serving from 4 March 1859 until resigning 3 March 1861 on the eve of his state's secession. After the Civil War, Nicholson served as Chief Justice of the Tennessee Supreme Court from 1870 until his death in Columbia, Tennessee, on 23 March 1876. "Alfred Osborn Pope Nicholson," *Biographical Directory of the United States Congress*, United States Congress.

Andrew Ewing was born in Nashville on 17 June 1813 and after graduating from the University of Nashville in 1832 went on to study law and was admitted to the bar in 1835. He was elected as a Democrat to the Thirty-First Congress, serving from 4 March 1849 to 3 March 1851, but declined renomination in 1850, returning instead to his Nashville legal practice. He was a delegate to the Democratic National Convention in 1860 and during the Civil War he served as judge of Gen. Braxton Bragg's military court. Ewing died in Atlanta, Georgia, on 16 June 1864 and is buried in the Nashville City Cemetery.

Chapter 2

1. Des Arc, incorporated in Prairie County in 1854, is located on the White River in the Delta region of eastern Arkansas. Des Arc quickly became a gateway between Memphis, Tennessee, and the rest of Arkansas, and was a principal distribution center for produce and lumber. The arrival of the Butterfield Overland Mail Company in the late 1850s further increasing the number of people traveling through the area. As river shipping declined, however, Des Arc was bypassed by railroads, interstate highways, and much of post-industrial society. Ted R. Worley, *Early History of Des Arc and Its People* (Des Arc, Ark.: White River Journal, 1957), 59.
2. Grandpa and Grandma were Hiram and Mary (Spinks) Kennedy, the parents of Orlando and Missie Palmer's mother, Martha Person "Patsy" Kennedy Palmer. Hiram E. Kennedy was born on 22 October 1792 at Mechanics Hill, Moore County, North Carolina, the son of David and Joanah Kennedy, and died at his Green Hill home on 20 August 1862. Mary H. (Spinks) Kennedy was born in Randolph County, North Carolina, on 20 January 1793 and died at Green Hill on 22 January 1875.
3. Elias Windsor Kennedy was born in Green Hill, Alabama, on 10 August 1831, the son of Hiram and Mary Kennedy. In 1852 he and his brother Enoch Riley Kennedy were seniors at LaGrange College in Florence, living in the home of their uncle John S. Kennedy. In 1850 Elias Kennedy resigned as editor of the *Florence Gazette*. Ten years later he was practicing law in Florence. In 1861 he enlisted as a private in the "Florence Guards" which was mustered into the Confederate army as Capt. S. A. M. Wood's Company K, Seventh Alabama Infantry, but by 20 November 1864 had been appointed as Braxton Bragg's quartermaster general with the rank of major. At the end of the war he moved to Louisville, Kentucky, where he and his nephew, Logan Paschal Kennedy, were cotton factors and commission merchants. He died in Louisville on 14 November 1875. He is buried in the Kennedy-Stutts Cemetery, Green Hill. Arthur Wyllie, *Confederate Officers* (n.p.: n.p., 2007), 285; James Edmonds Saunders, *Early Settlers of Alabama* (New Orleans, La.: L. Graham & Son, 1899), 174; Greensboro, Alabama, *Beacon*, 24 April 1857; *Catalogue of the Officers, Students and Libraries of LaGrange College, North Alabama, for the Collegiate Year 1851-'52* (Tuscumbia, Alabama, 1852); *List of Staff Officers of the Confederate States Army* (Washington, D.C.: Government Printing Office, 1891), 91.

4. Orlando Palmer was not alone in noting and reprehending his sister's despondent nature. On 8 September 1866 their aunt, Olive Kennedy, chided her, "if you are as gloomy all the time as you are when you write, you must get mighty lonesome." Rather, she advised, "you ought to be cheerful for Mr. Winston's sake. He is trying to make a start in life. All you both had left you by your parents has been taken away, and we all ought to give it up cheerfully, thinking it's the Lord's will."

5. The "Rector Guards" company was named in honor of Arkansas's governor, Henry Massie Rector. Rector was born on 1 May 1816, at Fontaine's Ferry near Louisville, Kentucky, but in 1835, at age nineteen, moved to Arkansas where he studied law and, in 1842, was appointed by President John Tyler as U. S. marshal for the district of Arkansas. In 1848 he was elected for the first of two terms to the Arkansas Senate; in 1852 he was chosen a Democratic presidential elector; from 1853 to 1857 he served as U.S. surveyor general for Arkansas. In 1854 Rector was elected to a term in the House of Representatives and in 1859 he was elected to the state Supreme Court.

In 1860 he was elected as governor on a pro-secession platform.

Rector was an ardent state's rights advocate and defied Confederate authority from Richmond, pledging on 8 May 1862 to "build a new ark and launch it upon new waters" if the Confederacy did not respond to Arkansas's abandonment in the face of a Federal invasion. Rector ran again for governor but was defeated on 6 October 1862. His application for a commission in the Confederate army was rejected, and he served as a volunteer in the state reserve for the rest of the war. Rector died in Little Rock on 12 August 1899.

"Black Republican" was, during the Civil War era, a slur hurled against the new Republican Party for its opposition to the expansion of slavery and its supposed agenda for African American social equality. In his famed Cooper Union speech, Republican candidate Abraham Lincoln charged that Southerner denounced his party "as reptiles, or, at the best, as no better than outlaws." They would, he said, "grant a hearing to pirates or murderers, but nothing like it to 'Black Republicans.'"

Timothy P. Donovan, Willard B. Gatewood, Jr., and Jeannie M. Whayne, eds., *The Governors of Arkansas: Essays in Political Biography* (Fayetteville: University of Arkansas Press, 1995); Michael B. Dougan, *Confederate Arkansas: The People and Policies of a Frontier State in Wartime* (Tuscaloosa: University of Alabama Press, 1976); Carl H. Moneyhon, "Governor Henry Massie Rector and the Confederacy: States' Rights versus Military Contingencies," *Arkansas Historical Quarterly* 73 (Winter 2014): 357–380; Abraham Lincoln, *Speeches and Writings, 1859–1865* (Washington, D.C.: Library of America, 1989), 120.

6. Cynthia (Cintha) Walker Palmer Kennedy, a sister of Orlando Palmer's father, Paschal W. Palmer, was born in Franklin County, Georgia, on 23 June 1820. She was married to William Wesley Kennedy and was the mother of Orlando Palmer's cousins, Oliver S. and Delia Kennedy. In 1860 she was a resident of Tippah County, Mississippi, but by 1870 she had returned to Green Hill, Lauderdale County, Alabama, where she died on 3 September 1894.
7. William Cummins Ratcliff was born in Arkansas County, Arkansas, on 12 March 1839. In 1859 he was graduated with honors from the Florence Wesleyan University where he no doubt met Orlando Palmer. Upon graduation he was appointed as a professor of mathematics, but in June of that year he moved to Little Rock, Arkansas, where he began to study law.

   During the Civil War he served as third lieutenant of Company A, Sixth Arkansas Infantry, and after the war was graduated in law at Washington and Lee University in 1872 and entered his father's Little Rock law firm. In 1876 he was secretary of the board of trustees of the Arkansas Female College and in 1899 he was the president of the Galloway Female College in Searcy. In 1877 he was elected as Pulaski County's representative in the Arkansas state legislature. He died in Little Rock on 20 September 1920. *Biographical and Historical Memoirs of Pulaski, Jefferson, Lonke, Faulkner, Grant, Saline, Perry, Garland, and Hot Springs Counties, Arkansas* (Chicago, Ill.: Goodspeed Publishing, 1898), 408; James Terry White, ed., *The National Cyclopaedia of American Biography*, (New York, N.Y.: James T. White and Company, 1898), 8:307; *Officers and Students of the Arkansas Female College* (Little Rock, Arkansas: P. A. Ladue, 1876), 6; "Traces of Old Galloway College Still Found at Harding," *Arkansas Gazette*, 14 June 1961; *Goodspeed Biographical and Historical Memoirs of Central Arkansas* (Chicago, Ill.: Goodspeed Publishing Company, 1889), 377.
8. R. T. Simpson was born in Alabama in or about 1837, but by 1860 he was practicing law in Prairie County, Arkansas. The firm was prepared to "practice in Prairie, White, Jackson, Monroe, St. Francis, and adjoining counties." Simpson enlisted as a private in the Tenth Arkansas Infantry on 1 July 1861. *Des Arc Weekly Citizen*, 23 October 1861.
9. "Aunt Mary" was Mary S. (Belk) Spinks, the wife of John E. Spinks. In 1860 she was living in Clarke County, Alabama.
10. Charles Wade Smith was born in Mississippi in 1821. On 29 December 1859 he was married to Rebecca "Babe" Perry, a native of Alabama, in Prairie County, Arkansas. He died in Arkansas in 1866.
11. "The Rector Guards," the company of Des Arc volunteers that would become Company D of the First Arkansas Infantry, was organized in March 1861 under the command of Capt. George Washington Glenn. Its uniform,

reported the *Des Arc Semi-Weekly Citizen*, was "exceedingly handsome," and its "close attention to the exercises of the drill is fast rendering them well trained in military affairs." The company was ordered to meet at the office of the mayor at 3:00 P.M. on 15 March 1861 by its orderly sergeant, George Murray. *Des Arc* (Arkansas) *Semi Weekly Citizen*, 15 March 1861.

12. John E. Spinks was elected as sergeant of Company A, Thirty-Eighth Alabama Infantry, and his son, William L. Spinks, was a corporal in the same company, but, given the number times that Orlando Palmer refers to him at home, it would appear that John Spinks's service was not of long duration.

    Elias Windsor Kennedy first enlisted as a private in the Seventh Alabama Infantry but was transferred to the quartermaster department in Chattanooga with the rank of captain.

13. Thomas Brown Winston was born near Hartsville, Tennessee, on 24 July 1839. In 1861 he was attending the Florence Wesleyan University (now the University of North Alabama) but on 30 May 1861, a week before his state seceded, he enlisted as a private in Company D, Ninth Tennessee Infantry, at Union City, Tennessee. Stuart W. Sanders, Maney's *Confederate Brigade at the Battle of Perryville* (Charleston, S.C.: Arcadia Publishing, 2014), 233; Jonathan Kennon Thompson Smith, comp., *Genealogical Abstracts from Reported Deaths: The Nashville Christian Advocate, 1905–1907* (Jackson, Tennessee: J. K. T. Smith, 2002), 63.

14. On 18 February 1861, Gov. Henry Massie Rector called for a special election to select delegates to a convention to decide whether Arkansas should secede. Voters elected a majority of anti–immediate secessionists, and when the convention met on 4 March 1861, majority of delegates blocked a move to secede immediately but approved a plebiscite for 5 August 1861. But when Abraham Lincoln called for volunteers after the bombardment of Fort Sumter on 12 April, Rector refused to send soldiers from Arkansas. "The people of this commonwealth are freemen, not slaves," he said, "and will defend to the last extremity their honor, lives and property against Northern mendacity and usurpation." Thereafter, the break with the Union was a foregone conclusion with the convention passing an ordnance of secession on 6 May 1861. Mark. K. Christ, ed., *The Die is Cast: Arkansas Goes to War, 1861* (Little Rock: Butler Center Books, 2010).

15. Orlando Palmer's uncle William Wesley Kennedy was born on 1 May 1816 in Mechanics Hill, North Carolina, the son of Hiram and Mary Spinks Kennedy. He was the husband of Cynthia Walker Palmer Kennedy and the father of Oliver Sylvester Kennedy. He died in Fort Worth, Texas, on 14 November 1878 and is buried in the Kennedy-Stutts Cemetery, Green Hill, Alabama.

16. B. F. Crittenden, a Lauderdale County physician, was born in Tennessee

in 1818. His son, Benjamin Franklin Crittenden, Jr., served as a corporal in Company F, Forty-Sixth Alabama Infantry.
17. *Des Arc* [Arkansas] *Semi-Weekly Citizen*, 4 June 1861.
18. *Des Arc* [Arkansas] *Semi-Weekly Citizen*, 28 May 1861.
19. "Letter from 'COP'!" 4 June 1861, *Des Arc* [Arkansas] *Semi-Weekly Citizen*.
20. Thomas H. Bradley was born on 25 July 1808 in Williamson County, Tennessee. In 1835, he joined the First Tennessee Volunteers and served in the Second Seminole War as his regiment's major and adjutant. In 1836, he moved to Crittenden County, Arkansas, and became a planter. He served one term in the Arkansas House of Representatives, 1850–1851, and, in 1860, as a Stephen A. Douglas delegate in the Democratic national convention.

    Bradley was elected to the Arkansas Secession Convention, but was initially opposed to secession, not changing his vote until the second convention on 6 May. Bradley was appointed brigadier general of Arkansas state troops in command of the Second Division of the state's militia. He was mistrusted due to his Unionist proclivities, and Col. Patrick R. Cleburne ignored his orders. A court-martial was called to investigate charges against him of drunkenness and cowardice, and although the court-martial never met and the charges were dropped, Bradley was relieved of his command and shortly after moved to Memphis where he died on 30 September 1864. Bruce S. Allardice, *More Generals in Gray* (Baton Rouge: Louisiana State University Press, 2006), 41; Ralph Wooster, "The Arkansas Secession Convention," *Arkansas Historical Quarterly* 13 (Summer 1954): 172–195; *Des Arc Semi-Weekly Citizen*, 7 June 1861.
21. *Des Arc* [Arkansas] *Semi-Weekly Citizen*, 7 June 1861.
22. Vernon L. Kennedy, the daughter of Mary Emeline and John Spinks Kennedy, was born in Florence, Alabama, in 1845.
23. William Joseph Hardee was born on 12 October 1815 at his family's Rural Felicity Plantation in Camden County, Georgia. He was graduated from the United States Military Academy at West Point, ranking twenty-sixth among the forty-five cadets in the class of 1838. He served in the Second U.S. Dragoons during the Second Seminole War and in the U.S.-Mexican War, winning brevet promotions through the rank of lieutenant colonel. Hardee returned to West Point as an instructor of tactics and served as commandant of cadets from 1856 to 1860, and in 1855 published *Rifle and Light Infantry Tactics for the Exercise and Manoeuvres of Troops When Acting as Light Infantry or Riflemen*, better known as *Hardee's Tactics*, which became the best-known drill manual of the Civil War

    Hardee resigned from the United States Army on 31 January 1861, and on 7 March accepted a commission as a colonel in the Confederate States

Army. He was soon promoted to major general and was assigned to the command of a brigade of Arkansas infantry in which he earned his nickname, "Old Reliable."

Hardee was transferred from Arkansas to Gen. Albert Sidney Johnston's Army of Central Kentucky in which he served as a corps commander with the rank of lieutenant general. He was wounded at the battle of Shiloh, but upon recovery returned to what was to become Gen. Braxton Bragg's Army of Tennessee, leading his corps at the siege of Corinth and during Bragg's invasion of Kentucky, commanding the army's Left Wing at the battle of Perryville.

At Murfreesboro in December 1862, Hardee's corps drove the right flank of Maj. Gen. William Rosecrans's army back to Stones River, but when Bragg once again abandoned an apparent tactical advantage and retreated out of Tennessee, his increasingly acrimonious disagreement with his commander's strategy led to Hardee's transfer to the command of the Department of Mississippi and East Louisiana. Following the battle of Chickamauga, however, he returned to the Army of Tennessee, then besieging the Union army at Chattanooga. With Maj. Gen. George Henry Thomas's victory at Missionary Ridge, and very much at Hardee's urging, Jefferson Davis relieved Bragg of command, giving Hardee temporary command of the Army of Tennessee. When Gen. Joseph E. Johnston took command in February 1864, Hardee was ordered to Alabama to reinforce Leonidas Polk's vain effort to check Sherman's Meridian Campaign but returned to Georgia to take part in the defense of Atlanta. Staunchly opposed to the seemingly mindless aggressive tactics of Lt. Gen. John Bell Hood, who had replaced Johnston, Hardee requested a transfer, and President Davis assigned him to command of the Department of South Carolina, Georgia, and Florida where he conducted a futile attempt to stem Sherman's March to the Sea. Following the battle of Bentonville, North Carolina, on 26 April 1865 he surrendered with the sad remnant of the Army of Tennessee.

After the war, Hardee moved to Selma, Alabama, where he became president of the Selma and Meridian Railroad. He died in Wytheville, Virginia, on 6 November 1873 and is buried in Selma's Live Oak Cemetery. Nathaniel Cheairs Hughes, *General William J. Hardee: Old Reliable* (Baton Rouge: Louisiana State University Press, 1965).

24. Thomas Carmichael Hindman was born on 28 January 1828 in Knoxville, Tennessee. With the coming of the U.S.-Mexican War he joined and was appointed adjutant of the Second Mississippi Volunteer Infantry which was assigned to garrison duty at Monterrey. After the war, he returned to Ripley, Mississippi, where began a career as a lawyer. In 1854 he was elected to the Mississippi House of Representatives as a Democrat. Hindman moved to

Helena, Arkansas, in 1856 where he opened a legal practice with his friend Patrick R. Cleburne and reentered politics, being elected to the U.S. House of Representatives in 1858 and reelected in 1860 on a pro-secession platform.

When Arkansas seceded, Hindman resigned from Congress to raise the Second Arkansas Infantry, of which was elected colonel. On 28 September 1861 he was promoted to the rank of brigadier general and was assigned to the command of a brigade in the Army of Mississippi. He sustained minor wounds at the battle of Shiloh, after which he was promoted to the rank of major general. In May 1862 he was reassigned to the command of the Trans-Mississippi Department.

Arkansas' defenses had been seriously depleted when Earl Van Dorn removed the Army of the West from the state to reinforce Albert Sidney Johnston's effort to halt the advance of U. S. Grant and Don Carlos Buell in Tennessee. Given the absence of resistance, Union general Samuel R. Curtis advanced out of Missouri and threatened the capture of Little Rock. Hindman built a new Confederate army to oppose him, but his declaration of martial law, his burning of cotton in on order to keep it from falling into Federal hands, and his aggressive use of the new Confederate conscription laws made him unpopular with many of the state's citizens who complained to the Davis administration that he had acted unconstitutionally. The Confederate war department replaced him as commander of the Trans-Mississippi with Lt. Gen. Theophilus H. Holmes, but Hindman retained command of the District of Arkansas.

On 7 December 1862 he fought the combined armies of James G. Blunt and Francis J. Herron to a tactical draw in the battle of Prairie Grove, but Hindman was forced to withdraw to the Arkansas River where his starving and ragged army, composed largely of unwilling draftees, disintegrated, again leaving the state virtually undefended. Hindman was relieved of command at his own request and, in July 1863, was assigned to the command of a division in the Army of Tennessee. He was seriously wounded at the battle of Chickamauga and again at Kennesaw Mountain after which he resigned from the army.

In June 1866, Hindman and his family moved to Mexico City and then to Carolata where he became a coffee planter and practiced law. Unsuccessful, he returned to Helena in 1867 where he again became active in Democratic politics.

On 28 September 1868, Hindman was shot and killed by an unknown assassin. He is buried in Helena's Maple Hill Cemetery. Diane Neal and Thomas W. Kremm, *Lion of the South: General Thomas C. Hindman* (Macon, Ga: Mercer University Press, 1993).

25. The 1860 Federal census lists two brothers, the sons of George W. and Mary A. Glenn, as residents of White River, Prairie County, Arkansas. John Edward Glenn was born in Newberry, South Carolina, on 29 November 1828. In 1860 he was a Des Arc attorney. He enlisted as a private in Company E, First Arkansas Infantry, but was soon elected first as first lieutenant of his company and then as lieutenant colonel of his regiment. His election, wrote "CAP" in a letter to the *Des Arc Citizen*, "caused great rejoicing among the Rector Guards, although we regretted very much the necessity of being separated from him, yet, we were proud to know that he was elevated to such a position, and was held in such estimation by the regiment at large. His gentlemanly deportment, his skill and experience as a military man, his many virtues endearing him to everyone he came into contact with, all contributed to make it a deserved and merited compliment." By 1880 he had moved to Nashville, Howard County, Arkansas. Glenn died at the Old Soldiers Home in Jacksonville, Florida, on 4 November 1905. He was the brother of George Washington Glenn, the captain of Company D, First Arkansas Infantry. In civil life, Captain Glenn was a physician and, in 1860, the owner of thirteen enslaved persons. He died in Little Rock on 15 February 1878. Bruce S. Allardice, *Confederate Colonels: A Biographical Register* (Columbia: University of Missouri Press, 2008), 164; *Des Arc* [Arkansas] *Semi-Weekly Citizen*, 31 July 1861.
26. The first battle of Manassas, or Bull Run as it is alternatively called, was fought in northern Virginia on 21 July 1861 between the Union army of Maj. Gen. Irwin McDowell and the combined Confederate forces of Generals P. G. T. Beauregard and Joseph E. Johnston. McDowell skillfully maneuvered his army across Bull Run and onto the Rebel left flank, driving it back until Brig. Gen. Thomas J. Jackson's brigade, just arrive from the Shenandoah Valley, made a stand on Henry House Hill, stemming the Federal advance and turning it to a rout and earning for its commander the sobriquet of "Stonewall." The Confederates, however, were as disorganized in victory as the Union forces were in defeat, and, also hampered by a lack of supplies and transportation as well as a crisis of divided command, and so failed to capitalize on their success. The Federal army escaped to Washington where it was reorganized by Maj. Gen. George B. McClellan, who, the following spring, led it back to Virginia. The battle, therefore, did not have the "tendency to shorten the war" that Palmer and many other Southerners hoped, but proved to be only the first of many bloody but indecisive battles.
27. At the same time, Col. Ulysses S. Grant, in his first Civil War campaign, was also chasing guerrillas in Missouri. When the pro-Confederate partisans

decamped before he could attack them, Grant learned that "the enemy had as much reason to fear my forces as I had his. The lesson was valuable." U. S. Grant, *Personal Memoirs* (New York, N.Y.: Charles L. Webster and Company, 1885), 1:248–50.

28. "Remlap" is Palmer spelled backward.
29. Plans for Hardee's brigade at Pitman's Ferry to move north into Missouri, there to unite with Brig. Gen. Gideon J. Pillow's force from western Tennessee and with that of Brig. Gen. Ben McCulloch, who was to advance from northwestern Arkansas, in a march to Saint Louis, failed when Hardee and Pillow refused to support each other in an attack on Ironton and Maj. Gen. Leonidas Polk, commander of the Confederate military district embracing the upper Mississippi River, withdrew his support from the project. Thomas W. Cutrer, *Ben McCulloch and the Frontier Military Tradition* (Chapel Hill: University of North Carolina Press, 1993), 220–221; *OR*, 3:612, 53:721–723.
30. Charles T. J. Banks was born in Alabama in 1827. On 24 March 1858 he was married to Nancy Caroline Tucker in Lauderdale, Mississippi. In July 1861 he enlisted in Company B, Thirteenth Alabama Infantry. Private Banks was killed at Leesburg, Virginia, on 1 January 1862. His son, Hugh R. Banks, was born in 1859 and died on 15 November 1862.

    Levi E. Briggs was a private in Company G, Thirteenth Alabama Infantry; J. G. Posey was a private in Company I, Thirteenth Alabama Infantry and Eli Posey, a private in Company H, Thirteenth Alabama Infantry, died of disease in Richmond, Virginia, on September 16, 1861. John Rigdon, *Historical Sketch and Roster of the Alabama 13th Infantry Regiment* (n.p., 2015).
31. Springfield is an alternate name for the battle of Wilson's Creek or Oak Hills, the first major battle west of the Mississippi River. In August 1861, Confederates under Brig. Gen. Ben McCulloch and Missouri State Guard troops under Maj. Gen. Sterling Price approached Brig. Gen. Nathaniel Lyon's Army of the West, camped at Springfield. Missouri. On 10 August, Lyon led his command in a preemptive strike against the Rebels camped along Wilson's Creek about ten miles southwest of Springfield. Lyon attempted to envelope the Southerners, positioning his own column on Oak Hill to the north and sending a column under Col. Franz Sigel around to their rear. While Price's Missourians held Lyon's column in check, McCulloch's troops drove Sigel's men from the field and then countermarched to join Price in an assault on the Federal line on Oak Hill. When Lyon was killed leading a counterattack, the Federal command devolved upon Maj. Samuel D. Sturgis who ordered a retreat to Springfield. William Garrett Piston and Richard W. Hatcher,

Wilson's Creek: The Second Battle of the Civil War and the Men Who Fought It (Chapel Hill: University of North Carolina Press, 2005).

32. Henry H. Hicks of Pulaski County served as the sergeant of Company A, Sixth Arkansas Infantry.
33. According to the return address on the envelope that enclosed this letter, by 21 November, Palmer was a lieutenant in Company G, First Arkansas Infantry.
34. Archibald Kennedy Patton was born on 24 May 1819 in Abbeville District, South Carolina. Despite Palmer's assessment of Patton's character, when he was killed in action at Shiloh, Cleburne reported that "he did his duty nobly in this battle and secured the love and confidence of every man in his regiment." He is buried in the Lower Long Cane cemetery, McCormick County, South Carolina. *OR*, 10:1, 584.
35. Chaplin Robert Franklin Bunting of the Eighth Texas Cavalry reported that the Unionist half of the local population had "fled before and on the arrival of our troops," abandoning all that they owned. "The people of this place were not driven out by our forces; it was their own choice to go," he insisted. Thomas W. Cutrer, ed., *Our Trust Is in the God of Battles: The Civil War Letters of Robert Franklin Bunting, Chaplain, Terry's Texas Rangers, C.S.A.* (Knoxville: Univ. of Tennessee Press, 2006), 5–6.

    "Southrons" was Sir Walter Scott's term for lowland Scots. In his 1820 novel *The Monastery: A Romance*, Halbert Glendinning tells Mary Avenel, "I wish a score of Southrons came up the glen this very day; and you would see one good hand, and one good sword, do more to protect you than all the books that were ever opened." Scott, avidly adopted by the "chivalry" of the region, greatly influenced the mind of the South. "But for the Sir Walter disease, the character of the Southerner—or Southron, according to Sir Walter's starchier way of phrasing it—would be wholly modern, in place of modern and medieval mixed, and the South would be fully a generation further advanced than it is. It was Sir Walter that made every gentleman in the South a Major or a Colonel, or a General or a Judge, before the war; and it was he, also, that made these gentlemen value these bogus decorations. For it was he that created rank and caste down there, and also reverence for rank and caste, and pride and pleasure in them. Enough is laid on slavery, without fathering upon it these creations and contributions of Sir Walter." Mark Twain, *Life on the Mississippi* (New York: N.Y.: H. O. Houghton and Co., 1874), 327–28.
36. The Eighth Texas Cavalry, popularly known as Terry's Texas Rangers, was mustered into Confederate service on 9 September 1861 and assigned to the army at Bowling Green, Kentucky, at the request of Gen. Albert Sidney

Johnston. Benjamin Franklin Terry was elected as the regiment's colonel and Thomas S. Lubbock, lieutenant colonel. With the deaths of Terry and Lubbock in December 1861, John Austin Wharton was elected colonel. When Wharton was promoted to brigadier general in the fall of 1862, command of the regiment devolved on Col. Thomas Harrison. The Terry Rangers distinguished themselves at the battles of Shiloh, Perryville, Murfreesboro, Chickamauga, and Chattanooga, in the Atlanta campaign, and as raiders in Kentucky and Tennessee under Lt. Gen. Nathan Bedford Forrest. The Rangers were also part of the hopelessly inadequate force under Gen. Joseph E. Johnston that attempted to slow Maj. Gen. William T. Sherman's inexorable "march to the sea" during the final months of the war. Cutrer, ed., *Our Trust Is in the God of Battles*.

37. Albert Sidney Johnston was born on 2 February 1803 in Washington, Kentucky. After attending Transylvania University in Lexington, Kentucky, where he met fellow student Jefferson Davis he received appointment to the United States Military Academy at West Point, graduating eighth of forty-one cadets in the class of 1826 and receiving a brevet as second lieutenant in the Second U.S. Infantry.

    In 1834, after service in the Black Hawk War, Johnston resigned his commission and moved to Texas where, in 1836, he enlisted as a private in Sam Houston's army during the Texas War of Independence, and on 5 August 1836 he was named adjutant general of the Army of the Republic of Texas with the rank of colonel. On 31 January 1837 he became senior brigadier general in command of the Texas Army. After serving as Secretary of War for the Republic of Texas from 1838 to 1840, Johnston resigned and returned to Kentucky, but during the U.S.-Mexican War he served under Brig. Gen. Zachary Taylor as the colonel of the First Texas Mounted Rifles, fighting at the battles of Monterrey and Buena Vista.

    After the war Johnston moved to "China Grove," a large plantation in Brazoria County, Texas, where he remained until December 1849 when President Zachary Taylor appointed him as paymaster of the U.S. Army with the rank of major. In 1855, President Franklin Pierce appointed him as colonel of the new Second U.S. Cavalry. Johnston commanded the U.S forces in the so-called Utah War, November 1857, which installed Alfred Cummings as governor of the Utah territory in place of Brigham Young. For this service he received a brevet promotion to brigadier general and, in December 1860, he was appointed to the command of the Department of the Pacific.

    At the outbreak of the Civil War, Johnston resigned his commission to accept from his old classmate and friend, President Jefferson Davis, command the Western Military Department, that area of the Confederacy west of the Allegheny Mountains, with the rank of general. But with fewer than 40,000 men spread throughout Kentucky, Tennessee, Arkansas, and Missouri—10,000 of whom were in the Missouri State Guard under Maj. Gen. Sterling Price—his resources were stretched thin.

Following the Confederate defeat at the Mill Springs and the loss of Fort Henry and Fort Donelson, Johnston abandoned first his forward position at Bowling Green, Kentucky, and then the vital Confederate industrial center at Nashville, retreating with the Army of Central Kentucky to Corinth, Mississippi, where, with the aid of Gen. P. G. T. Beauregard, he sought to concentrate Confederate forces for a counterstroke.

Hoping to destroy U. S. Grant's isolated army at Pittsburg Landing on the Tennessee River before it could be reinforced by Maj. Gen. Don Carlos Buell's Army of the Ohio, Johnston marched from Corinth with his Army of Mississippi on 3 April 1862, intent on surprising Grant's force on the following day. Despite maddening delays, the Confederates launched a surprise attack against Grant at Shiloh on 6 April, overrunning the Union camps and driving the Federals back to the Tennessee. As the assault lost momentum during the afternoon, however, Johnston rode to the front of personally rallied his faltering troops. At about 2:30 P.M. he was wounded behind his right knee, the bullet severing his popliteal artery, and soon thereafter Johnston died from blood loss. Although Beauregard continued the offensive until nightfall, that night Don Carlos Buell arrived with 20,000 fresh troops and a counterattack the following day drove the Confederates from the field.

Johnston was the highest-ranking fatality of the war on either side, and his death was a severe blow to Confederate morale, with Jefferson Davis believing his loss to be "the turning point of our fate." Johnston was buried in New Orleans, but in 1866 the Texas Legislature passed a joint resolution of to have his body reinterred at the Texas State Cemetery in Austin. Charles P. Roland, *Albert Sidney Johnston: Soldier of Three Republics* (Austin: University of Texas Press, 1964).

38. Palmer refers to the battle of Belmont, fought on 7 November 1861 in Mississippi County, Missouri. On 3 September 1861, Maj. Gen. Leonidas Polk had moved Confederate forces into neutral Kentucky and occupied Columbus, a strategic position on the bluffs overlooking the Mississippi River. Three days later Brig. Gen. Ulysses S. Grant, with the nucleus of what would become the Army of the Tennessee, seized Paducah, Kentucky. Grant determined to attack the isolated garrison of Belmont, Missouri, 2,700 men

under Brig. Gen. Gideon J. Pillow, directly across the river from Columbus. On 6 November, Grant's 3,114 men aboard six steamboats escorted by the gunboats *Lexington* and *Tyler* departed Cairo, Illinois. Grant's troops overran and destroyed the Confederate camp, but the scattered Confederate forces quickly reorganized and were reinforced from Columbus. They counterattacked, supported by heavy artillery fire from across the river. Grant retreated to his boats and steamed upriver to Paducah. Tom Winston's Ninth Tennessee Infantry was, as was the largest part of Polk's army, held in reserve in Columbus and took no part in the fighting at Belmont. Nathaniel Cheairs Hughes, *Battle of Belmont: Grant Strikes South* (Chapel Hill: University of North Carolina Press, 1991).

39. When Federal forces invaded Tennessee, the Confederate position at Columbus was outflanked, forcing the Rebels to withdraw in March 1862. Union troops held Columbus for the remainder of the war.

40. On 18 September 1861 Brig. Gen. Simon Bolivar Buckner's division of the Army of Central Kentucky occupied Bowling Green and began its fortification, and by mid-October more than 12,000 Confederate troops garrisoned the strategically important town. Kentucky secessionists held a "Sovereignty Convention" in nearby Russellville, passing an ordnance of secession on 20 November 1861, and naming Bowling Green as the state's capital. Within months, however, the Confederates were driven from Kentucky. The evacuation of Bowling Green began on 11 February and Confederate troops set fire to the town's business district, railroad depots, warehouses, and bridges. Federal troops seized the town on 14 February with Brig. Gen. Ormsby Mitchel placed in command of the garrison. Bowling Green remained under Union control for the remainder of the Civil War.

41. William Wesley Kennedy, born on 1 May 1816 at Mechanics Hill, Moore County, North Carolina, was the son of Hiram and Mary Kennedy and was the husband of Cynthia W. Palmer. He died on 14 November 1875 and is buried in Fort Worth, Texas. He was the brother of Enoch Riley Kennedy and of Elias Windsor Kennedy, and was the father of Oliver Sylvester Kennedy.

42. Twenty-one-year-old William H. Cook enlisted as a private in Company I, Eighth Mississippi Infantry, on 1 August 1861. He was hospitalized at Tullahoma, Alabama, on 10 November 1862 and died of an unspecified disease four days later.

43. In 1860 twenty-five-year-old William L. Spinks was a teacher in Clarke, Alabama. He was a corporal in Company A, Thirty-Eighth Alabama Infantry. On 16 May 1870 he married Mary E. Norwood.

Chapter 3

1. Department of the Navy, *OR Navies*, series 1, 22:537; "Cincinnati '*Gazette*' Narrative," *The Rebellion Record: A Diary of American Events* (New York, N.Y.: D. Van Nostrand, 1865), 121–122.
2. John B. Jones, *A Rebel War Clerk's Diary*, (Philadelphia, Pa.: J. B. Lippincott, 1886), 110; John S. Sledge, *These Rugged Days: Alabama in the Civil War* (Tuscaloosa: University of Alabama Press, 2017), 41–44.
3. *OR Navies*, series 1, 22:469.
4. *New York Times*, 13 February 1862.
5. *The Rebellion Record: A Diary of American Events* (New York, N.Y.: D. Van Nostrand, 1865), 99.
6. In the summer of 1862, following the battle of Shiloh, Maj. Gen. Don Carlos Buell was advancing on Chattanooga, and in June Maj Gen. Ormsby MacKnight Mitchell's division occupied Huntsville, Alabama. One of Mitchell's regiments, the Tenth Kentucky Infantry under the command of Col. John Marshall Harlan, occupied Florence until the Army of the Ohio was compelled to countermarch to intercept Braxton Bragg's incursion into Kentucky. Stephen D. Engle, *Don Carlos Buell: Most Promising of All* (Chapel Hill: University of North Carolina Press, 2014), 219, 258; John C. Carter, ed., *Welcome the Hour of Conflict: William Cowan McClellan and the 9th Alabama* (Tuscaloosa: University of Alabama Press, 2014), 140.
7. Palmer expected to be discharged from the army in April or May 1862, having volunteered for one year of service on 8 May 1861, but the First Conscription Act, passed by the Confederate Congress on 26 April 1862, made every white male between the ages of eighteen and thirty-five liable to three years of military service. His discharge, therefore, was not forthcoming.
8. William Rufus Chisholm was born in Nashville, Tennessee, on 9 May 1837, but by 1860 was living at Green Hill, Alabama. He was the captain of Company A of Col. Philip Dale Roddey's Fourth Alabama Cavalry. He died in Florence, Alabama, on 31 August 1878.
9. *The Spectator* was a literary journal founded in 1711 by the writers Joseph Addison and Richard Steele, intended, as they wrote, "to enliven morality with wit, and to temper wit with morality." *The Spectator* sought to refine and reform the tastes of English society, and its prose style was and remains considered exemplary. The journal's readership was large, because, as one of its essays claimed, "every middle-class household with aspirations to looking like its members took literature seriously" were subscribers. Women, especially, were among the periodical's more avid readers because it sought to prepare them for "a more elevated life and conversation." Steele recom-

mended that ladies consider it "as a part of the tea-equipage" and read it each morning. Although it lasted only one year, going out of publication in 1712, *The Spectator*, sold in eight bound volumes, continued to be popular well into the nineteenth century.

10. The battle of Mill Springs, also known as Somerset, Logan's Crossroads, or Fishing Creek, was fought on 19 January 1862. In November 1861, Brig. Gen. Felix Zollicoffer advanced from Cumberland Gap into central Kentucky, establishing winter quarters at Mill Springs. Brig. Gen. George H. Thomas, planning to drive the Confederates across the Cumberland River, arrived at Logan's Crossroads on 17 January 1862, but while the Federals were awaiting reinforcements, they were attacked by a Confederate force under the general command of Maj. Gen. George B. Crittenden. Although the Confederate assault was initially successful, additional Union troops under Brig. Gen. Albin Schoepf came to Thomas's relief, turning the tide of battle. Union resistance stiffened, Zollicoffer was killed, and a second Confederate attack was repulsed. Union counterattacks forced the Rebels from the field, driving them back to Murfreesboro, Tennessee. Mill Springs was the first significant Union victory of the war. Stuart W. Sanders, *The Battle of Mill Springs, Kentucky* (Mount Pleasant, South Carolina: Arcadia Publishing, 2015).

11. Maj. Gen. George B. Crittenden reported that the Sixteenth Alabama Infantry, which had been assigned as his division's reserve, "did, at this critical juncture, most eminent service," and Brig. Gen. William Henry Carroll reported that "Colonel Wood brought his men forward with the steadiness of veterans and formed them in battle array with the coolness and precision of a holiday parade." The regiment reported nine killed and five wounded at Mill Springs. OR, 7:105–110–16.

12. William Basil Wood was born in Nashville, Tennessee, in 1820 but the following year his family moved to Florence, Alabama, where he became an attorney as well as a preacher in the Methodist Church. Wood served as judge of the County Court of Lauderdale County from 1844 to 1850, as an elector on the Bell and Everett ticket in 1860, and was elected circuit judge in 1863, but remained in the army as commander of the Sixteenth Alabama Infantry, a regiment in the brigade of his brother, Brig. Gen. Sterling A. M. Wood, until the close of the war. In retreat from Fishing Creek, he, with many members of his regiment, contracted typhoid fever. He was granted sick leave and was not able to rejoin the regiment until the following November at Estell's Springs, Tennessee. He led his regiment at the battles of Triune and Murfreesboro, but in May 1863 he was appointed presiding judge of Lt. Gen. James Longstreet's corps and was transferred to the Army of Northern Virginia.

After the war he was elected as circuit judge, but was removed by Alabama's provisional governor, Lewis Eliphalet Parsons, as "an impediment to reconstruction." Reelected in 1866, he was again removed from the bench by the Reconstruction Acts of 1868. Elected again in 1874, he served until 1880. James Edmonds Saunders, *Early Settlers of Alabama* (New Orleans, La.: L. Graham and Son, 1899), 172.

13. Fort Henry, on the Tennessee River, fell to Union forces on 6 February 1862. Maj. Gen. U. S. Grant had landed two divisions upstream from the Rebel bastion with the intention of assaulting it from the north while the flotilla of gunboats under Flag Officer Andrew Hull Foote bombarded it from the river. A combination of heavy rain, which caused the river to rise and threaten the fort with inundation, and effective fire from Foote's boats, however, caused Brig. Gen. Floyd Tilghman, the fort's commandant, to surrender to Foote before Grant arrived. This important Union victory opened the Tennessee River as far south as Muscle Shoals and Florence, Alabama.

    On 12 February, Grant's army proceeded overland twelve miles to attack Fort Donelson on the Cumberland River. On 14 February, Foote's gunboats attempted to reduce the fort with gunfire, but were forced to withdraw after sustaining heavy damage from the fort's batteries. Grant then proceeded to besiege Fort Donelson, surrounding it by the fifteenth. The Rebel commander, Brig. Gen. John B. Floyd, ordered his second-in-command, Brig. Gen. Gideon Johnson Pillow, to open an escape route to Nashville, but once a breech in Grant's siege line was established Floyd unaccountably ordered Pillow's men back to their fortifications.

    On 16 February, Floyd and Pillow escaped the beleaguered fort, with its command devolving upon Brig. Gen. Simon Bolivar Buckner who later that day accepted Grant's demand of unconditional surrender. The loss of these two forts resulted in the loss of all of Kentucky as well as much of Tennessee, including the strategically vital city of Nashville. Benjamin Franklin Cooling, *Forts Donelson and Henry: The Key to the Confederate Heartland* (Knoxville: University of Tennessee Press, 1987).

14. George M. Murray was the original second lieutenant of Company I, Fifteenth Alabama Infantry, but became his company's captain and was promoted to lieutenant colonel 8 May 1862. He died at Knoxville, Tennessee, on 7 November 1862 of what was identified as typhoid pneumonia.

15. Here Palmer slightly misquotes John Milton's description of Eve in *Paradise Lost*:

    > "For contemplation hee and valour formd,
    > For softness shee and sweet attractive Grace,
    > Hee for God only, shee for God in him."

16. Catherine A. E. "Katie" Pate was born on 2 September 1844 in Ripley, Mississippi. There, on 22 November 1861, she married William Henry "Tip" Davis who served as a private in Company B, Thirteenth Alabama Infantry, and who was "discharged for disability" at the end of the Peninsula Campaign in spring, 1862. By June 1865 when the first of their two children was born the couple was living in Florence, Alabama, where she died in 1870.
17. A Stephen Little from Lauderdale County, serving as a private in Company I of Col. William B. Wood's Sixteenth Alabama Infantry. He died in the Confederate hospital, Lauderdale Springs, Mississippi, on 10 August 1862. On 22 July 1866, Delia Kennedy married Michael Jayne Danaher. Although born in Pennsylvania, an M. J. Danaher served as ordnance sergeant of the Thirteenth Tennessee Infantry.
18. Georgia Cheatham Foster was born on in Tennessee on 17 November 1843. She was the daughter of William Lytle Foster and a granddaughter of Ephraim Hubbard Foster, a Senator from Tennessee. Her mother, Susan Cheatham, was a daughter of Richard Cheatham, who served several terms in the Tennessee House of Representatives and was a one-term United States congressman and was a sister of Maj. Gen. Benjamin Franklin Cheatham. Georgia Kennedy died in Fort Worth on 8 December 1919. Christopher Losson, *Tennessee's Forgotten Warriors: Frank Cheatham and His Confederate Division* (Knoxville: University of Tennessee Press, 1989); application for membership in the Daughters of the American Revolution, Oliver S. Kennedy papers, Special Collections Library, University of Texas at Arlington.
19. Benjamin Franklin Foster, Jr., was born on 28 November 1841 in Davidson County, Tennessee. Foster served as a private in Sterling Wood's Seventh Alabama Infantry. He died on 4 September 1898 in Davidson County, Tennessee, where he is buried in the Murrell Cemetery.

    Benjamin Franklin Foster, Sr., a resident of Florence, Alabama, was born on 25 October 1802 in Davidson County, Tennessee. He was the uncle of William Lytle Foster and the great uncle of Georgia C. (Foster) Kennedy. In 1860 he enslaved sixteen men and women. He died on 16 July 1887 in Wichita, Kansas.
20. The incomplete remains of this letter are fragmented, disordered, and badly faded.
21. The action that Kennedy predicted did not come to pass. Not until the battle of Shiloh, 6–7 April 1862, was the Sixteenth Alabama engaged.
22. Alexander Donelson Coffee was the son of John R. Coffee who commanded a brigade of Tennessee militiamen at the battle of New Orleans and who, with Secretary of War John Eaton, negotiated the treaty with the Choctaw

that led to the Indian Removal Act of 1830. He was born on 3 June 1821 in Florence, Alabama, and served as the captain of Company C, Sixteenth Alabama Infantry. He died in Florence on 9 May 1901 and is buried there in the Coffee family cemetery.

23. Thomas McHenry Sloss of Lauderdale County served as a private in the "Florence Guards," Company K, Seventh Alabama Infantry.

24. Marion and Peter were two of the men enslaved on the Kennedy farm.

25. The Fifteenth Arkansas was heavily engaged in the battle of Shiloh, taking part in the ill-fated attack on Col. Ralph Pomeroy Buckland's brigade of Sherman's division. The charge was repulsed with heavy loss and the regiment's major, J. T. Harris, was killed. On 7 April, the second day of the battle, Cleburne's brigade, with its left outflanked, fell back, along with the rest of the Confederate army, until Braxton Bragg ordered it to counterattack the advancing Federals. Cleburne protested but complied. The attack was repulsed, and Cleburne reported that "the Fifteenth Arkansas was the only regiment that rallied anywhere near the disaster." Palmer received a superficial wound to the leg or foot. Larry J. Daniel, *Shiloh: The Battle that Changed the Civil War* (New York, N.Y.: Simon and Schuster, 1997), 162–63, 282–83; *OR*, 10:1, 584.

26. Martha Carter was born in Ripley, Mississippi, on 23 March 1846. On 24 February 1870 she married R. L. Boone. She died on 14 December 1878 and is buried in Ripley.

27. Annie Davidson of Ripley, Mississippi, married Raleigh Richardson White, a Ripley physician, in Tippah County, Mississippi, in 1863. She died on 23 February 1902 and is buried in the Hillcrest Cemetery, Temple, Texas.

28. On 8 November 1861, the USS *San Jacinto*, commanded by Captain Charles Wilkes, intercepted the British mail packet RMS *Trent* and removed two Confederate envoys, James Murray Mason and John Slidell, bound for Britain and France to urge the Confederacy's case for diplomatic recognition and to request financial and military support. The *Trent* Affair threatened a war between the United States and Great Britain, with the British government sending troops to Canada. The American ambassador, Charles Francis Adams, described the mood in England. "The passions of the country are up and a collision is inevitable if the Government of the United States should, before the news reaches the other side, have assumed the position of Captain Wilkes in a manner to preclude the possibility of explanation. . . . Ministers and people now fully believe it is the intention of the [U.S.] Government to drive them into hostilities."

The Lincoln administration wisely ended the incident by releasing Mason and Slidell, and on 14 January 1862 the two envoys resumed their voyage to Britain. The British accepted their release as a diplomatic victory, and the diplomatic crisis was largely defused.

Nevertheless, hopes for British and French intervention on the behalf of the Confederacy remained alive, and three days before Palmer wrote this letter, the *Richmond Enquirer* had offered the opinion that "foreign recognition of our independence will go very far towards hastening its recognition by the government of the United States. Our independence once acknowledged, our adversaries must for very shame disgust themselves with the nonsense about 'Rebels,' 'Traitors,' &c" and look upon our Independence . . . as *un fait accompli*." *Richmond Enquirer*, 6, 18 June 1862. For an excellent summation of the issue of European recognition of the Confederacy, see James M. McPherson, "The Saratoga Campaign that Wasn't," in *This Mighty Scourge: Perspectives on the Civil War* (New York, N.Y.: Oxford University Press, 2009), 65–76. Norman B. Ferris, *The Trent Affair: A Diplomatic Crisis*. (Knoxville: University of Tennessee Press, 1977).

29. John Spinks Kennedy, a Florence attorney, was born on 1 October 1818 at Mechanics Hill, Moore County, North Carolina, but moved with his family to Green Hill, Alabama, in 1828. He was admitted to the bar in 1831 and was, in the same year, elected to the state legislature. In 1847 he was elected to the first of three terms as solicitor of the Florence circuit. He was a Breckenridge elector in 1860, and with the outbreak of the Civil War he volunteered as a private in Capt. Sterling A. Wood's "Florence Guards," which became Company K of the Seventh Alabama Infantry. He served as assistant commissary with the rank of captain. At the end of the war, he and his family moved to Tuscaloosa, Alabama, where he became a successful businessman and where he died on 2 May 1899. The *Tuscaloosa Times*, May 1899; James Edmonds Saunders, *Early Settlers of Alabama* (New Orleans, La.: L. Graham and Son, 1899).

30. In the spring 1862 Maj. Gen. Thomas J. "Stonewall" Jackson executed a brilliant campaign in Virginia's Shenandoah Valley, marching 17,000 men 646 miles in forty-eight days and fighting battles at Kernstown, McDowell, Front Royal, Winchester, Cross Keys, and Port Republic, against three Union armies totaling 52,000 men under Nathaniel Prentiss Banks, John C. Frémont, and James Shields, threatening Washington and preventing the Lincoln administration from reinforcing Maj. Gen. George B. McClellan's army, then threatening the Confederate capital. At the close of the campaign, Jackson marched his Army of the Valley to Richmond in time to reinforce Robert E. Lee in the Seven Days Battles. Peter Cozzens, *Shenandoah 1862: Stonewall Jackson's Valley Campaign* (Chapel Hill: The University of North Carolina Press, 2008); Gary W. Gallagher, ed., *The*

Shenandoah Campaign of 1862 (Chapel Hill: University of North Carolina Press, 2010).

31. In March 1862, Maj. Gen. George B. McClellan landed his 121,500-man Army of the Potomac at Fortress Monroe near the tip of the peninsula formed by Virginia's York and James rivers with the intention of capturing the Confederate capital at Richmond from the east before Gen. Joseph E. Johnston's 43,000 man army could march from Culpeper to its defense. Brig. Gen. John B. Magruder's so-called Warwick Line between the two rivers checked McClellan's advance and forced him to lay siege to Yorktown, costing him valuable time. Johnston, having arrived on McClellan's front, began a withdrawal up the Peninsula, fighting rearguard actions first at Williamsburg and then, in an attempt to save the capital, at Seven Pines or Fair Oaks on 31 May. The battle was inconclusive, but Johnston was severely wounded and was replaced in command of the Confederate army by Robert E. Lee who seized the initiative and, from 25 June until 1 July, launched a series of attacks collectively known as the Seven Days Battles. McClellan, although maintaining an overwhelming numerical superiority, retreated down the Peninsula to Malvern Hill where he reembarked his army and sailed back to Washington. Steven Sears, *To the Gates of Richmond: The Peninsula Campaign* (New York, N.Y.: Ticknor & Fields, 1992); Gary Gallagher, ed., *The Richmond Campaign of 1862: The Peninsula and the Seven Days* (Chapel Hill: University of North Carolina Press, 2000).

    Palmer's statement that "the whole Mississippi is now in possession of the enemy" was not quite true. Despite the capture of New Orleans in April 1862, Rebel garrisons still held Vicksburg, Mississippi, and Port Hudson, Louisiana, leaving the portion of the river between those two points in Confederate hands.

32. John E. Spinks was the brother of Orlando Palmer's grandmother. He was married to Mary S. (Belk) Spinks, and in 1870 was residing in Clarke County, Alabama.
33. An E. B. Stainback, a planter in Washington County, Mississippi, served as the second lieutenant of Company F, Third Mississippi State Troops.
34. Andrew Brown, a Florence native, was elected second lieutenant of Company B, Thirty-Third Alabama Infantry. W. E. Matthews, "Diary and Regimental History of the 33rd Regiment of Alabama Infantry." Alabama Department of Archives and History, Montgomery, Alabama.
35. Oliver S. Kennedy Papers, Special Collections Libraries, University of Texas at Arlington.
36. *OR*, 16:1, 950.

37. William Mecklenburg Polk, *Leonidas Polk: Bishop and General* (New York, N.Y.: Longman's, Green, and Company, 1893), 156; Kenneth Noe, *Perryville: This Grand Havoc of Battle* (Lexington: University of Kentucky Press, 2001).
38. James M. Holcombe was appointed as surgeon of the Fifteenth Arkansas Infantry on 4 December 1862. On 31 January 1863 he was appointed senior surgeon of the First Brigade of Maj. Gen. Benjamin Franklin Cheatham's Division. Joseph Jones, "Roster of the Medical Officers of the Army of Tennessee During the Civil War Between the Northern and Southern States, 1861–1865," *Southern Historical Society Papers*. 215.
39. Robert Montrose Bostwick was born 21 January 1834 in Mecklenburg County, North Carolina, but in 1837 moved with his parents to Marshall Co., Mississippi. In 1857 he earned an M.D. degree from the University of Louisville and established a practice in Hardeman County, Tennessee.

    On 13 May 1861 he enlisted as a private in Company K, 154th Tennessee Infantry, but by 1 July 1862 had been detailed as a hospital steward. On 16 May 1864 he was assigned as assistant surgeon of the Thirteenth and the One-hundred and Fifty-Fourth Tennessee Infantry regiments of Maj. Gen. Benjamin Franklin Cheatham's division. He was seriously wounded in the fighting at Lovejoy's Station near Atlanta, 20 August 1864.

    After the war he practiced medicine in Memphis where he died on 28 March 1903. F. T. Hambrecht and J. L. Koste, *Biographical Register of Physicians Who Served the Confederacy in a Medical Capacity*; A. J. Vaughan, *Personal Record of the Thirteenth Regiment, Tennessee Infantry* (n.p., 2012).
40. Camp Dick Robinson, named for a local landowner, was located seven miles north of Lancaster, Kentucky. Upon entering Kentucky, Maj. Gen. Braxton Bragg directed that the Confederate depot at Danville "be transferred as rapidly as practicable to Bryantsville and Camp Dick Robinson, where all supplies will in the future be concentrated." Bragg then ordered the establishment of "a camp of instruction for new troops . . . at or near the site of Old Camp Dick Robinson, to be known as Camp Breckinridge." Some ten days later following the battle of Perryville, Bragg began his withdrawal from Kentucky and on 13 October his troops evacuated Camp Breckinridge which was promptly occupied by Federal forces. United States War Department, *The War of the Rebellion: A Compilation of the Official Records of the Union and Confederate Armies* (Washington: 1880–1901), Series 1, 4: 251–53, 52 (1), 186; Series 1, 16, (2), 815, 883, 887, 52 (2), 367; Donald A. Clark, *The Notorious "Bull" Nelson: Murdered Civil War General* (Carbondale: Southern Illinois University Press, 2011).
41. Logan Paschal Kennedy was Orlando's and Missie's cousin, the son of John

Spinks and Mary Emiline Kennedy. He was born on 22 November 1846 in Lauderdale County, Alabama, and died in Washington, D.C., in November 1934.

42. Sterling A. M. Wood was a native of Florence, and his father, Alexander Hamilton Wood, was the town's first mayor. He served as the first colonel of the Sixteenth Alabama Infantry and was wounded by friendly fire at Shiloh. When he was promoted to brigadier general on January 7, 1862, he was given command of the Fourth Brigade of Maj. Gen. Simon Bolivar Buckner's Third Division of Maj. Gen. William Joseph Hardee's Corps of the Army of Mississippi. The brigade consisted of the Third Confederate Infantry, the Sixteenth Alabama, the Thirty-Third Alabama, the Forty-Fourth Tennessee, and Thirty-Second, Thirty-Third, and Forty-Fifth Mississippi. Palmer served as Wood's adjutant from October 9, 1862, until January 1, 1863. S. A. M. Wood papers, Alabama Department of Archives and History, Montgomery, Alabama; *The Florence* (Alabama) *Times*, 26 May 1922.

43. Sylvanus William "Doc" Perry was born on 10 July 1846 at Pittsboro, Chatham County, North Carolina. As a private in Company D, Ninth Tennessee Infantry, he was wounded and captured at Perryville and killed in action at the battle of Chickamauga. James R. Flemming, *The Confederate Ninth Tennessee Infantry* (Gretna, La.: Pelican Publishing), 230.

44. Although Palmer claimed to "think it best at all times to tell the simple truth," he seems here to be dissimulating in order to spare his sister's feelings. According to his service record, Thomas B. Winston was wounded and captured at Perryville. He was disabled by his wounds, but following his exchange was detailed as a forage agent under his wife's uncle, Elias Kennedy, in April 1863. Flemming, *The Confederate Ninth Tennessee*, 233.

45. Missie apparently forwarded both George and Marion to her brother, as he writes of them both "getting along finely" in his letter of 19 November 1862.

46. William Preston was born in Louisville, Kentucky, on 16 October 1816 and in 1838 received a law degree from Harvard. He practiced in Louisville until the outbreak of the U.S.-Mexican War in which he served as the lieutenant colonel of the Fourth Kentucky Volunteers after which he was elected to the Kentucky House of Representatives and then to the state senate. He was twice elected to Congress, serving until 1858 when President James Buchanan appointed him as Envoy Extraordinary and Minister Plenipotentiary to Spain. He resigned as ambassador in 1861 at the outbreak of the Civil War.

Preston served as a colonel and volunteer aide to Gen. Albert Sidney Johnston, and on 18 April 1862, following Johnston's death at Shiloh, he was commissioned a brigadier general and assigned to Breckinridge's corps. On 30 September 1862, Preston reported to Braxton Bragg for service in the Kentucky campaign. After leading a brigade consisting primarily of Kentucky troops at Murfreesboro and during the Chickamauga campaign, he was severely critical of Bragg's failure to capitalize on the Rebel victory at Chickamauga and urged President Davis to replace him in command of the army of Tennessee. As a result, on 7 January 1864, Davis reassigned him as Envoy Extraordinary and Minister Plenipotentiary to Mexico.

After the war, Preston again served as a member of the Kentucky's House of Representatives in 1868 and 1869. William Preston died in Louisville on 21 September 1887. Peter J. Sehlinger, *Kentucky's Last Cavalier: General William Preston, 1816–1887* (Lexington: University Press of Kentucky, 2004).

47. A William W. Leftwich served as captain of Company I, Fourth Alabama Infantry.
48. Margaret Ann Whitesides, the daughter of William Button and Margaret Rankin Whitesides of Shelbyville, Kentucky, was twenty-four years of age in 1860. Maggie Whitesides married William H. Ward in Todd County, Kentucky, on 5 February 1873.
49. Braxton Bragg was born on 22 March 1817 in Warrenton, North Carolina, and was graduated fifth of fifty cadets from the West Point Class of 1837. As a junior officer in the Third U.S. Artillery, he served in the Second Seminole War in Florida and received three brevet promotions for distinguished service in the U.S.-Mexican War but resigned from the U.S. Army in 1856 to become a sugar planter in Louisiana. He was a corps commander at Shiloh, where he launched several costly and unsuccessful frontal assaults against the Hornet's Nest, which he attacked for hours with piecemeal frontal assaults.

After the battle of Shiloh, Jefferson Davis appointed Bragg a full general and as commander of the Western Department and the Army of Mississippi. Earl Hess, *Braxton Bragg: The Most Hated Man in the Confederacy* (Chapel Hill: University of North Carolina Press, 2016).
50. Of Joseph Eggleston Johnston's arrival, Capt. Daniel E. Coleman wrote, "his presence will no doubt put fresh zeal into the troops. He is regarded as one of the great chieftains of our age." Johnston was born on 3 February 1807 near Farmville, Virginia, and was graduated from the U.S. Military Academy at West Point in 1829, finishing thirteenth in a class of forty-six cadets. He served in the Black Hawk War before resigning from the army to study civil engineering, but rejoined the army on 7 July 1838, as a topographical engineer, earning a brevet promotion to the rank of captain in the war against the Seminoles. During the Mexican War he was wounded at Cerro Gordo in April 1847 and again at Chapultepec in September 1847, earning the brevet rank of colonel.

In the 1850s Johnston supervised topographical surveys and river improvements in the West, and on 28 June 1860, Secretary of War John B. Floyd appointed him quartermaster general with the rank of brigadier general. With Virginia's secession, Johnston resigned from the U.S. Army and accept a commission as a brigadier general in the Confederate army with command of the army in the Shenandoah Valley. When Irwin McDowell advanced toward P. G. T. Beauregard's army at Manassas Junction, Johnston reinforced him by rail and led is brigades in the Confederate victory in the first battle of Bull Run, for which he was promoted to the rank of general and given command of the army defending the Confederate capital at Richmond. When the Union Army of the Potomac under George B. McClellan advanced up the Peninsula in the spring of 1862, Johnston withdrew before him, fearing that Union naval superiority threatened his flanks and rear with amphibious operations on the York or the James River. President Davis, however, urged him to fight, and on 31 May 1862, he attacked the right wing of McClellan's Army of the Potomac, isolated from the rest of the army by the rain-swollen Chickahominy River. The battle of Seven Pines failed to destroy McClellan's isolated units, and Johnston was severely wounded.

When Robert E. Lee, who ascended to command due to Johnston's injury, proved more successful at repulsing McClellan's advance and saved Richmond, in November 1862, after he had recovered from his wounds, Davis transferred Johnston, with whom he bitterly disagreed over strategy and tactics, to command of the Department of the West where he had the fruitless task of coordinating the operations of Braxton Bragg's and John C. Pemberton's armies. In May 1863, as Ulysses S. Grant threatened Vicksburg, Davis ordered Johnston to salvage the situation, but as he had few troops to command and as William T. Sherman had positioned his corps between Vicksburg and such a force as Johnston had been able to amass at Jackson, he was unable to prevent Grant's capture of the strategically vital city.

Bragg resigned after the loss of the battle of Chattanooga in November 1863, and when Sherman moved into Georgia following the Federal victory, Davis reluctantly named Johnston commander of the Army of Tennessee. In May 1864 Sherman began his campaign to capture Atlanta, with Johnston repeatedly forcing him to either outflank strong Confederate positions or to frontally assault the well-fortified Confederates at Resaca, New Hope Church, and Kennesaw Mountain. Johnston, in addition to inflicting disproportionate casualties on the Federal army, hoped to draw Sherman deep into Georgia, where he might isolate his forces and interdict his dangerously extended line of supply. Davis, however, fearful that Johnston intended to evacuate Atlanta without a fight, relieved him of command on 17 July 1864, in favor of John Bell Hood, an aggressive fighter.

In February 1865, following Hood's loss of Atlanta and his staggering casualties at Franklin and Nashville, Davis reappointed Johnston to command of the remnant of the Army of Tennessee. The forlorn Confederate strategy was for Johnston to delay Sherman's juggernaut in North Carolina for long enough for Lee to extricate himself from Grant's pursuing force in Virginia and unite his army with that of Johnston to confront Sherman. Grant, however, ran the Army of Northern Virginia to ground at Appomattox Court House where in surrendered on 9 April 1865. With all hope of a Confederate victory lost, Johnston surrendered to Sherman on 26 April.

In 1878 Johnston was elected to the U.S. House of Representatives, but, disliking politics, served only a single term. In 1885 President Grover Cleveland appointed him to the U.S. railroad commission. In 1874 Johnston published his *Narrative of Military Operations*, in which he continued his feud with Jefferson Davis, with Beauregard, and with everyone else whom he felt to have slighted him during the war. Johnston died on 21 March 1891 and is buried at Green Mount Cemetery in Baltimore. Norman M. Shapiro, ed., "The Daniel E. Coleman Diary," 1; Craig L. Symonds, *Joseph E. Johnston: A Civil War Biography* (New York, N.Y.: W. W. Norton & Company, 1994).

51. John Austin Wharton was born near Nashville, Tennessee, on 3 July 1828 but moved with his family to Texas as an infant. In 1850, Wharton was graduated from South Carolina College (now the University of South Carolina), whereupon he returned to Texas and was licensed to practice law. In 1860 Wharton served as a Breckinridge presidential elector and later represented Brazoria County at the state Secession Convention. When the war began, Wharton was elected captain of Company B, Eighth Texas Cavalry. He rose to command the regiment after the deaths of Col. Benjamin F. Terry and Lt. Col. Thomas S. Lubbock. Wharton led his men with distinction at the battle of Shiloh, where he was wounded. His leadership during Braxton Bragg's 1862 Kentucky invasion earned him promotion to the rank of brigadier general on 28 November 1862, and his behavior at the battle of Chickamauga earned him promotion to the rank of major general. In February 1864, Wharton was assigned as chief of cavalry in Maj. Gen. Richard Taylor's Trans-Mississippi Department where he again distinguished himself in the Red River campaign. On 6 April 1865, while visiting Maj. Gen. John B. Magruder's headquarters at the Fannin Hotel in Houston, Wharton was killed by fellow officer George W. Baylor in a personal quarrel that grew out of "an unpleasant misunderstanding over military matters." Wharton is buried in the State Cemetery in Austin.

Thomas W. Cutrer, ed., "'Emphatically a General of Cavalry': A Tribute to Maj. Gen. John Austin Wharton from Chaplain Robert Franklin Bunting," Terry's Texas Rangers," *Military History of the West*, 30, (2004), 13–32.

52. Bragg ordered Col. John Hunt Morgan to move north with his cavalry and operate along Rosecrans's line of communication and to prevent him from foraging for supplies. The action at Hartsville, a crossing point on the Cumberland River about forty miles upstream from Nashville, was an incident in Morgan's raid to the north, before Rosecrans had the bulk of his infantry forces on the move.

    Under the cover of darkness in the early morning of 7 December 1862, Morgan crossed the river at Hartsville with about 1,300 men and attacked the camp of Col. Absalom B. Moore's brigade. Although outnumbered by about 1,000 troops, Morgan's attack took the Union camp by surprise, and when one of Moore's units broke and ran, the Federals fell back. By 8:30 A.M., the Confederates had surrounded the Union soldiers, convincing Colonel Moore to surrender.

    Morgan inflicted 58 casualties at the cost of 139 Confederate; however, he also left the battlefield with 1,844 Union prisoners and a wagon train loaded with captured equipment and supplies. Gen. Joseph E. Johnston called this a "brilliant feat" and recommended that Morgan be appointed brigadier general. Jefferson Davis, then at Murfreesboro, promoted Morgan in person. James A. Ramage, *Rebel Raider: The Life of General John Hunt Morgan* (Lexington: University Press of Kentucky, Louisville, 1986); Edison H. Thomas, *John Hunt Morgan and His Raiders* (Lexington: University Press of Kentucky, 1985).

53. Georgia C. Foster, the daughter of William Lytle and Susan Long Foster, was born 17 November 1843 in Nashville, Tennessee. On 27 January 1863 she married Orlando Palmer's cousin, Oliver Sylvester Kennedy, in Lauderdale County, Alabama. By 1880 the couple were living in Fort Worth, Texas, where she died on 8 December 1919.

54. Robert Jackson Andrews, born 10 August 1842 in Florence, Alabama. He enlisted as a private in Company E, Twenty-Seventh Alabama Infantry, on 1 December 1861 and achieved the rank of captain. He died on 10 June 1918 and is buried in the Florence Cemetery.

55. Of a review of Wood's brigade held on 9 February, "for the benefit of some ladies from North Alabama," Capt. Daniel Coleman wrote, "It seemed to inspire and cheer the men very much. The ladies seemed charmed and spoke encouraging words to us." Shapiro, ed., "The Daniel E. Coleman Diary," *The Huntsville Historical Review* 26:2 (summer-fall 1999), 5.

Lt. Alfred Moore, also of Wood's brigade, informed his brother that he knew "several women in town and have had a good time so far with several of them." He had, he boasted, "managed to squeeze nearly all of my female acquaintances in Tennessee." Alfred Moore to brother, 2 August 1863, Harrison, Tennessee. Alabama Department of Archives and History.

56. C. D. Hooks of Lauderdale County served as a musician in Col. William B. Wood's Sixteenth Alabama Infantry.
57. Daniel E. Coleman was the captain of Company B, Thirty-Third Alabama Infantry, and a member of Palmer's brigade. Shapiro, ed., "The Daniel E. Coleman Diary," *The Huntsville Historical Review* 26:2 (summer-fall 1999), 1–44.
58. James J. Bailey was the captain of Company F, Sixteenth Alabama Infantry.
59. The true reason for the Confederate president's visit to Murfreesboro was not to review the troops but to review the performance of their commander, Braxton Bragg, whose senior officers were becoming increasingly vocal in their condemnation of his apparent incompetence. Although Davis was, himself, disillusioned with Bragg, he saw few options with whom to replace him and so left the command structure as it was. William C. Davis, *Jefferson Davis: The Man and His Hour* (New York, N.Y.: HarperCollins, 1991), 491–94.
60. Robert Coleman Foster, Jr., a Nashville attorney, was born on 1 November 1796. He "served one term as recorder in that city, during which time he was known as 'fifty dollars and costs,' because it was his habit to impose that fine upon every man who had the misfortune to be accused of drunkenness." He died at Courtland on 28 December 1871 and is buried in Florence, Alabama. Robert Coleman Foster III served as a brigadier general of Tennessee state troops. *Memphis Daily Appeal*, 1 January 1872; Bruce S. Allardice, *More Generals in Gray* (Baton Rouge: Louisiana State University Press, 1995), 92–93
61. On 21 December 1861 Wharton informed Wood that he was "preparing to attack the enemy." Hardee wished "to know the strength of the army Wharton is fighting," saying that "he cannot send General Wood's forces far away, and says his men will soon be prepared to fight."

    Four days later, Robert Franklin Bunting, the chaplain of Terry's Texas Rangers, reported that the left wing of Bragg's army "had been protected by Gen. Wharton's Brigade for over a month" when it was driven in by the advance of Rosecrans's army. ALS, Hardee to Wharton, 21 December 1861. Gider Lehrman Collection, The Gider Lehrman Institute of American History. Cutrer, ed., *Our Trust Is in the God of Battles*, 107–8.

62. Simon Bolivar Buckner was born on 1 April 1823, near Munfordville, Kentucky, and was graduated from the U.S. Military Academy at West Point. He served in the U.S.-Mexican War and thereafter at various army posts until 1855 when he resigned his commission to become manager of family property in Chicago. At the outbreak of the Civil War he worked to build up the state guard of Kentucky and to ensure the neutrality of the state, but eventually he espoused the secessionist cause and was commissioned a brigadier general in the Confederate Army.

Ordered to reinforce Fort Donelson, Tennessee, he found the military situation hopeless and on 16 February 1862 surrendered unconditionally to Ulysses S. Grant. After his exchange he served the Confederacy in many capacities and was a lieutenant general when the war ended.

In 1868 Buckner returned to Kentucky, became editor of the *Louisville Courier*, and eventually recovered his family's property in Chicago. After some years in private business, he entered politics as a Democrat and served as governor of Kentucky from 1887 to 1891. In 1896 Buckner ran unsuccessfully for the vice presidency on the presidential ticket of John M. Palmer, as a gold Democrat, in opposition to the Free Silver majority. Buckner died near Munfordville on 8 January 1914. Arndt M. Stickles, *Simon Bolivar Buckner: Borderland Knight* (Chapel Hill: University of North Carolina Press, 1940).

63. The Sixteenth Alabama Infantry, Oliver S. Kennedy's regiment, was commanded by Col. William Basil Wood, a founder of Florence, Alabama, and a brother of the brigade commander, Brig. Gen. Sterling A. M. Wood. *The Florence Times*, 11 April 1891; *Northern Alabama: Historical and Biographical* (Birmingham, Ala.: Smith and De Land, 1888), 311–12, 529–31.

64. This piece of doggerel appeared in *The* (Cassville, Ga.) *Standard*, 17 June 1852.
"But, after all, I don't believe
My heart will break with woe;
If she's a mind to love that chap,
Why, bless her, let her go."

65. Panthea Narcissa Kennedy was born in Tippah County, Mississippi, in or about 1843, the daughter of William Wesley and Cynthia Walker Palmer Kennedy and the sister of Oliver S. Kennedy. On 30 December 1858 she married George Washington Payne who served as a private in Company A, Eighteenth Mississippi Cavalry, and who died in 1865. She later married Sylvester Sherwood, a New Yorker, who died on 21 November 1882. Panthea Kennedy Sherwood died in Denton, Texas, on 24 October 1915.

66. Enoch Riley Kennedy, a Methodist preacher, a farmer, and a miller, was born in Moore County, North Carolina, on 23 November 1823, the son of Hiram and Mary Kennedy. In 1860 he was the owner of one enslaved black

man, age twenty-one. He was married to Louisa Jane Chisholm on 25 December 1845 and was the father of six children. Among the Palmer papers is an undated bill of sale for two black men, Jessie and Bill, from E. R. Kennedy to O. S. Palmer and "Miss Palmer." Enoch Riley Kennedy died on 8 April 1886 and is buried in the Kennedy-Stutts Cemetery, Green Hill, Lauderdale County, Alabama.

67. In the margin of this letter O. S. Palmer wrote, "I have just learned that Lt. Andrews gave your money to Sally Kennedy."
68. Charles S. Hunt was the colonel of the Ninth Tennessee Infantry.

    Thomas B. Winston was not listed among the officers of the Ninth Tennessee, but in his wife's obituary notice, he is identified as "Captain Winston" and his photograph in the Palmer collection is identified as "Capt. Winston." James R. Fleming, *The Confederate Ninth Tennessee Infantry* (New Orleans. La.: Pelican Press, 2005); unidentified newspaper clipping, Orlando Palmer papers, Wilbur Smith Research Archive, Museum of Regional History, Texarkana, Texas.
69. The rumor that Lincoln's secretary of state, William H. Seward, and Maj. Gen Ambrose Burnside, had resigned and were willing to recognize Confederate independence was, of course, an entire fabrication.
70. The battle of Sharpsburg or, more commonly, Antietam Creek, was fought on 17 September 1862 between Gen. Robert E. Lee's Army of Northern Virginia and Maj. Gen. George B. McClellan's Army of the Potomac. Concurrently with Bragg's incursion into Kentucky, Lee's army had, for the first time, crossed the Potomac River into Maryland, hoping to win Southern independence by winning a decisive battle in Union territory. Although outnumbered on the field by 87,164 to 38,000—a ratio of more than two to one—Lee's army fought the Federals to a bloody draw, but on the nineteenth withdrew into Virginia, having failed to achieve its objective. The battle was the costliest single day in all American history, having amassed at total of 22,717 dead, wounded, or missing. Stephan Sears, *Landscape Turned Red: The Battle of Antietam* (New York: Ticknor and Fields, 1983).
71. The rumor that Nathan Bedford Forrest won a battle at Corinth in December 1862 was false, as he was at that time raiding deeply into western Tennessee. He did, however, on 18 December capture Col. Robert G. Ingersoll and 147 of his men, two cannon, and a sizable amount of supplies near Lexington, and on 19 December he destroyed a section of the Tennessee and Ohio Railroad vital to the supply of Grant's operations against Vicksburg. Brian Steel Wills, *A Battle from the Start: The Life of Nathan Bedford Forrest* (New York, N.Y.: HarperCollins, 1992), 81–88.
72. Capt. James J. Bailey was the quartermaster of the Sixteenth Alabama

Infantry. According to his biographer, "he was a good officer and continued to the bitter end, and in the last act of the drama, in North Carolina, he was ready to go into the ranks with his musket." James Edmonds Saunders, *Early Settlers of Alabama* (New Orleans, La.: L. Graham and Son, 1899), 114.

73. "Certificate," Orlando Palmer Papers, Wilbur Smith Research Archive, Museum of Regional History, Texarkana, Texas.
74. Peter Cozzens, *No Better Place to Die: The Battle of Stones River* (Champaign: University of Illinois Press, 1989). For first person accounts of the battle of Murfreesboro or Stones River from members of Sterling A. M. Wood's brigade, see Maj. J. F. Cameron, Third Confederate Infantry, OR, 20:1, 906–29, and Alfred Moore, the adjutant of the Thirty-Third Alabama Infantry, letter to mother, Alabama Department of Archives and History.
75. While camped at Murfreesboro, the Fifteenth Arkansas had been united with the Thirteenth Arkansas. The Thirteenth/Fifteenth Arkansas Infantry reported sixty-eight casualties at Murfreesboro, after which it was further consolidated with the First (Fagan's-Colquitt's) Arkansas Infantry.

Chapter 4

1. Dulcinea, the object of Don Quixote's affection in Miguel de Cervantes' classic novel, is merely a figment of the knight errant's imagination, for he believes he must have a lady, because, in his view, chivalry requires it. Dulcinea, in his mind, is the model of female perfection: "Her rank must be at least that of a princess," he says, "since she is my queen and lady, and her beauty superhuman, since all the impossible and fanciful attributes of beauty which the poets apply to their ladies are verified in her; for her hairs are gold, her forehead Elysian fields, her eyebrows rainbows, her eyes suns, her cheeks roses, her lips coral, her teeth pearls, her neck alabaster, her bosom marble, her hands ivory, her fairness snow, and what modesty conceals from sight such, I think and imagine, as rational reflection can only extol, not compare."
2. Oliver Sylvester Kennedy married Georgia Cheatham Foster in Lauderdale County, Alabama, on 27 January 1863. In June 1863 he resigned from his regiment due to the lingering effects of his Perryville wound and was assigned to the commissary department. Oliver S. Kennedy Papers, University of Texas at Arlington.
3. Two young women named Polk were living in the area of Florence in 1863: Sina, born in 1839, and Margaret, born in 1840.
4. Capt. Mumford E. Dixon of the Third Confederate Infantry regiment of Cleburne's Division echoed Palmer's opinion. "The is one thing we all know,

or think so anyway, that is we will whip Yankees whenever and wherever we fight. Our confidence in ourselves and in General [Johnston] is unshaken." "Captain Mumford H. Dixon Diary," Special Collections, Robert W. Woodruff Library, Emory University.

5. A great many Foster families with a large number of nubile daughters lived in Lauderdale County.

   Ann Foster was born in Tennessee in or about 1840, the daughter of Benjamin F. and Agnes E. Foster. In 1860 she was living with her family in Florence, Alabama.

   Jayne Lytle Foster was the thirteen-year-old daughter of William Lytle Foster and the younger sister of Georgia C. (Foster) Kennedy. Which, if either, was the object of Palmer's affection must now be a matter of conjecture.

6. Palmer was not the only soldier who deplored Bragg's leave policy. "It is surprising to see how many apply for 'leaves of absence,'" wrote Lt. Alfred Moore, the adjutant of the Thirty-Third Alabama Infantry, Wood's brigade, "and none are scarcely ever approved, a few for 4 or 5 days." Although Lieutenant Moore claimed to be "the only officer in the regiment that can say of himself, he never was absent at any time or lost a day's duty," the generals "never consider these things when granting leaves of absence." Alfred Moore to brother, 2 August 1863, Harrison, Tennessee. Alabama Department of Archives and History.

7. Artimisia Palmer and Thomas Brown Winston were married at her grandmother's home in Green Hill on 25 February 1863.

8. On 7 April 1863, Rear Admiral Samuel Francis Du Pont led nine ironclads in a naval assault against the harbor defenses of Charleston, South Carolina, commanded by Gen. P. G. T. Beauregard. Du Pont's slow monitors were late getting into position for the attack, and once the fleet and the Rebel batteries were in range of one another in less than two hours the Confederate gunners fired more than 2000 rounds, of which 520 struck Union vessels while the Union fleet got off only 154 shots. Most of the Federal ships were damaged to some degree, with Keokuk hit 90 times, including 19 shots at or below the waterline. Barely afloat, it withdrew from the fight. When the tide turned, Du Pont suspended the operation. His ships had been unable to penetrate even the first line of harbor defense. Stephen R. Wise, *Gate of Hell: Campaign for Charleston Harbor, 1863* (Columbia: University of South Carolina Press, 1994).

9. Maj. Gen. Earl Van Dorn, believing that Federal forces had abandoned Franklin, Tennessee, led his cavalry division on a reconnaissance in force to

determine whether, in fact the Federals were gone. On 10 April, as the Rebel cavalrymen neared the city they met increasing strong resistance, with Forrest's brigade losing and retaking one of its batteries. Van Dorn returned to Spring Hill, having demonstrated that Maj. Gen. Gordon Granger still held Franklin in force. Casualties to both sides in the running fight were minor. Brian Steel Wills, *A Battle from the Start: The Life of Nathan Bedford Forrest* (New York, N.Y.: HarperCollins, 1992), 107–9; Robert G. Hartje, *Van Dorn: The Life and Times of a Confederate General* (Nashville, Tenn.: Vanderbilt University Press, 1967), 297–301.

10. Sidney Posey Allington was born in Florence on 20 April 1839. He served as a private in the Sixteenth Alabama Infantry. He died in Florence in 1919. John C. Rigdon, *Historical Sketch and Roster of the Alabama 16th Infantry Regiment* (N.p.: CreateSpace Independent Publishing Platform, 2015).

11. Alexander M. Hannay, a native of County Wightown, Scotland, immigrated to Florence, Alabama. A tailor by trade, he was "accepted and respected by his neighbors," served on a jury appointed on 1 April 1850, and on the same day filed for U.S. citizenship. The court found that "he has behaved as a man of good moral character attached to the principles of the United States and well disposed to the good order of the same" and declared him "a citizen of the United States of America with all the rights privileges and amenities thereunto belonging." On 1 April 1852, however, he pled guilty to a charge of assault and battery and was fined $5.00 plus costs." In 1860 he was serving as an alderman. Circuit Court Records, Lauderdale County; *Florence Times Daily*, 6 March 2008.

12. The earliest regulations for the uniform of the Confederate States Army specified that staff officers' buttons "will be of bright gilt, convex, rounded at the edge—a raised eagle at the center, surrounded by thirteen stars. Exterior diameter of large size buttons, one inch; of small size, half inch." New Orleans *Picayune*, 25 May 1861.

13. Philip Dale Roddey was born in Moulton, Lawrence County, Alabama, in or about 1826. Having achieved financial success despite an impoverished childhood, Roddey raised and was elected to command of a cavalry company. On 4 May 1862, Braxton Bragg wrote that "Roddey is invaluable," and on 21 August 1862, added that, Roddey had led "another brilliant dash upon a superior force of the enemy, resulting in the capture of 123 prisoners." In October 1862, he was promoted to colonel with command of the Fourth Alabama Cavalry, which was to serve under Nathan Bedford Forrest and Joseph Wheeler, principally in Tennessee and Alabama.

In December 1862, Roddey was promoted to brigadier general and appointed commander of the District of Northern Alabama. Roddey fought a delaying action against Grenville Dodge during Abel D. Streight's 1863 raid across Alabama and Georgia, earning him the sobriquet, "Defender of North Alabama."

In April 1864, Roddey's brigade was transferred to the Department of Alabama, Mississippi, and East Louisiana, and remained in Alabama during John Bell Hood's 1864 Nashville campaign. After Hood's failure, Roddey joined Forrest in vainly attempting to check Maj. Gen. James H. Wilson's March 1865 raid into south Alabama. Most of Roddey's command was captured at the disastrous battle at Selma, Forrest's last fight. The remnant surrendered at Pond Springs (now Wheeler), Alabama, in May 1865.

After the war, Roddey moved to Tuscaloosa, Alabama, but later relocated to New York City, where he became a successful commission merchant. A scandalous affair with a wealthy young heiress, whom he allegedly defrauded, forced him to decamp to London, where he died on 19 July 1897. His body was returned to Tuscaloosa for burial. Ezra J. Warner, *Generals in Gray: Lives of the Confederate Commanders* (Baton Rouge: Louisiana State University Press, 1959), 262.

14. Grenville M. Dodge was born on 12 April 1831 in Danvers, Massachusetts. In 1851 he graduated from Norwich University with a degree in civil engineering and was, for the next ten years, a surveyor for several western railroads. He commanded a brigade at the battle of Pea Ridge, Arkansas, for which he was promoted to brigadier general, and given command of the garrison of Corinth, Mississippi. He served as Grant's chief of intelligence through the Vicksburg campaign and subsequently commanded a division in the Army of the Tennessee, but proved his greatest worth in repairing the railroads, bridges, and telegraph lines destroyed by the retreating Confederates.

On 18 April 1863 Dodge led an expedition to northern Alabama, screening the advance of Abel D. Streight's disastrous raid. In December, his forces engaged in a skirmish near Rawhide, twelve miles north of Florence, Alabama. Promoted to major general, Dodge commanded a corps during the Atlanta campaign until a severe head wound removed him from active duty.

Following the war, he served in the United States House of Representatives and was instrumental in the construction of the Transcontinental Railroad. Grenville Dodge died at Council Bluffs, Iowa, on 3 January 1916. His biographer, Stanley P. Hirshon, has stated that Dodge, "by virtue of the range of his abilities and activities," could be considered "more important in the national life after the Civil War than his more famous colleagues and friends, Grant, Sherman, and Sheridan." Stanley P. Hirshon, *Grenville M. Dodge: Soldier, Politician, Railroad Pioneer* (Bloomington: Indiana University Press, 1967.

15. Joseph "Fighting Joe" Wheeler was born near Augusta, Georgia, on 10 September 1836 and was graduated from the United States Military Academy at West Point with the class of 1859. At the outbreak of the Civil War he was serving with the Regiment of Mounted Rifles in the New Mexico Territory, but resigned his commission to accept command of the Nineteenth Alabama Infantry, which he led at the battle of Shiloh and the siege of Corinth. In September 1862 he was transferred to the command of a cavalry brigade of the Army of Mississippi. During the Kentucky Campaign, Wheeler fought at the battle of Perryville and commanded the rearguard screening the army's withdrawal and was promoted to brigadier general on 30 October.

In December, when the Army of the Cumberland began its advance against Bragg's army at Murfreesboro, Wheeler led a raid behind the Union army, destroying hundreds of wagons and capturing more than 700 prisoners. After the battle of Stones River, Wheeler again struck the Union supply lines at Harpeth Shoals on 12–13 January 1863, burning three steamboats and capturing more than 400 prisoners, for which he received promotion to a major general on 20 January 1863.

In July 1864, during Sherman's Atlanta Campaign, Wheeler, with fewer than 5,000 cavalrymen, defeated two columns of Federal horsemen attempting interdict the Macon and Western Railroad supplying John Bell Hood's army defending Atlanta.

After the fall of Atlanta, Wheeler's cavalry became virtually the only force opposing the March to the Sea, and continued the futile resistance during the Sherman's drive into North Carolina. Following the surrender of Lee's and Johnston's armies in April and May 1865, Wheeler escorted President Jefferson Davis in his attempt to escape to the trans-Mississippi, but was captured and imprisoned for two months, first at Fort Monroe and then in solitary confinement at Fort Delaware, where he was paroled on 8 June.

After the war, Wheeler became a planter and a lawyer near Courtland, Alabama, and in 1880, was elected to the first of eight terms in the United States House of Representatives.

In 1898, with the outbreak of the Spanish-American War, President William McKinley appointed Wheeler a major general of volunteers and to the command of the cavalry division that included Theodore Roosevelt's "Rough Riders." At the head of his division he took part in the battles of battle of Las Guasimas and San Juan Hill and in the siege of Santiago and was a senior member of the commission that negotiated an end to the war.

During the Philippine–American War he commanded a brigade in Arthur MacArthur's division, and on 16 June 1900 was commissioned a brigadier general in the regular army. With the end of the war, he commanded the Department of the Lakes until his retirement on 10 September 1900,

Wheeler died in Brooklyn, New York, on 25 January 1906 and is buried in the Arlington National Cemetery. He was the author of several books, including *A Revised System of Cavalry Tactics, for the Use of the Cavalry and Mounted Infantry, C.S.A.* (1863) and *The Santiago Campaign* (1898). John P. Dyer, *From Shiloh to San Juan: The Life of "Fightin' Joe" Wheeler* (Baton Rouge: Louisiana State University Press, 1961).

16. In March 1863, Maj. Gen. William S. Rosecrans ordered Col. Able D. Streight to conduct a raid across northern Alabama and into northwest Georgia to interdict the Western and Atlantic Railroad, supplying the Army of Tennessee. Streight's provisional brigade totaled approximately 1,700 soldiers mounted on mules, many of which were old or unbroken, leading the Rebels to term it the "Jackass Cavalry." On 19 April 1863, Streight's brigade left Nashville on steamboats and steamed up the Tennessee River to Eastport, Mississippi. Two days later, Streight rendezvoused with Brig. Gen. Grenville Dodge and his 8,000 cavalrymen and moved toward Tuscumbia, but there the two Union commands separated, with Streight riding toward Moulton and Dodge headed north in an effort to screen the "Jackass Cavalry's" raid from the 500 Confederate cavalrymen commanded by Maj. Gen. Nathan B. Forrest and by Col. Phillip Roddey. Streight left Tuscumbia on 26 April closely pursued by Rebel cavalry in a heavy rainstorm that made roads virtually impassable.

    Streight temporarily checked Forrest's pursuit at Day's Gap near Sand Mountain and pressed on toward Gadsden, but pressure from Forrest's horsemen prevented his men from resting. On the afternoon of 2 May, the Federals crossed Black Creek, burning the bridge behind them. Streight planned to fight his pursuers at Rome, but, with the guidance of 16-year-old Emma Sansom, Forrest located a ford and quickly overtook the poorly mounted Federals. Moreover, when local citizens held the bridge over the Coosa River into Rome, Streight abandoned his plan and turned west toward Centre, Alabama, but the Confederates overtook and surrounded him at Cedar Bluff. Streight's belief that he was greatly outnumbered—a belief that Forrest reinforced with bluff and stratagem—was compounded by the fact that much of his ammunition had become hopelessly soaked. Under these circumstances, on 3 May 1863, Streight surrendered his command. Wills, *A Battle from the Start*, 109–119.

17. Chancellorsville, Robert E. Lee's masterpiece battle, was fought on 30 April-6 May 1863 south of the Rappahannock River near Fredericksburg, Virginia, and in the Wilderness of Spotsylvania. Maj. Gen. Joseph Hooker,

commanding the 133,868-man Army of the Potomac, planned a bold strike, dividing his army in two, leaving approximately one-third of his men under Maj. Gen. John Sedgwick to demonstrate against Lee's fortifications on Marye's Heights while he led the remaining force upstream to cross on Lee's rear and either force the Rebels from their strong position and into the open or to crush them between the army's two wings. Astute reconnaissance by Maj. Gen. James Ewell Brown "Jeb" Stuart's cavalry, however, discovered Hooker's threat to Lee's rear, and, with supreme audacity, the Confederate commander left only a reinforced division to hold the heights above Fredericksburg while he marched with the rest of his 60,298-man army into the Wilderness to confront Hooker head on. On 2 May, when Stuart discovered that Hooker's right flank was vulnerable to attack, Lee dispatched Lt. Gen. Thomas Johnathan "Stonewall" Jackson with his entire corps—more than half of Lee's disposable force—on a bold flanking march around the Federal right, catching Hooker entirely by surprise and routing his right wing.

Hoping to crush the Federal army against the Rappahannock before it could rally, Jackson's men pushed Hooker's divisions as hard as the tangled terrain of the Wilderness would allow, but Confederate units became disrupted in the jungle-like environment and by sundown had lost their momentum. In an attempt to rally his men and keep the pressure on the retreating Federals, Jackson himself rode beyond the Confederate front, and in the gathering twilight was accidently shot by his own men. During the night, Hooker's demoralized army retreated across the Rappahannock. Jackson's left arm was amputated, and he seemed to be moving toward recovery when he was overcome by pneumonia, dying on 10 May, a devastating blow to Confederate hopes. Stephen Sears, *Chancellorsville* (New York, N.Y.: Houghton Mifflin Harcourt, 1996); Gary Gallagher, ed., *Chancellorsville: The Battle and Its Aftermath* (Chapel Hill: University of North Carolina Press, 1996).

18. So badly mauled was the Army of the Cumberland in the fight at Stones River that it was unable to renew its offensive for nearly half a year, the longest hiatus between campaigns by a major army in the war. Not until 24 June 1863 did William S. Rosecrans launch his so-called Tullahoma campaign. But when he again moved south, he did so with skill and apparent ease, outflanking Bragg's line on the Duck River and in one week driving him eighty miles, almost bloodlessly, back into Chattanooga. Then, on 16 August, Rosecrans again outmaneuvered Bragg, crossing the Tennessee River below Chattanooga and, thus threatening the Rebel line of supply, forced Bragg to abandon Chattanooga without a fight. David A. Powell and Eric J. Wittenberg, *Tullahoma: The Forgotten Campaign that Changed the Course of the Civil War, June 23–July 4, 1863* (El Dorado Hills, Calif.: Savas Beatie, 2020).

19. Jackson, Mississippi, the state's capital, an important manufacturing center and the intersection of two strategically vital railroads, was located forty-four miles east of Vicksburg, which it supplied by way of the Southern Railroad of Mississippi.

    On 30 April–1 May 1863, Maj. Gen. Ulysses S. Grant crossed to the east bank of the Mississippi River, downstream from Vicksburg, and turned north, threatening to interdict the Southern Railroad. Gen. Joseph E. Johnston was given the impossible task of assembling an army at Jackson and breaking the siege of Vicksburg, but by the second week of May he had rightly concluded that the situation was hopeless and so ordered the evacuation of Jackson. Under the cover of a rearguard action conducted by Brig. Gen. John Gregg on 14 May, the small force that Johnston had accumulated at Jackson decamped, and by late that afternoon the Union flag once again flew over the state capitol.

    Grant immediately marched toward now isolated Vicksburg, leaving Sherman to destroy railroad facilities, foundries, factories, gins, mills, and other public property as well as putting to the torch many private homes, leaving in his wake a scene of desolation and ruin.

    The fall of Vicksburg, 4 July 1863, had a chilling effect on civilian morale. "The people throughout the country are very much depressed in spirits since the capture of Vicksburg and Lee's retreat from Pa.," Lt. Alfred Moore of Wood's brigade wrote to his brother. The army, however, continued to believe in its ultimate success. "I see no earthly use of being low spirited," Moore continued, "as we are destined in the end to be victorious no matter what disasters may now happen to us." Edwin C. Bearss and Warren Grabau, *The Battle of Jackson, May 14, 1863* (Baltimore, Md.: Gateway Press, 1981); Alfred Moore to brother, 2 August 1863, Harrison, Tennessee, Alfred Moore letters, Alabama Department of Archives and History, Montgomery, Alabama.

20. Clement Laird Vallandigham was born on 29 July 1820, in New Lisbon, Ohio, and after completing a law course set up a practice in Dayton, Ohio. In 1845 he was elected to the first of two terms in the Ohio legislature. He was then elected to the United States House of Representatives, serving until 1863. On 14 January 1863, as a leader of the "Copperhead" faction of the anti-war Democrats, Vallandigham delivered a speech in the House stating his opposition to Lincoln's violations of civil liberties, "which have made this country one of the worst despotisms on earth," and criticizing the Emancipation Proclamation, charging that "war for the Union was abandoned; war for the Negro openly begun."

    After Maj. Gen. Ambrose E. Burnside issued General Order Number 38, warning that the "habit of declaring sympathies for the enemy" would not be tolerated in the Military District of Ohio, Vallandigham was arrested, tried by a military court, and sentenced to confinement in the military prison at Fort Warren, Massachusetts, "during the continuance of the war."

The Lincoln administration voided the sentence, ordering him sent through the lines to the Confederacy instead. From there, Vallandigham went to Windsor, Ontario, where he declared himself a candidate for governor of Ohio, winning the Democratic nomination *in absentia* but losing the general election.

In the spring of 1864, Vallandigham, as a leader of the Sons of Liberty, conspired with agents of the Confederate government to form a Northwestern Confederacy, consisting of the states of Ohio, Kentucky, Indiana, and Illinois. Accused of plotting a revolt against the Federal government, he was again tried for conspiracy.

As a delegate for Ohio, Vallandigham attended the 1864 Democratic National Convention where he declared the war a failure and demanded an immediate end of hostilities. Thereafter he returned to Ohio where he lost campaigns for the Senate and the House of Representatives and then resumed his law practice. He died in 1871 in Lebanon, Ohio, after accidentally shooting himself while representing a defendant in a murder case. Thomas C. Mackey, *Opposing Lincoln: Clement L. Vallandigham, Presidential Power, and the Legal Battle over Dissent in* Wartime (Topeka: University Press of Kansas, 2020).

21. John S. Sledge, *These Rugged Days: Alabama in the Civil War* (Tuscaloosa: University of Alabama Press, 2017), 59.
22. Len Eagleburger, *The Fighting 10th: The History of the 10th Missouri Cavalry, US* (n.p.: AuthorHouse, 2004).
23. Moses Wright Hannon was born in Baldwin County, Georgia, on 14 December 1827 and in 1847 moved to Montgomery, Alabama, where he became a wealthy merchant. He was elected captain of Company B, First Alabama Cavalry, and was promoted to lieutenant colonel on 3 December 1861. He raised and, on 5 November 1862, was appointed colonel of the Fifty-Third Alabama Cavalry. This regiment performed guard duty around Tuscumbia, Alabama, until April 1863 when it was assigned to the brigade of Philip Dale Roddey in northern Alabama.

On 15 August 1863, Hannon's regiment was transferred to the Army of Tennessee. During the Atlanta campaign, he commanded a brigade in Brig. Gen. William Y. C. Humes's division and, in June 1864, was transferred to the division of Brig. Gen. John H. Kelly of Joseph Wheeler's cavalry corps.

In August 1864, Hannon's brigade captured a Union wagon train and more than 1,000 head of cattle. For this exploit, Gen. John Bell Hood promoted Hannon to brigadier general, but he never received official confirmation from the President or the Senate.

His brigade opposed Sherman's March to the Sea and the Union drive into the Carolinas, until the battle of Monroe's Crossroads, near Kinston, North Carolina, where, on 10 March 1865, Hannon was wounded and disabled for the remainder of the war.

In 1870, Hannon moved to Texas to become a planter. He died on 3 June 1897 at Oakwood, Leon County, Texas, and is buried in Oakwood Cemetery. Bruce S. Allardice, *More Generals in Gray* (Baton Rouge: Louisiana State University Press, 1995), 214–15.

24. With the Davis administration's approval, Robert E. Lee determined to end what was becoming an unwinnable war of attrition with a decisive victory on Northern soil. In mid-June 1863 his army forded the Potomac River, marched rapidly across Maryland, and entered Pennsylvania. On 1 July it encountered the Army of the Potomac, then under the command of Maj. Gen. George Gordon Meade, at the crossroads village of Gettysburg where, in a three-day battle that has been characterized as "the highwater mark of the Confederacy," it was repulsed and forced to retire into Virginia. Lee was never again able to seize the strategic offensive, and from that point until the end of the war fighting only defensive battles in response to Union initiatives.

25. Joseph Kennedy was the son of William Wesley and Malinda Richardson Kennedy, born in Lauderdale County, Alabama, in 1840. In 1860 he was residing in McNairy County, Tennessee.

26. This is most likely William M. Simpson, born on 14 April 1831 in Florence, Alabama. On 29 November 1858 he married Clara Adeline Collier in Lauderdale, Alabama. Simpson was elected captain of Company E of Maj. S. H. Colm's First Battalion, Tennessee Infantry. He died on 3 June 1897 and is buried in Florence.

27. Lucius Eugene Polk was born in Salisbury, North Carolina, on 10 June 1833, but, at the age of two, moved with his family to the vicinity of Columbia, Tennessee. After attending the University of Virginia, 1850–1851, he moved to Helena, Arkansas, where he became a planter.

In 1861, Polk enlisted as a private in Patrick R. Cleburne's Company B, Fifteenth Arkansas Infantry, the "Yell Rifles." He was wounded in the face at Shiloh, after which he was promoted to colonel and given command of the Fifteenth Arkansas. When Cleburne was promoted to division commander,

Polk was appointed brigadier general to date from 13 December 1862 and led his brigade in the battles of Murfreesboro, Chickamauga, and Chattanooga and in the Atlanta Campaign. On 19 August 1863 he married Sally Moore in Lauderdale County, Alabama. In June 1864, Polk lost a leg to a Union artillery shell (his fourth wound during the war) at the battle of Kennesaw Mountain and was discharged from service.

He returned to Columbia and in 1884 served as a delegate to the Democratic National Convention in Chicago. In 1887 he was elected to the Tennessee Senate. Polk died in Columbia and is buried at St. John's Church Cemetery at nearby Ashwood.

28. Early in the battle of Perryville, according to Private W. E. Matthews of Company B, Thirty-Third Alabama Infantry, Wood "fell or was thrown from his horse and left the field; and the regiments that went into the fight were without the aid of a Brigadier, no one assuming the command that I know of or saw." W. E. Matthews, "Diary and Regimental History of the 33rd Regiment of Alabama Infantry." Alabama Department of Archives and History, Montgomery, Alabama.

29. William M. Simpson was born on 14 April 1831 in Florence, Alabama, where he became a prosperous merchant with the firm of Simpson, McAlester & Co. He entered the Confederate army early in the war as a lieutenant in Company G, Twenty-Seventh Alabama Infantry. He was promoted to the rank of captain and served as adjutant on the staffs of S. A. M. Wood and L. E. Polk. Simpson died in Nashville, Tennessee, 3 June 1897, but is buried in the Florence Cemetery. His brother, First Lieut. John Cotton Simpson, Jr., was killed in the first battle of Manassas, 21 July 1861. *Nashville Banner*, 6 June 1897.

30. In his official report on the battle of Chickamauga, Patrick Cleburne wrote that "Captain O. S. Palmer, assistant adjutant-general of Wood's brigade, was conspicuous for his coolness and attention to duty on the field, and has my thanks." *O.R.* 30:2, 157.

31. Bragg's failure to crush Rosecrans' discomfited army after its rout at Chickamauga, in combination with his unseemly retreat from Perryville and Stones River and his abandonment of Tennessee, caused his senior commanders to loudly question his competence. As a result, Jefferson Davis traveled to Georgia to contain what seemed to be becoming a generals' mutiny. When he arrived at army headquarters on 9 October, he found that Bragg's four corps commanders as well as Bedford Forrest were calling for his replacement. Nevertheless, the rank and file of the army were fervent in their enthusiasm for Davis, shouting for an impromptu speech when he arrived at Chickamauga Station. In response, Davis declared that "man never spoke as you did on the field of Chickamauga, and in your presence I dare not speak.

Yours is the voice that will win the independence of your country and strike terror to the heart of a ruthless foe." Addressing the Army of Tennessee more formally on 10 October, Davis applauded the army for its "glorious victory on the field of Chickamauga," but reminded the men that "obedience was the first duty of a soldier" and that "prompt, unquestioning obedience" of superiors "could not be too highly commended." With the army's continued "devotion, sacrifice, and harmony," he confidently predicted, they would soon "plant our banners permanently on the banks of the Ohio." Brooks D. Simpson, ed., "Jefferson Davis: Speech at Missionary Ridge, October 10, 1863," *The Civil War: The Third Year Told by Those Who Lived It* (Washington, D.C.: The Library of America, 2023), 547.

32. Following Gettysburg, the Army of Northern Virginia moved back up the Shenandoah Valley. George Gordon Meade's Army of the Potomac crossed the Potomac in cautious pursuit. The Federals crossed the Blue Ridge Mountains and marched along the Manassas Gap Railroad, and for a time, considered an attack on Lee's flank near Manassas Gap, but Maj. Gen. William H French, leading the expedition, became overcautious and backed away from the initiative. Jeffery William Hunt, *Meade and Lee After Gettysburg: The Forgotten Final Stage of the Gettysburg Campaign, from Falling Waters to Culpeper Court House, July 14–31, 1863* (El Dorado Hills, Calif.: Savas Beatie, 2017).

33. Mark Perrin Lowrey, who William J. Hardee called "the parson soldier, who preached to his men in camp and fought with them in the field with equal earnestness and effect," was born on 30 December 1828 in McNairy County, Tennessee, but in 1843 moved with his family to Farmington, Mississippi.

During the Mexican War, Lowrey enlisted as a private in the Second Mississippi Volunteers but did not see action, and after his discharge he became a Southern Baptist preacher.

On 6 December 1861, Lowrey was elected colonel of what was to become the Thirty-Second Mississippi Infantry. He was severely wounded in the left arm at the battle of Perryville but remained on the field. After six weeks of recuperation, he rejoined the army in time to participate in the battle of Murfreesboro. He was promoted to brigadier general on 4 October 1863, but ill health caused him to resign from the army on 14 March 1865.

After the war, Lowrey returned to Mississippi where, in 1873, although he had received no formal education, he founded and became president of the Blue Mountain College. Lowrey, who Patrick Cleburne called "the bravest man in the Confederate Army," died at Middleton, Tennessee, on 27 February 1885. Rev. J. William Jones, ed., *Southern Historical Society Papers*, vol. 31, 156; Larry Wells Kennedy, "The Fighting Preacher of the Army of Tennessee"

(PhD dissertation, Mississippi State University, 1976); Mark Perrin Lowrey, Unpublished Autobiography, 30 September 1867, Archives of the National Alumnae Association of Blue Mountain College, Blue Mountain, Mississippi.

34. Earl Hess, *Braxton Bragg: The Most Hated Man in the Confederacy* (Chapel Hill: University of North Carolina Press, 2016); James L. McDonough, *Chattanooga: A Death Grip on the Confederacy* (Knoxville: University of Tennessee Press, 1989), 183.

35. Capt. Daniel E. Coleman of the Thirty-Third Alabama confessed to his diary on 25 November that "while Cleburne's division had won imperishable fame on this trying day and done its whole duty, yet on the account of the disgraceful conduct of the troops on the other parts of the field we have to retire." On the retreat to Chickamauga, he maintained, "Cleburne's division alone seems to maintain any order." Shapiro, ed., "The Daniel E. Coleman Diary," *The Huntsville Historical Review* 26:2 (summer-fall 1999), 35.

36. On 26 November, Captain Coleman wrote that Cleburne's division served as the army's rearguard, "being the only one in which real order is left." After 10:00 P.M. Federal skirmishers closed on the division's rear "and we determined to check him." In a spirited skirmish a mile east of Ringgold "we worsted the enemy considerably—successfully checking his advance and gaining new favor for the Division." Cleburne's division of 4,175 men formed a line at Ringgold Gap, Georgia, on November 27, and the Fifteenth Arkansas was prominent in the fighting that stopped a 12,300-man Union corps and allowed the rest of the Confederate army to escape. Cleburne wrote of the Fifteenth, which captured two stands of colors during the battle: "In a fight where all fought nobly I feel it my duty to particularly compliment this regiment for its courage and constancy." Shapiro, ed., "The Daniel E. Coleman Diary," *The Huntsville Historical Review* 26:2 (summer-fall 1999), 36; *OR*, 31:2, 756

37. Lowrey reported that at Taylor's Ridge he "was deprived of the valuable services of Capt. O. S. Palmer until the close of the engagement, he being with the Sixteenth Alabama Regiment."

Capt. M. H. Dixon, commander of the Third Confederate Infantry, reported that "from a position behind what I learned to be Taylor's Ridge, covering the road and railroad bridge, the regiment advanced in line of battle some 300 or 400 yards to the summit of the hill. Our sharpshooters encountered the enemy's, and immediately after he appeared in line of battle, making his way up the opposite steep. The firing was opened on both sides, and continued for about three-quarters of an hour, the enemy pressing with great obstinacy and perseverance in the face of the continuous fire until he was within 30 or 40 yards of our line, the more adventurous and daring leading to within that number of feet. These were mostly killed or wounded and captured. After sustaining, as he must have done, a heavy loss the enemy broke and fled down the hill." *OR*, 31:2, 769–770.

38. In the fighting at Ringgold Gap, in which "the officers fought with pistols and with rocks, and so close was the fight that some of the enemy were knocked down with the latter missiles and captured," Cleburne reported, the Union assault was repulsed and "hurled down the hill, with the loss of many killed on the spot." The colors of the Seventy-Sixth Ohio Infantry and most of the prisoners were captured by the Fifteenth Arkansas. *OR*, 31:2, 756–57.

39. Frank Moore, ed. *The Rebellion Record: A Diary of American Events* (New York, N.Y.: D. Van Nostrand, 167), volume 10, 388.

40. This report was not entirely true. Leonidas Polk was born on 10 April 1806 in Raleigh, North Carolina, and was graduated from the U.S. Military Academy at West Point with the class of 1827, ranking eighth in a class of thirty-eight cadets. Within six months, however, he resigned his commission to enroll in the Virginia Theological Seminary and was ordained as a priest in the Episcopal Church in 1831.

In 1832, Polk moved to his family's plantation in Maury County, Tennessee, becoming the county's largest slaveholder. Concurrently, he served as priest of St. Peter's Church in Columbia, Tennessee. In September 1838 he was appointed Missionary Bishop of the Southwest and in October 1841 was elected first Bishop of Louisiana. Bishop Polk was the leading founder of the University of the South at Sewanee, Tennessee, which he envisioned as a national university for the South and a New World equivalent of England's Oxford and Cambridge.

At the outbreak of the Civil War, Polk offered his services to his friend and former West Point classmate, Jefferson Davis, who on 25 June 1861, commissioned him as a major general and assigned him to the command Department No. 2. When asked if he was putting off the gown of an Episcopal bishop to take up the sword of a Confederate general, he replied, "I am buckling the sword over the gown."

Polk committed one of the great blunders of the war by violating Kentucky's neutrality by seizing Columbus, Kentucky, in September 1861.

Resentful of serving under his former West Point roommate, Albert Sidney Johnston, he submitted his resignation to Jefferson Davis in November, but the president declined to accept it.

Polk commanded I Corps of Johnston's Army of the Mississippi at Shiloh and continued in that role under Gen. P. G. T. Beauregard and during Bragg's invasion of Kentucky. Polk's corps constituted the main attacking force against Maj. Gen. Don Carlos Buell's Army of the Ohio at the battle of

Perryville, but Polk was reluctant to attack the small portion of Buell's army that faced him until Bragg arrived at the battlefield.

Polk waged a year-long campaign to have Bragg relieved of command. Bragg, for his part, wrote to Davis, "Gen'l Polk by education and habit is unfit for executing the plans of others. He will convince himself his own are better and follow them without reflecting on the consequences," and after the battle of Chickamauga, Bragg relieved Polk of command and ordered him court-martialed for disobeying orders. The President dismissed the charges but transferred Polk, who had been promoted to lieutenant general in October 1862, to command of the Department of Mississippi and East Louisiana and then the Department of Alabama and East Mississippi. Polk unsuccessfully attempted to oppose Sherman's raid against Meridian, Mississippi, in February 1864. In May, he was ordered to report with his 20,000-man Army of Mississippi to Joseph E. Johnston to resist Sherman's advance toward Atlanta. On 14 June 1864, while scouting the Federal position near Marietta, Georgia, Polk was killed by an artillery shell. Joseph H. Parks, *General Leonidas Polk, C.S.A.: The Fighting Bishop* (Baton Rouge: Louisiana State University Press, 1962).

Daniel Harvey Hill, who was born on 12 July 1821 in York District, South Carolina, was graduated from the United States Military Academy in 1842 and was appointed to the First United States Artillery. In the U.S. war with Mexico, he received brevets through major for his leadership at the battles of Contreras, Churubusco, and Chapultepec.

In 1849, Hill resigned from the army to become a professor of mathematics at Washington College (now Washington and Lee University); in 1854 he joined the faculty of Davidson College, North Carolina; and in 1859 he became superintendent of the North Carolina Military Institute in Charlotte.

With his state's secession, Hill was elected colonel of the First North Carolina Infantry, and on 10 July 1861 he was promoted to brigadier general and in the spring of 1862, to major general and assigned to the command of a division in the Army of Northern Virginia, which he led through the Peninsula campaign and in the battle of Sharpsburg. Although a close a friend of his brother-in-law, Thomas J. Jackson, Hill and Robert E. Lee failed to cooperate, and after minimal involvement at Fredericksburg, Chancellorsville, and Gettysburg, Hill was reassigned as a lieutenant general to the command of a corps in Braxton Bragg's Army of Tennessee. Hill, however, became one of Bragg's severest critics and was relieved of his command and reverted to major general. He saw little active service thereafter but ended the war as a division commander under Joseph E. Johnston.

From 1866 to 1869, Hill edited *The Land We Love*, a magazine of Southern history and culture. In 1877 he was named president of the University of Arkansas and in 1885 he became the president of the Military and Agricultural College of Milledgeville, Georgia. Hill died at Charlotte on 24 September 1889 and was buried in the Davidson College Cemetery. Hal Bridges, *Lee's Maverick General: Daniel Harvey Hill* (New York, N.Y.: McGraw-Hill, 1961).

41. On 2 February 1864, Capt. Daniel E. Coleman recorded in his diary that in a raid on Athens, Alabama, some forty miles east of Florence, the Federals "brutally assailed my Mother's house, sacked and pillaged it, and drove the family from home. Oh, Lord!" he asked, "what creatures have we to deal with! Are they human beings or are they fiends?" Norman M. Shapiro, ed., "The Daniel E. Coleman Diary," *The Huntsville Historical Review* 26:2 (summer-fall 1999), 37.
42. Susie G. Kennedy was born in Alabama on 1 December 1863 and passed away on 4 May 1911 in Fort Worth, Texas. She never married.

Chapter 5

1. Calvin F. Carson of Florence was the captain of Company C, Sixteenth Alabama Infantry. He particularly distinguished himself at the battle of Murfreesboro where, according to Patrick Cleburne's report, he "remained fighting after he was wounded." *OR*, 22:1, 679.
2. On 30 September 1863, teen-aged Sallie Independence Foster of Florence recorded in her diary that Sherman's army "passed through today" and "camped on the male college hill and in the college." Although clearly disconcerted by this turn of events, she noted that "they have beautiful music." Sallie Independence Foster diary, Sallie Independence Foster Collection, Collier Library, University of North Alabama Archives and Special Collections.
3. Just after Christmas 1863, Joseph E. Johnston took command of the 40,000 to 50,000 dispirited soldiers of the Army of Tennessee encamped at Dalton, Georgia. Soon, the regular arrival of trains from Atlanta on the Western and Atlantic Railroad, bringing food, clothing, shoes, and weapons dramatically improved the army's morale.
4. As Union armies approached northern Alabama, the guerrilla war intensified. Daniel E. Sutherland, *A Savage Conflict: The Decisive Role of Guerrillas in the American Civil War* (Chapel Hill: University of North Carolina Press, 2009); Wade Pruitt, *The Bugger Saga: The Civil War Story of Guerilla and Bushwhacker Warfare in Lauderdale County, Alabama, and Southern Middle Tennessee* (Columbia, Tenn.: P-Vine Press, 1982).

5. Mary S. (Belk) Spinks was the wife of John E. Spinks, then living in Clarke County, Alabama.
6. Susie Agnes Kennedy was born on 1 December 1863 and died on 4 May 1911 in Fort Worth, Texas, where she is buried in the Oakwood Cemetery. County, Texas, United States of America

    Sarah Elizabeth "Sallie" Palmer, a sister of Paschal Palmer, was born 29 September 1836 in Lauderdale County, Alabama. On 26 May 1862 she married James M. "Roe" Griffin and following his death in 1864 she married William Rowland Stansell. Sallie Palmer died on 7 September 1916 in Alabama.
8. James M. "Roe" Griffin was born in Davidson County, Tennessee, in 1835, but by 1850 was living in Tippah County, Mississippi. He served as the ordnance sergeant of the Forty-Second Mississippi Infantry and was killed in a personal affray on 13 March 1864. He was married to Sarah Elizabeth "Sallie" Palmer, a sister of Paschal Palmer.

    John Dederick Palmer of Tippah County served as the second lieutenant of Company H, Thirty-Fourth Mississippi Infantry. He was a brother of Paschal W. Palmer and was married to Caroline Cristina "Cynthia" Borugher.
9. From Vicksburg, Maj. Gen. William T. Sherman led a raid on Meridian, Mississippi, a strategically important city about 150 miles to the east at the junction of the Mobile and Ohio Railroad and the Southern Railroad. Sherman began his campaign on 3 February 1864, intending "to break up the enemy's railroads at and about Meridian, and to do the enemy as much damage as possible."

    His army consisted of four divisions—a total of 20,000 infantry and some 5,000 cavalry and artillery. His adversary, Lt. Gen. Leonidas Polk, had only half as many men, and they were widely scattered. Meeting only slight resistance, by 9 February Sherman was in Morton, having covered more than half the distance from Vicksburg to Meridian in less than a week. There he destroyed "the railroad buildings, machine-shops, turning-table, several cars, and one locomotive." By 14 February, Confederate resistance had evaporated, and Sherman's lead elements were in Meridian.

    Sherman instructed his men to "do the enemy as much damage as possible," and in five days they destroyed more than one-hundred miles of railroad, more than sixty bridges, twenty locomotives, and eight bridges. Meridian, Sherman reported, "with its depots, store-houses, arsenal, hospitals, offices, hotels, and cantonments no longer exists." He then returned to Vicksburg on 28 February. *O.R.*, 32,1: 174; Buck T. Foster, *Sherman's Mississippi Campaign* (Tuscaloosa: University Alabama Press, 2006).
10. For six months following the Confederate defeat at Missionary Ridge, the

Army of Tennessee remained at Dalton, sheltered behind the Rocky Face and Dug Gap mountain ranges. As Palmer surmised, on 22 February a reconnaissance in force of about 25,000 soldiers from George H. Thomas's Army of the Cumberland probed Joseph E. Johnston's strength to determine whether the absence of two divisions detached to reinforce Leonidas Polk in Mississippi made the Confederates vulnerable to attack. In several days of intense skirmishing, Johnston's army demonstrated that it was still capable of repelling a major Union assault and Thomas retreated to Chattanooga, having lost 300 killed or wounded. Johnston's casualties amounted to 140. Albert Castel, *Decision in the West: The Atlanta Campaign of 1864* (Topeka: University Press of Kansas, 1992), 131–135.

11. This child, Orlando Winston, seems not to have lived, as no record of his birth seems to be extant. However, three children of Thomas and Missie Winston did survive childhood. All were born at Blue Mountain, Mississippi. Mary Kennedy "Mattie," was born in 1866 and died single in Texarkana, Arkansas, 6 December 1909. Vernon Lillian, born in 1877, who lived with her widowed mother at 802 Hazel Street, Texarkana, Arkansas, was teacher and principal of the Whitaker Street School and Highland Park School in Texarkana, Texas. She died unmarried on 26 March 1954 in Texarkana, where she was buried in the Woodlawn Cemetery. Artimisia, known as "Mittie" or "Missia," was born in 1879. Like her father and her sister, she was an educator, becoming principal of the Texarkana Junior High School. Of the three daughters, only she was married—to Yancey E. Montgomery on 24 June 1902—and was the mother of two children. She died in 1967. *Texarkana City Directory*, (1924), 305; Iola Edwards Field, "Miss Vernon Winston: Childhood through College," typescript, 1949, Wilbur Smith Research Archive, Museum of Regional History, Texarkana, Texas, 1–3.

12. This is the first of Palmer's letters to be written in pencil, further evidence of the declining fortunes of the Southern Confederacy.

13. For two months and seventy miles, Maj. Gen. William T. Sherman's ponderous advance through northwest Georgia was characterized by a series of flanking maneuvers against Gen. Joseph E. Johnston's Army of Tennessee, with each turning the Rebels out of heavily fortified positions with minimal casualties but offering no significant strategic result. On 27 June 1864, Sherman changed his tactics and launched his army's most significant frontal assault of the Atlanta campaign at Kennesaw Mountain, near Marietta, Georgia. Maj. Gen. John A. Logan assaulted Pigeon Hill while Maj. Gen. George H. Thomas attacked Cheatham Hill at the center of the Confederate line. Both were repulsed with heavy losses. Maj. Gen. John M. Schofield,

however, threatened the Confederate left flank, prompting Johnston to again withdraw toward Atlanta. Although a tactical victory for the Confederates, the battle Kennesaw Mountain failed to halt Sherman's advance and led to Johnston's removal as commander of Army of Tennessee. Earl J. Hess, *Kennesaw Mountain: Sherman, Johnston, and the Atlanta Campaign* University of North Carolina Press, 2013).

14. William Lytle Foster, the father of Georgia C. (Foster) Kennedy, was born on 24 July 1820 in Mansfield, Henry County, Tennessee to Ephraim Hubbard Foster and Jane Mebane Lytle. He was married to Susan Long Cheatham and became the father of three daughters. He died on 4 March 1889 and is buried in the Nashville City Cemetery.

15. Alexander White was a Talladega attorney, born in 1816.

16. In 1860, George Washington Foster's holdings in Lauderdale County included three plantations, Courtview, Woodland, and Oak Grove, amounting to 6,281 acres of land and 100 enslaved people. A George Washington Foster was elected captain of Company C, Second Alabama Infantry, but was killed in action at battle of Corinth. Robert S. Steen, *History of Foster House, Courtview, Rogers Hall and Early City of Florence* (Florence: University of North Alabama, 2006).

17. Thomas Jefferson Foster was born in Nashville, Tennessee, on 11 July 1809, the son of Robert C. Foster. In 1833 Foster moved to Courtland, Lawrence County, Alabama, where he became a prosperous planter. At the outbreak of the Civil War, he raised and was elected colonel of the Twenty-Seventh Alabama Infantry, which was to become a part of the garrison of Fort Henry, a bastion the construction of which he had strongly advocated for the protection of the vital Tennessee River valley. He and his regiment were captured with the fall of the fort to Ulysses S. Grant on 6 February 1862. Following his exchange, he was elected to represent Alabama in the First and Second Confederate Congresses. In 1865 he was elected to the United States House of Representatives, but was denied his seat as an impediment to reconstruction. He died on 24 February 1887. Ezra J. Warner and W. Buck Yearns, *Biographical Register of the Confederate Congress* (Baton Rouge: Louisiana State University Press, 1975), 89; *Moulton* [Alabama] *Advertiser*, 24 February 1887.

18. This report, if not entirely true, did contain a large element of fact. By the last week of July 1864, Union forces had interdicted three of the four railroads leading into Atlanta, leaving only the Macon and Western Railroad to supply Hood's army. In order to sever this final lifeline, Sherman sent Maj. Gen. George H. Stoneman and 5,000 cavalry riding south from Decatur and, from his right, Brig. Gen. Edward McCook with about 4,000

troopers, the two columns to converge at Lovejoy's Station. Stoneman also received permission to attack Macon and Andersonville to free the more than 30,000 Union prisoners there. This permission was premised, however, on Stoneman first destroying the Macon and Western Railroad and the Confederate cavalry under Maj. Gen. Joseph Wheeler. Stoneman rode out of Decatur on 27 July, but instead of the rendezvous at Lovejoy's Station, his objective, contrary to Sherman's orders, was Macon. Wheeler brushed aside the division that Stoneman had left to block the Rebel cavalry and, after detaching troops to deal with McCook, took up the pursuit of Stoneman's main column. The outnumbered Confederates struck McCook from behind, convincing him that he was surrounded. McCook cut his way out, but the fragments of his command fled piecemeal toward Marietta, leaving behind hundreds of their comrades as prisoners.

Stoneman reached Macon on 30 July to find it defended at the Ocmulgee River by a collection of Georgia Reserves and local militia companies. Failing to force a crossing, Stoneman turned south with the intention of riding to Florida, but reports of Southern cavalry threatening the river crossings in that direction convinced him to turn back. On 31 July, he encountered three of Wheeler's brigades at Sunshine Church, and, supposing himself outnumbered, ordered two of his brigades to escape while he remained with the third to cover their retreat. That afternoon, Stoneman and more than 700 of his men surrendered.

As historian William Marvel has written, "Instead of closing Hood's supply line, forcing the evacuation of Atlanta, and freeing tens of thousands of prisoners, Stoneman's raid had resulted in the virtual elimination of two Union cavalry divisions." David Evans, *Sherman's Horsemen: Union Cavalry Operations in the Atlanta Campaign* (Bloomingdale, Indiana University Press, 1996), 291–355; John P. Dyer, *From Shiloh to San Juan: The Life of "Fightin' Joe" Wheeler* (Baton Rouge: Louisiana State University Press, 1961), 141–44; William Marvel, *Andersonville*: The Last Depot (Chapel Hill: University of North Carolina Press, 1994), 158–160.

19. On 10 August, Wheeler's cavalry crossed the Chattahoochee River in an attempt to destroy the Western and Atlantic Railroad supplying Sherman's army from Chattanooga. Wheeler's men entered Dalton, Georgia, but were unable to capture the nearby fort. He then crossed the Tennessee River above Knoxville and began a raid into east Tennessee. Riding west, he temporarily disrupted the Nashville and Chattanooga Railroad and then returned south through Franklin, recrossing the Tennessee at Tuscumbia on 2 September. Dyer, *From Shiloh to San Juan*, 148–52.

20. In consequence of its devastating casualties, the First/Fifteenth was further consolidated with the Fifth/Thirteenth, and the Second/Twenty-Fourth Arkansas, to be commanded by Col. Peter V. Green, formerly the commander of the Fifth Arkansas Infantry. *OR*, 38:3, 714.
21. *OR*, 38:3, 736.
22. *OR*, 38:3, 714–15.
23. Sherman quoted in Charles Carleton Coffin, *Freedom Triumphant: The Fourth Period of the War of the Rebellion* (New York, N.Y.: Harper and Brothers, 1891), 76.
24. Forrest quoted in John Allan Wyeth, *Life of Nathan Bedford Forrest* (New York: Harper & Brothers Publishers, 1899), 544. Cheatham and Hood quoted in Wiley Sword, *Embrace an Angry Wind: The Confederacy's Last Hurrah: Spring Hill, Franklin, and Nashville* (New York, N.Y.: HarperCollins, 1992), reprinted as *Shrouds of Glory* (Topeka: University Press of Kansas, 1993), 178–180.
25. John Bell Hood, *Advance and Retreat: Personal Experiences in the United States Army and Confederate States Army* (New Orleans, La.: Hood Orphan Memorial Fund, 1880; reprint, Richard N. Current, ed. Bloomington: Indiana University Press, 1959), 270.
26. Daniel E. Sutherland, ed., *Reminiscences of a Private: William E. Bevens of the First Arkansas Infantry* (Fayetteville: University of Arkansas Press, 1992), 208–9.
27. This flag was captured at Jonesboro, Georgia, 1 September 1864 but was returned to the state after the war and is presently in the collection of the Old State House Museum, Little Rock, Arkansas. "W. E. Mat[t]hews [Preston] Diary and Regimental History," Alabama Department of Archives and History, Montgomery, Alabama
28. William J. Hardee, "Sketch of Maj.-Gen. Patrick R. Cleburne," Rev. J. William Jones, ed., *Southern Historical Society Papers*, XXXI, (Richmond, Va., January-December 1903), 161.
29. Sutherland, ed., *Reminiscences of a Private*, 211.
30. Palmer was replaced as brigade adjutant by Capt. W. J. Milner. Irving A. Buck, *Cleburne and His Command* (Jackson, Tenn.: McCowat-Mercer Press, 1958), 282–83; *Confederate Veteran*, (January 1922), 30:1, 31.

Afterword

1. Wiley Sword, *Embrace an Angry Wind: Spring Hill, Franklin, and Nashville* (New York, N.Y.: HarperCollins, 1992); Stanley Horn, *The Decisive Battle*

of Nashville (Baton Rouge: Louisiana State University Press, 1956); James Lee McDonough and Thomas L. Connelly, *Five Tragic Hours: The Battle of Franklin* (Knoxville: University of Tennessee Press, 1983); James Lee McDonough, *Nashville: The Western Confederacy's Final Gamble* (Knoxville: University of Tennessee Press, 2004).

2. Samuel R. Watkins, *Company Aytch, Maury Grays, First Tennessee Regiment; Or, a Side Show of the Big Show* (Nashville, Tenn.: Cumberland Presbyterian Publishing House, 1882), 209.
3. Because Thomas's army was composed of elements of the Army of the Cumberland, the Army of the Ohio, the Army of the Tennessee, and other commands, the force in Nashville had no official name.
4. Grant quoted in John Russell Young, *Around the World with General Grant* (New York, N.Y.: The American News Company, 1879).
5. Watkins, *Company Aytch*, 218.
6. In 1911 Kennedy sold much of the property near which the Castle stands to the city of Fort Worth to be inundated by Lake Worth, the city's reservoir. This gothic structure is said to be haunted. *Fort Worth City Directory*, 1878–1879; *Houston Post*, 27 February 1909.
7. Iola Edwards Field, "Miss Vernon Winston: Childhood through College," typescript, 1949, Wilbur Smith Research Archive, Museum of Regional History, Texarkana, Texas, 1–3.
8. Unidentified newspaper clipping dated 6 August 1884; "An Act to Incorporate Blue Mountain Academy, in Tippah County," *Journal of the Senate of the State of Mississippi* (1896), 274, 446; obituary, Mrs. T. B. Winston, unidentified newspaper clipping, Palmer Papers, Wilbur Smith Research Archive, Texarkana Museum of Regional History; Thomas Brown Winston obituary, undated clipping from the *Texarkana Gazette*, Palmer Papers, Wilbur Smith Research Archive, Texarkana Museum of Regional History.

Bibliography

Primary Sources

Unpublished Manuscripts

Armstrong, Charles Jacob. "Diary of Sergeant Charles Jacob Armstrong, Co. C, 33rd Alabama Infantry." Alabama Department of Archives and History, Montgomery, Alabama.

Captain Mumford H. Dixon Diary, Special Collections, Robert W. Woodruff Library, Emory University.

Diary of Lt. William Tanner Huddleston, Company A, Fifteenth Arkansas Infantry.

"Family Register." Kennedy Family Bible. Copy in Palmer papers, Wilbur Smith Research Archive, Museum of Regional History, Texarkana, Texas.

Kennedy, Larry Wells. "The Fighting Preacher of the Army of Tennessee" (PhD dissertation, Mississippi State University, 1976.

Kennedy, Orlando S. "United Confederate Veterans Descriptive List." Southwest Collection, Special Collections Library at Texas Tech University, Lubbock, Texas.

Lowrey, Mark Perrin. Unpublished Autobiography. 30 September 1867. Archives of the National Alumnae Association of Blue Mountain College, Blue Mountain, Mississippi.

Matthews, W. E. Preston. "Diary and Regimental History of the 33rd Regiment of Alabama Infantry." Alabama Department of Archives and History, Montgomery, Alabama.

Alfred M. Moore letters. Alabama Department of Archives and History, Montgomery, Alabama.

Oliver S. Kennedy letters, Special Collections Library, University of Texas at Arlington.

Orlando S. Palmer papers, Wilbur Smith Research Archive, Museum of Regional History, Texarkana, Texas.

S. A. M. Wood papers, Alabama Department of Archives and History, Montgomery, Alabama.

Sallie Independence Foster Collection, Collier Library, University of North Alabama Archives and Special Collections.

Published Books

Beck, Brandon H., ed. *Third Alabama! The Civil War Memoir of Brigadier General Cullen Andrews Battle, CSA.* Tuscaloosa: University of Alabama Press, 2000.

Bierce, Ambrose. "What Occurred at Franklin." *The Collected Works of Ambrose Bierce.* New York, N.Y.: Neale Publishing Company, 1909.

Brown, Norman D., ed. *One of Cleburne's Command: The Civil War Reminiscences and Diary of Capt. Samuel T. Foster, Granbury's Texas Brigade, C.S.A.* Austin: University of Texas Press, 1980.

Buck, Irving A. *Cleburne and His Command.* Jacksonville, Tenn.: McCowat-Mercer Press, 1959.

Carter, John C., ed. *Welcome the Hour of Conflict: William Cowan McClellan and the 9th Alabama.* Tuscaloosa: University of Alabama Press, 2014.

Catalogue of the Officers, Students and Libraries of LaGrange College, North Alabama, for the Collegiate Year 1851-'52. Tuscumbia, Alabama, 1852.

Christ, Mark K., ed. *Getting Used to Being Shot At: The Spence Family Civil War Letters.* Fayetteville: University of Arkansas Press, 2002.

Crute, Joseph H. Jr. *Confederate Staff Officers.* Powhatan, Va.: Derwent Books, 1982.

Cutrer, Thomas W., ed. *Our Trust Is in the God of Battles: The Civil War Letters of Robert Franklin Bunting, Chaplain, Terry's Texas Rangers, C.S.A.* Knoxville: University of Tennessee Press, 2006.

Department of the Navy. *Official Records of the Union and Confederate Navies in the War of the Rebellion.* Washington, D.C.: Government Printing Office, 1921.

Downey, Clifford, ed. *The War Time Papers of R. E. Lee.* New York, N.Y.: Bramhall House, 1961.

Grant, U. S. *Personal Memoirs.* New York, N.Y.: Charles L. Webster and Company, 1885.

Hammock, John C. *With Honor Untarnished: The Story of the First Arkansas Infantry Regiment, Confederate States Army.* Little Rock: Pioneer Press, 1961.

Hughes, Nathaniel Cheairs, Jr., ed. *Liddell's Record: St. John Richardson Liddell, Brigadier General, C.S.A., Staff Officer and Brigade Commander, Army of Tennessee.* Baton Rouge: Louisiana State University Press, 1987.

Hood, John Bell. *Advance and Retreat: Personal Experiences in the United States Army and Confederate States Army.* New Orleans, La.: Hood Orphan Memorial Fund, 1880; reprint, Richard N. Current, ed. Bloomington: Indiana University Press, 1959.

Jones, John B. *A Rebel War Clerk's Diary at the Confederate States Capital.* Philadelphia, Pa.,: J. B. Lippincott, 1886.

Lincoln, Abraham. *Speeches and Writings, 1859–1865*. Washington, D.C.: Library of America, 1989.
The Rebellion Record: A Diary of American Events. New York, N.Y.: D. Van Nostrand, 1865.
Sutherland, Daniel E., ed. *Reminiscences of a Private: William E. Bevens of the First Arkansas Infantry, C.S.A.* Fayetteville: University of Arkansas Press, 1992.
United States War Department. *The War of the Rebellion: A Compilation of the Official Records of the Union and Confederate Armies*. Washington, D.C.: Government Printing Office, 1880–1901.
Vaughan, Alfred Jefferson. *Personal Record of the Thirteenth Regiment, Tennessee Infantry.* n.p., 2012.
Watkins, Samuel R. *Company Aytch, Maury Grays, First Tennessee Regiment; Or, a Side Show of the Big Show*. Nashville, Tenn.: Cumberland Presbyterian Publishing House, 1882,

Published Articles

Cutrer, Thomas W., ed., "'Emphatically a General of Cavalry': A Tribute to Maj. Gen. John Austin Wharton from Chaplain Robert Franklin Bunting, Terry's Texas Rangers." *Military History of the West*, vol. 30, (2004), 13–32.
Jones, J. William, ed. "Sketch of Maj.-Gen. Patrick R. Cleburne." *Southern Historical Society Papers*, vol. 31, 156.
Mahon, John K., ed. "The Journal of A. B. Meek and the Second Seminole War, 1836." *Florida Historical Quarterly*. 38:4 (April 1960), 302–318.
Moore, Frank, ed. "Expedition to Florence, Alabama." *The Rebellion Record: A Diary of American Events*. New York, N.Y.: D. Van Nostrand, 1865, 119-20.
Noyes, Edward, ed. "Excerpts from the Civil War Diary of E. T. Eggleston." *Tennessee Historical Quarterly*. Vol. 17, No. 4 (December 1958), 336–358.
Shapiro, Norman M., ed. "The Daniel E. Coleman Diary." *The Huntsville Historical Review* 26:2 (summer-fall 1999), 1–44.

Secondary Sources

Books

Allardice, Bruce S. *More Generals in Gray*. Baton Rouge: Louisiana State University Press, 1995.
Bearss, Edwin C., and Warren Grabau. *The Battle of Jackson, May 14, 1863*. Baltimore, Md.: Gateway Press, 1981.
Brewer, Willis. *Alabama, Her History, Resources, War Record, and Public Men: From 1540 to 1872*. Montgomery, Ala.: Barrett and Brown, 1872.

Bridges, Hal. *Lee's Maverick General: Daniel Harvey Hill*. New York, N.Y.: McGraw-Hill, 1961.
Castel, Albert. *Decision in the West: The Atlanta Campaign of 1864*. Topeka: University Press of Kansas, 1992.
Christ, Mark. K., ed. *The Die is Cast: Arkansas Goes to War, 1861*. Little Rock: Butler Center Books, 2010.
Connelly, Thomas Lawrence. *Army of the Heartland: The Army of Tennessee, 1861–1862*. Baton Rouge: Louisiana State University Press, 1967.
———. *Autumn of Glory: The Army of Tennessee, 1861–1862*. Baton Rouge: Louisiana State University Press, 1971.
Cooling, Benjamin Franklin. *The Decisive Battle of Nashville*. Knoxville: University of Tennessee Press, 1988.
———. *Forts Donelson and Henry: The Key to the Confederate Heartland*. Knoxville: University of Tennessee Press, 1987.
Cozzens, Peter. *No Better Place to Die: The Battle of Stones River*. Champaign: University of Illinois Press, 1989.
———. *Shenandoah 1862: Stonewall Jackson's Valley Campaign*. Chapel Hill: The University of North Carolina Press, 2008.
———. *The Shipwreck of Their Hopes: The Battles for Chattanooga*. Champaign: University of Illinois Press, 1994.
———. *This Terrible Sound: The Battle of Chickamauga*. Champaign: University of Illinois Press, 1992.
Daniel, Larry J. *Shiloh: The Battle that Changed the Civil War*. New York, N.Y.: Simon and Schuster, 1997.
Davis, William C. *Battle at Bull Run: A History of the First Major Campaign of the Civil War*. Baton Rouge: Louisiana State University Press, 1977.
———. *Jefferson Davis: The Man and His Hour*. New York, N.Y,: HarperCollins, 1991.
DeLand, T. A., and A. Davis Smith. *A History of Lauderdale County Alabama*. Birmingham: Northern Alabama Historical and Biographical, 1888.
Dougan, Michael B. *Confederate Arkansas: The People and Politics of a Frontier State*. Tuscaloosa: University of Alabama Press, 1976.
Dyer, John P. *From Shiloh to San Juan: The Life of "Fightin' Joe" Wheeler*. Baton Rouge: Louisiana State University Press, 1961.
Engle, Stephen D. *Don Carlos Buell: Most Promising of All*. Chapel Hill: University of North Carolina Press, 2014.
Evans, David. *Sherman's Horsemen: Union Cavalry Operations in the Atlanta Campaign*. Bloomingdale, Indiana University Press, 1996.
Ferris, Norman B. *The Trent Affair: A Diplomatic Crisis*. Knoxville: University of Tennessee Press, 1977.

Bibliography

Gallagher, Gary W., ed. *Chancellorsville: The Battle and Its Aftermath*. Chapel Hill: University of North Carolina Press, 1996.
———. *The Richmond Campaign of 1862: The Peninsula and the Seven Days*. Chapel Hill: University of North Carolina Press, 2000.
———. *The Shenandoah Campaign of 1862*. Chapel Hill: University of North Carolina Press, 2010.
Gatewood, Willard B., Jr., and Jeannie M. Whayne, eds. *The Governors of Arkansas: Essays in Political Biography*. Fayetteville: University of Arkansas Press, 1995.
Goodspeed Biographical and Historical Memoirs of Central Arkansas. Chicago, Ill.: Goodspeed Publishing Company, 1889.
Hershon, Stanley P. *Grenville M. Dodge: Soldier, Politician, Railroad Pioneer*. Bloomington: Indiana University Press, 1967.
Hess, Earl J. *Braxton Bragg: The Most Hated Man in the Confederacy*. Chapel Hill: University of North Carolina Press, 2016.
———. *Kennesaw Mountain: Sherman, Johnston and the Atlanta Campaign*. Chapel Hill: University of North Carolina Press, 2013.
———. *Storming Vicksburg*. Chapel Hill: University of North Carolina Press, 2020.
———. *War in the West: Victory and Defeat from the Appalachians to the Mississippi*. Chapel Hill: University of North Carolina Press, 2012.
History of Texas, together with a Biographical History of Tarrant and Parker Counties. Chicago, Ill.: Lewis Publishing Company, 1895.
Holt, Michael F. *The Election of 1860: A Campaign Fraught with Consequences*. Topeka: University Press of Kansas, 2017.
Horn, Stanley F. *The Decisive Battle of Nashville*. Baton Rouge: Louisiana State University Press, 1956.
Hughes, Nathaniel Cheairs. *Battle of Belmont: Grant Strikes South*. Chapel Hill: University of North Carolina Press, 1991.
———. *General William J. Hardee: Old Reliable*. Baton Rouge: Louisiana State University Press, 1965.
Hunt, Jeffery William. *Meade and Lee after Gettysburg: The Forgotten Final Stage of the Gettysburg Campaign, from Falling Waters to Culpeper Court House, July 14–31, 1863*. El Dorado Hills, Calif.: Savas Beatie, 2017.
Ivey, William. *North Carolina Schools of Longrifles 1765–1865*. N.p.: Ivey, 2010.
Jones, James Pickett. *Yankee Blitzkrieg: Wilson's Raid through Alabama and Georgia*. Athens: University of Georgia Press, 1976.
Knight, James R. *The Battle of Franklin: When the Devil Had Full Possession of the Earth*. Charleston, S.C.: The History Press, 2009.
Lauderdale County Heritage Book Committee. *The Heritage of Lauderdale County, Alabama*. Clanton, Ala.: Heritage Publishing Consultants, 1999.

List of Staff Officers of the Confederate States Army. Washington, D.C.: Government Printing Office, 1891.

Losson, Christopher. *Tennessee's Forgotten Warriors: Frank Cheatham and His Confederate Division.* Knoxville: University of Tennessee Press, 1989.

Mackey, Thomas C. *Opposing Lincoln: Clement L. Vallandigham, Presidential Power, and the Legal Battle over Dissent in Wartime.* Topeka: University Press of Kansas, 2020.

Marvel, William. *Andersonville: The Last Depot.* Chapel Hill: University of North Carolina Press, 1994.

McDonald, William Lindsey. *A Walk Through the Past: People and Places of Florence and Lauderdale County, Alabama.* Gloucester, Va.: Bluewater Publishing, 2003.

McDonough, James Lee. *Chattanooga: A Death Grip on the Confederacy.* Knoxville: University of Tennessee Press: 1984.

———. *Nashville: The Western Confederacy's Final Gamble.* Knoxville: University of Tennessee Press, 2004.

McDonough, James Lee, and Thomas L. Connelly. *Five Tragic Hours: The Battle of Franklin.* Knoxville: University of Tennessee Press, 1983.

McIlwain, Christopher Lyle. *Civil War Alabama.* Tuscaloosa: University of Alabama Press, 2020.

McPherson, James M. *This Mighty Scourge: Perspectives on the Civil War.* New York, N.Y.: Oxford University Press, 2009.

Neal, Diane, and Thomas W. Kremm. *Lion of the South: General Thomas C. Hindman.* Macon, Ga: Mercer University Press, 1993.

Noe, Kenneth. *Perryville: This Grand Havoc of Battle.* Lexington: University of Kentucky Press, 2001.

Northern Alabama: Historical and Biographical. Birmingham, Ala.: Smith and De Land, 1888.

Officers and Students of the Arkansas Female College. Little Rock, Ark.: P. A. Ladue, 1876.

Parks, Joseph H. *General Leonidas Polk: The Fighting Bishop.* Baton Rouge: Louisiana State University Press, 1962.

———. *John Bell of Tennessee.* Baton Rouge: Louisiana State University Press, 1950.

Polk, William Mecklenburg. *Leonidas Polk: Bishop and General.* London: Longman's, Green, and Company, 1893.

Piston, William Garrett, and Richard W. Hatcher. *Wilson's Creek: The Second Battle of the Civil War and the Men Who Fought It.* Chapel Hill: University of North Carolina Press, 2005.

Powell, David A., and Eric J. Wittenberg. *Tullahoma: The Forgotten Campaign that Changed the Course of the Civil War, June 23-July 4, 1863*. El Dorado Hills, Calif.: Savas Beatie, 2020.

Pruitt, Wade. *The Bugger Saga: The Civil War Story of Guerilla and Bushwhacker Warfare in Lauderdale County, Alabama, and Southern Middle Tennessee*. Columbia, Tenn.: P-Vine Press, 1982.

Ramage, James A. *Rebel Raider: The Life of General John Hunt Morgan*. Lexington: University Press of Kentucky, Louisville, 1986.

Rigdon, John. *Historical Sketch and Roster of the Alabama 13th Infantry Regiment*. n.p., n.d., 2015.

Robinson, Blackwell P. *The History of Moore County—1747–1847*. Southern Pines, N.C.: Moore County Historical Association, 1956.

Roland, Charles P. *Albert Sidney Johnston: Soldier of Three Republics*. Austin: University of Texas Press, 1964.

Sears, Steven. *Chancellorsville*. New York, N.Y.: Houghton Mifflin Harcourt, 1996.

———. *Landscape Turned Red: The Battle of Antietam*. New York: Ticknor and Fields, 1983.

———. *To the Gates of Richmond: The Peninsula Campaign*. New York, N.Y.: Ticknor & Fields, 1992.

Sanders, Stuart W. *The Battle of Mill Springs, Kentucky*. Charleston, S.C.: Arcadia Publishing, 2015.

———. *Maney's Confederate Brigade at the Battle of Perryville*. Charleston, S.C.: Arcadia Publishing, 2014.

Saunders, James Edmonds. *Early Settlers of Alabama*. New Orleans, La.: L. Graham & Son, 1899.

Sehlinger, Peter J. *Kentucky's Last Cavalier: General William Preston, 1816–1887*. Lexington: University Press of Kentucky, 2004.

Sledge, John S. *These Rugged Days: Alabama in the Civil War*. Tuscaloosa: University of Alabama Press, 2017.

Steen, Robert S. *History of Foster House, Courtview, Rogers Hall and Early City of Florence*. Florence: University of North Alabama, 2006.

Sutherland, Daniel E. *A Savage Conflict: The Decisive Role of Guerrillas in the American Civil War*. Chapel Hill: University of North Carolina Press, 2009.

Sword, Wiley. *Embrace an Angry Wind: The Confederacy's Last Hurrah: Spring Hill, Franklin, and Nashville*. New York, N.Y.: HarperCollins, 1992, reprint, Topeka: University Press of Kansas, 1993.

Symonds, Craig L. *Joseph E. Johnston: A Civil War Biography*. New York, N.Y.: W. W. Norton & Company, 1994.

———. *Stonewall of the West: Patrick Cleburne and the Civil War*. Topeka: University Press of Kansas, 1997.

Thomas, Edison H. *John Hunt Morgan and His Raiders*. Lexington: University Press of Kentucky, 1985.
Thrasher, Christopher. *Suffering in the Army of Tennessee: A Social History of the Confederate Army of the Heartland from the Battles for Atlanta to the Retreat from Nashville*. Knoxville: University of Tennessee Press, 2021.
Walker, Scott. *Hell's Broke Loose in Georgia: Survival in a Civil War Regiment*. Athens: University of Georgia Press, 2005.
Walther, Eric H. *William Lowndes Yancey and the Coming of the Civil War*. Chapel Hill: University of North Carolina Press, 2006.
Warner, Ezra J., and W. Buck Yearns. *Biographical Register of the Confederate Congress*. Baton Rouge: Louisiana State University Press, 1975.
Warren, Polly C., comp. *Lauderdale County, Alabama, Civil War Records*. Columbia, Tenn.: P-Vine Press, 1978.
White, James Terry ed. *The National Cyclopaedia of American Biography*. New York, N.Y.: James T. White and Company, 1898.
Wills, Brian Steel. *A Battle from the Start: The Life of Nathan Bedford Forrest*. New York, N.Y.: HarperCollins, 1992.
Wise, Stephen R. *Gate of Hell: Campaign for Charleston Harbor, 1863*. Columbia: University of South Carolina Press, 1994.
Woods, James M. *Rebellion and Realignment: Arkansas's Road to Secession*. Fayetteville: University of Arkansas Press, 1987.
Woodworth, Steven E., ed. *The Chickamauga Campaign*. Carbondale: Southern Illinois University Press, 2010.
Worley, Ted R. *Early History of Des Arc and Its People*. Des Arc, Ark.: White River Journal, 1957.
Wyeth, John Allan. *Life of Nathan Bedford Forrest*. New York: Harper & Brothers Publishers, 1899.
Wyllie, Arthur. *Confederate Officers*. n.p.: n.p.
Young, John Russell. *Around the World with General Grant*. New York, N.Y.: The American News Company, 1879.

Secondary Sources

Articles

Fisher, Noel C. "'Prepare Them for My Coming': General William T. Sherman, Total War, and Pacification in West Tennessee." *Tennessee Historical Quarterly*. 51, No. 2 (summer 1992): 75–86.
Moneyhon, Carl H. "Governor Henry Massie Rector and the Confederacy: States' Rights versus Military Contingencies." *Arkansas Historical Quarterly* 73 (Winter 2014): 357–380.

Watts, J. Carter. "History of Jefferson Guards and the Fifteenth Arkansas Regiment." *Jefferson County Historical Quarterly*, 11, No. 4 (1983): 25–42.

Wooster, Ralph. "The Arkansas Secession Convention." *Arkansas Historical Quarterly* 13 (Summer 1954): 172–195.

Unpublished Articles and Typescripts

Field, Iola Edwards. "Miss Vernon Winston: Childhood through College," typescript, 1949, Wilbur Smith Research Archive, Museum of Regional History, Texarkana, Texas, 1–3.

Index

Allington, Sidney Posey, 108, 192n10
Anderson, Joseph Briggs, 14, 158n9
Anderson's Crossroads, Tennessee, 124
Andersonville, Georgia, 209n18
Atlanta, Georgia, campaign for, 145, 146, 147, 153, 184n50, 194n15, 207n13
Atlanta and Chattanooga Railroad, 146

Bailey, James J., 82, 89, 137, 187n58, 190n73
Banks, Charles T. J. "Charlie," 43, 169n30
Banks, Nathaniel Prentiss, 68, 179n30
battle, experience of, 64
Beauregard, Pierre Gustave Toutant, 56, 70, 106, 115, 168n26, 172n37, 184n50, 191n8, 203n40
Bell, John, 14, 158n10, 160n19, 175n12
Belle, enslaved African American child, 82
Belmont, Missouri, battle of, 48, 172n38
Benteen, Frederick, 117
Bevens, William E., 149
Blue Mountain Academy, Tippah County, Mississippi, 154
Bostwick, Robert Montrose, 73, 181n39
Bowen William D., 117
Bowling Green, Kentucky, 20, 46, 48–49, 50, 51, 53, 56, 58, 170n36, 172n37, 173n40
Bradley, Thomas H., 35–36, 165n20
Bragg, Braxton, 4, 70, 71, 78, 80, 81, 85, 90, 101, 104, 123, 127, 128, 132, 161n20, 101n3, 165n23, 174n6, 178n25, 181n40, 182n46, 183nn49–50, 185n51, 186n52, 187n59, 189n71, 191n6, 192n13, 196n18, 200n31, 204n40, 205n40
Bragg's Kentucky Campaign, 72–73
Breckinridge, John C., 11, 127, 182n46, 185n51
Briggs, Levi E., 43, 169n30
Brooks, John Jesse Westmorland ("Uncle Jesse"), 16, 26, 32, 68, 76, 86, 88, 102, 141, 142, 158n13
Brooks, Olive Elizabeth Kennedy ("Aunt Ollie" and "Aunt Ollie"), 16, 32, 62, 68, 102, 105, 107, 111, 113, 120, 121, 126, 131, 159n13
Brown, Andrew, 69, 180n34
Buckner, Simon Bolivar, 4, 77, 86, 173n40, 176n13, 182n42, 188n62
Buell, Don Carlos, 58, 70–71, 90, 167, 172n37, 174n6, 204n40
Burnside, Ambrose, 89, 189n70, 197n20

Camp Breckinridge, Kentucky, 181n40
Camp Dick Robinson, Kentucky, 73, 181n40
Camp Rector, Arkansas, 35
Carson, Calvin F., 135, 205n1
Carter, Martha "Mattie," 67, 178n26
Chancellorsville, battle of, 112, 196n17, 204n40
Chattanooga, siege and battle of, 123, 125, 126, 127, 128, 129, 140, 152, 166n23, 171n36, 184n50, 196–97n18, 200n27, 207n10
Chattanooga, Tennessee, 70, 72, 80, 83, 100, 124, 147, 173n6, 209–10n19

Index

Cheatham, Benjamin F., 145, 148, 149, 151, 181nn38–39
Chickamauga, battle of, 123, 124, 126, 128, 129, 149, 11n36, 183n46, 185n51, 200nn30–31, 201n31
Chisholm, William Rufus, 57, 174n8
Churchill, Thomas J., 70
Cleburne, Patrick R., 4, 39, 41, 42, 44, 45, 46, 47, 52, 68, 70, 72, 86, 87, 127, 128, 129, 130, 140, 149–50, 165n20, 167n24, 169n34, 178n25, 191n4, 299n27, 200n30, 202nn33, 35–36, 203n38, 205n1
Coffee, Alexander Donelson, 66, 177n22
Coleman, Daniel E., 82, 88, 183n50, 186n55, 187n57, 202nn35–36, 205n41
Colquittt, John W., 147
Columbia, Tennessee, 13, 47, 148, 149, 150, 152, 160n20, 199n27, 200n27, 203n40
Columbus, Kentucky, 48, 49, 59, 62, 172n38, 173n39, 203n40. *See also* Belmont, battle of
Compton's Hill, 152
Confederate patriotism and loyalty to Southern cause, 3, 7, 33, 40, 43, 59, 62, 63–64, 65–66, 72, 75, 140, 141, 143
Cook, William H., 52, 173n42
Corinth, Mississippi, 48, 56, 65, 66, 69, 78, 89, 110, 116, 166, 172, 189n72, 193n14, 194n15, 208n16
Cornyn, Florence M., 116–17
Crittenden, George B., 175nn10–11
Crittenden, Kentucky, 72
Crittenden, Mary, 88
Crittenden, Mrs. B. F., 32, 164n16
Crittenden County, Arkansas, 165
Cumberland County, North Carolina, 156n
Cumberland Ford, Tennessee, 72

Cumberland Gap, 73, 175n10
Cumberland River, 73, 81, 151, 175n10, 176n13, 186n52
Cumberland School of Law, Lebanon, Tennessee, 2, 11, 157n1

Dalton, Georgia, 128, 132, 137, 138, 141, 142, 147, 205n3, 207n10, 209n19
Davidson, Annie, 18, 50, 67, 111, 114, 178n27
Davidson College, North Carolina, 204n40
Davidson County, Tennessee, 177n18, 206n8
Davie, George N., 73
Davis, Jefferson, 29, 69, 75, 83, 128, 147, 166, 167, 171, 172n37, 182nn46–49, 184n50, 186n52, 196n15, 199n24, 200n31, 203n40
Davis, Sallie, 89, 102, 107, 108, 113, 114, 115, 119, 120–21, 131
Davis, William Henry "Tip," 177n16
Decatur, Alabama, 61, 62, 115, 209n18
depression (mental illness), 5, 23, 33, 41, 69, 72, 88, 89, 118, 120, 126, 138, 162n4
Des Arc, Arkansas, 2, 21, 22, 26, 29, 32, 34, 36, 38, 41, 42, 44, 46, 161n1, 163n11, 168n25
Des Arc Citizen, 26, 35
"Dixie" (song), 102
Dodge, Grenville M., 110, 116, 192n13, 193n14, 195n16
Donelson, Daniel P., 73
Duck River, 148, 152, 196n18

enslaved people, self-liberation, 146
Estell Springs, Tennessee, 75
European intervention, 67, 178n28
Everett, Edward, 14, 19, 158n10, 160n19, 175n12
Ewing, Andrew, 19, 160n20

Fishing Creek, battle of. *See* Mills Springs
Florence, Alabama, 1, 2, 8, 9, 12, 14, 29, 55–56, 57, 62, 77, 80, 81, 83, 89, 108, 116–17, 123, 131, 134, 142, 146, 147, 151, 154, 155n1, 159nn13–14, 165n22, 174nn6–8, 175n12, 176n13, 177nn16–19, 178n22, 179n29, 180n34, 182n42, 186n54, 187n60, 188n63, 190, 3, 191n5, 192nn10–11, 193n14, 199n26, 200n29, 205n41, 205nn1–2
Florence, Kentucky, 70, 72
Florence guards (Alabama militia company), 29, 161n3, 178n23, 179n29
Foote, Andrew Hull, 55, 176n13
Forrest, Nathan Bedford, 88, 106, 110, 111, 149, 151, 152, 171n36, 189n72, 192nn9–13, 195n16, 200n31
Fort Delaware, Delaware, 194n15
Fort Donelson, Tennessee, 56, 172n37, 176n13, 187n62
Fort Henry, Tennessee, 35, 59, 172n37, 176n13, 208n17
Fort Monroe, Virginia, 194n15
Fort Sumter, South Carolina, 29, 164n14
Fort Warren, Massachusetts, 198n20
Fort Worth, Texas, 153, 173n41, 177n18, 186n53, 205n42, 211n6
Foster, Benjamin Franklin "Frank," 63, 77, 79, 103, 123, 146, 177n19
Foster, Ephraim Hubbard, 177n18, 208n14
Foster, George Washington, 146, 208n16
Foster, Georgia Cheatham "Georgie," 8, 9, 62, 63, 64, 65, 68, 68, 81, 82, 83, 86, 105, 111, 113, 122, 132, 139, 145, 153, 177nn18–19, 186n53, 190n2, 191n5, 208n14
Foster, Robert Coleman, 83, 187n60, 208n17

Foster, Sallie Independence, 151, 205n2
Foster, Thomas Jefferson, 146, 208n17
Foster, William Lytle, 103, 145, 177n18, 208n14

George, enslaved African American, 74, 76, 79, 86, 89, 102, 105, 107, 113, 115, 120, 126, 141, 155, 182n45
Gettysburg, battle of, 123, 199n24, 201n32
Giles County, Tennessee, 12, 14, 157n3
Glenn, George Washington, 41, 163n11, 168n25
Glenn, John Edward, 38, 46, 168n25
Govan, Daniel Chevilette, 147, 153
Grant, Ulysses S., 56, 115, 123, 127–28, 130, 151–52, 167n24, 168n27, 172nn37–38, 176n13, 184n50, 188n62, 189n72, 193n14, 197n19, 208n17
Green Hill, Alabama, 1, 2, 22, 148
Greenville, Missouri, 41
Greenville, South Carolina, 157n6
Griffin, James Monroe "Roe" ("Uncle Roe"), 46, 139, 206nn6–7

Halleck, Henry W., 70
Hannay, Alexander M., 108, 115, 192n11
Hardee, William Joseph, 3, 38, 39, 41–40, 43, 52, 68, 71, 90, 127, 132, 149, 165n23, 169n29, 182n42, 187n61, 201n33
Hardee flag, 149
Harpeth River, 148, 149
Hicks, H. H., 44, 170n32
Hill, Daniel Harvey, 130, 204n40
Hindman, Thomas Carmichael, 38, 130, 166n24
Holcombe, James M, "Bob," 73, 181n38
Holly Springs, Mississippi, 57
Hooker, Joseph, 112, 113, 127, 196n17
Hunt, Charles S., 88, 189n69

Index

Iuka, Mississippi, 63, 64, 65

Jackson, Mississippi, 80, 84, 89, 115, 116, 184n50, 196n17, 196n19
Jackson, Thomas Jonathan "Stonewall," 68, 112, 168n26, 179n30, 204n40
Jesse (African American man enslaved by Orlando and Artisima Palmer), 82, 89, 102, 126
Johnston, Albert Sidney, 4, 46, 48, 56, 62, 166, 167, 170n36, 180n37, 182n46, 203n40
Johnston, Joseph E., 4, 68, 78, 81, 83, 101, 115, 116, 138, 140, 166, 168n26, 180n31, 183n50, 186n52, 191n4, 194n15, 197n19, 204n40, 205n3, 207nn10–13
Jones, John Beauchamp, 56
Jonesboro, Georgia, 210n27

Kendrick, Jennie, 22, 52, 114
Kennedale, Texas, 153
Kennedy, Alexander, 2
Kennedy, Cynthia Walker Palmer. *See* Cynthia Walker Palmer
Kennedy, David Lewis ("Uncle David"), 2, 15, 159n11
Kennedy, Delia, 15, 22, 26, 27, 28, 30, 32, 52, 60, 61, 79, 81, 82, 86, 87, 88, 102, 103, 105, 111, 113, 114, 121, 133, 139, 142, 144, 147, 159n12, 163n6, 177n17
Kennedy, Elias Windsor ("Uncle Elias"), 2, 18, 19, 22, 26, 29, 30, 33, 37, 50, 58, 67, 68, 77, 100, 106, 113, 114, 115, 118, 120, 137, 139, 141, 144, 145, 159n16, 161n3, 164n12, 173n41, 182n44
Kennedy, Georgia Cheatham Foster. *See* Georgia Cheatham Foster
Kennedy, Hiram ("Grandpa"), 1, 2, 14, 15, 16, 22, 23, 26, 28, 30, 32, 34, 37, 38, 48, 50, 58, 68, 132, 139, 161n2

Kennedy, Joanna, 2
Kennedy, John Alexander, 1
Kennedy, Johnathan Spinks ("Uncle Spinks"), 2, 9, 29, 30, 32, 58, 65, 68, 86, 88, 132, 137, 139, 142, 165n22, 179n29
Kennedy, Joseph ("Cousin Joe"), 118, 199n25
Kennedy, Logan Paschal, 161n3, 181–82n41
Kennedy, Mary Spinks ("Grandma"), 1, 14, 15, 23, 26, 28, 30, 32, 33, 34, 38, 60, 68, 74, 81, 102, 105, 106, 107, 111, 121, 126, 131, 136, 137, 138, 141, 144, 161n2
Kennedy, Oliver Sylvester, 7, 8–9, 19, 25, 26, 28, 29, 31, 32, 34, 37, 45, 50, 59, 62, 63, 64, 65, 68, 69, 77, 78, 79, 80, 82, 83, 87, 100, 101, 103, 105, 108, 111, 113, 122, 123, 132, 139, 145, 153, 156n10, 159n12, 163n6, 173n41, 186n53, 188nn63–65, 190n2
Kennedy, Panthea Narcissa, 87, 188n65
Kennedy, Vernon L., 30, 32, 36, 165n22
Kennedy, William Wesley ("Uncle Wesley"), 8, 52, 88, 169n12, 163n6, 173n41, 188n65
Kennedy, Willis P. "Willie," 32, 74, 164n15
Kennedy Gun Factory, 1–2
Knoxville, Tennessee, 71, 72, 73, 166n24, 176n14

LaGrange, Georgia, 140, 146
LaGrange College (Wesleyan College, Florence, Alabama), 18, 155n5, 161n3
Lane, Joseph, 14
Lauderdale County, Alabama, 1, 3, 5, 6, 8, 29, 71, 78, 80, 106, 107, 116, 117, 124, 132, 136, 138, 139, 156n4, 159nn11–16, 163n6, 164nn15–16,

226

169n30, 175n12, 177n17, 178n23, 182n41, 186n53, 187n56, 189n66, 190n2, 191n5, 192n11, 199nn25–26, 200n27, 206nn4–6, 208n16
Lauderdale Springs, Mississippi, 177n17
Lawrenceburg, Tennessee, 11, 13, 79, 157n3
Lebanon, Tennessee, 2, 11, 14, 119, 121, 158n9
Lee, Stephen D., 149
Leftwich, William W., 77, 182n47
Lige (an enslaved African American), 141
Lincoln, Abraham, 29, 47, 49, 50, 66, 68, 127, 151, 158n6, 160n19, 162n5, 164n14, 178n28, 179n30, 189n70, 197n20
Little Rock, Arkansas, 25, 36, 159n12, 162n5, 162n7, 167n24, 168n25
Logan, John A., 152, 208n13
love, courtship, romance, and flirtation, 6, 52, 72, 77, 79, 82, 86, 87, 89, 99, 100, 101, 102, 103, 104–5, 106, 114, 118, 120, 122, 131, 141, 143–44
Lowery, Mark Perrin, 3, 126, 147, 156n6, 201n33, 202n37

Madison, Arkansas, 21
Madison County, Florida, 159n11
mail service, 5, 41, 76, 79, 99, 109, 113, 117, 121, 123, 124
Marion (an African American enslaved by Orlando Palmer), 7, 67, 74, 76, 86, 89, 102, 105, 107, 113, 115, 120, 126, 141, 156n1, 177n24, 182n45
Martin, William H., 147
Mayfield, Tennessee, 12
McClellan, George B., 68, 152, 168n26, 179n30, 180n31, 184n50, 189n71
McClellan, William Cowan, 56

McCook, Edward, 209n18
McCormick County, South Carolina, 170n34
McCulloch, Ben, 169nn29–31
Mechanics Hill, North Carolina, 1
Memphis, Tennessee, 22, 48, 59, 68, 161n1, 165n20, 181n39
military units (Confederate)
   First Arkansas Infantry (*see* Fifteenth Arkansas Infantry)
   Second Alabama Infantry, 208n16
   Fourth Alabama Cavalry, 174n8
   Fourth Alabama Infantry, 183n47
   Seventh Alabama Infantry, 29, 161n3, 164n12, 177n19, 178n23, 179n29
   Eighth Texas Cavalry, 47, 170n36
   Ninth Alabama Infantry, 56
   Thirteenth Alabama Infantry, 169n30, 177n16
   Fifteenth Arkansas Infantry, 40
   Fifteenth Alabama Infantry, 176n14
   Sixteenth Alabama Infantry, 8, 86, 175nn11–12, 177n17, 178n22, 182n42, 187nn56–58, 188n63, 192n10, 205n1
   Nineteenth Alabama Infantry, 194n15
   Twenty-Seventh Alabama Infantry, 186n54, 200n29, 208n17
   Thirty-Third Alabama Infantry, 90, 158n6, 180n34, 191n6, 200n28
   Thirty-Eighth Alabama Infantry, 164n12, 173n43
   Forty-Sixth Alabama Infantry, 164n16
   One-Hundred and Fifty-Fourth Tennessee Infantry, 73
Mills Springs, battle of, 8, 175n10, 175n12
Milner, Joseph, 18, 159n16
Milner, W. J., 210n30
Milner and Kennedy Wool Factory, 2

Missionary Ridge, 3, 126, 127, 128, 129, 166n23, 201n31, 207n10
Mobile, Alabama, 146
Mobile and Ohio Railroad, 66, 206n9
Moore, Absalom B., 186n52
Moore, Alfred M., 90, 158n6, 187n55, 191n6, 197n19
Morgan, John Hunt, 4, 81, 186n52
Murfreesboro, battle of, 79–80, 90, 128, 149, 166n23, 190n75
Murfreesboro, Tennessee, 71, 73, 78, 81, 82, 87, 101, 108, 125, 151, 190n76
Murray, George M., 60, 61, 67, 164n11, 176n14
Mussel Shoals, Alabama, 56, 176n13

Nashville, battle of, 151, 185n50, 193n13
Nashville, Tennessee, 13, 18, 19, 49, 59, 73, 76, 78, 81, 83, 85, 86, 90, 107, 146, 147, 148, 149, 151, 152, 158n7, 160n20, 172n37, 174n8, 175n12, 176n13, 185n51, 186n53, 187n60, 195n16, 200n29, 208nn14–17
Nashville and Chattanooga Railroad, 152, 210n19
Nashville and Louisville Railroad, 85
Neely, Mollie, 25
Nelson, William "Bull," 70
Nicholson, Alfred Osborne Pope, 19, 160n20

Palmer, Artimisia "Missie," 1, 3, 155n1, 191n7
Palmer, Cynthia Walker ("Aunt Cynthia"), 8, 25, 45, 46, 52, 57, 60, 139, 159n12
Palmer, John ("Uncle John"), 46, 67, 132, 139
Palmer, Martha Person "Patsy" (Kennedy), 1
Palmer, Paschal W., 1

Pate, Catherine A. E. "Katie," 38, 50, 51, 52, 60, 176n16
Patton, Archibald Kennedy, 45, 52, 170n34
Peach Orchard Hill, 152
Peninsula Campaign and Seven Days battle, 68
Perry, Rebecca "Babe," 28, 163n10
Perry, Sylvanus William "Doc," 74, 100, 109, 111, 114, 123, 125, 182n43
Perryville, battle of, 3, 70, 72–74, 89, 90, 149, 166n23, 171n36, 181n40, 182n44, 190n2, 194n15, 200nn28–31, 201n33, 204n40
Peter, an enslaved African America, 67, 178n24
Phelps, Seth, 55
Pillow, Gideon J., 43, 169n29, 173n38, 16n13
Pitman's Ferry, Arkansas, 38, 39, 41, 42, 169n29
Pocahontas, Arkansas, 39, 42, 44
Polk, James K., 13, 158n8
Polk, Leonidas, 71, 90, 121, 130, 140, 145, 166n23, 169n29, 172n38, 201n40, 206n9, 207n10
Polk, Lucius Eugene, 199n27, 200n29
Polk, William Mecklenburg, 71
Posey, Eli, 43
Prairie County, Arkansas, 3, 24, 161n1, 163nn8–10, 168n25
Prairie Grove, battle of, 167n24
Preston, William, 4, 75, 182n46
Pulaski, Tennessee, 12, 13, 148, 157n4
Pulaski County, Tennessee, 163n7, 170n32

Ratcliff, William Cummings, 25, 44, 163n7
reading and literature, 5, 19, 23–24, 26, 27, 33, 36, 57, 58, 122
Rector, Henry Massie, 162n5, 164n14

Index

Rector Guards (Arkansas militia company), 3, 24, 35, 36, 162n5, 163n11, 168n25
Richmond, Kentucky, battle of, 70, 72, 149
Richmond, Virginia, 56, 67, 116, 128, 162, 169n30, 179n30, 180n31, 184n50
Richmond Enquirer, 179n28
Ringgold Gap, Georgia, 128, 129, 149, 202n36, 203n38
Ripley, Mississippi, 15, 48, 56, 60, 67, 87, 123, 132, 142, 156n1, 166n24, 176n16, 178nn26–27
Roddey, Philip Dale, 110, 116, 117, 139, 174n8, 192n13, 195n16, 198n23
Rogers, Lee, 12
Rogersville, Alabama, 25
Rose, Solon E., 12, 157n4
Rosecrans, William S., 90, 101, 106, 123, 127, 130, 152, 166, 186n52, 187n61, 194n16, 196n18, 200n31

Schofield, John McAllister, 148, 152, 153, 207n13
Seward, William H., 89, 189n70
Shiloh, battle of, 3, 8, 56, 66, 67, 73, 149, 166n23, 167n24, 170n34, 171n36, 172n37, 173n6, 177n21, 182n42, 182, 46, 183n49, 185n51, 194n15, 200n27, 204n40
Simonton, Anna, 12, 157n3
Simonton, William, 12
Simpson, R. T., 26, 29, 30, 31, 163n8
Simpson, William M., 99, 102, 122, 142, 144, 199n26
Simpson, William M., 120, 200n29
slavery, 7, 82, 88, 116, 127, 146, 156n1, 157n6, 162n5, 170n35
Sloss, Thomas Henry "Tom," 66, 178n23
Smith, Charles Wade, 28, 163n10

Smith, Edmund Kirby, 70–71
Smithfield, North Carolina, 153
social values, 37, 56, 57
Spinks, John E., 164n12, 180n32, 1811–82n41, 206n5
Spinks, Mary S. Belk ("Aunt Mary"), 26, 30, 138, 143, 163n9
Spinks, Oliver, 32
Spinks, William L., 52, 164n12, 173n43
Spring Hill, Tennessee, 148
Springfield, Missouri, battle of. *See* Wilsons Creek, battle of
St. Louis, Missouri, 40, 169n29
Stainbach, E. B., 69, 180n33
Stewart, Alexander P., 148, 149, 152

Taylor's Ridge, Georgia, 129, 202n37
Terry's Texas Rangers. *See* Eighth Texas Cavalry
Texarkana, Texas/Arkansas, 154, 207n11
Thomas, George Henry, 127, 128, 130, 148, 151, 152, 166n23, 175n10, 207n10, 208n13, 211n3
Tippah County, Mississippi, 1, 8, 38, 101, 137, 154, 155n1, 159n12, 163n6, 178n27, 188n65, 206n8, 211n8
Tupelo, Mississippi, 4, 66, 69, 71, 72, 73, 153

Union loyalists in Alabama, 5, 55, 138, 144

Vallandigham, Clement Laird, 116, 197n20
Van Dorn, Earl, 107, 167n24, 192n9
Vicksburg, siege of, 102, 116, 118, 123, 127, 184n50, 193n14, 197n19, 206n9

Walker, William H. T., 127, 145
Watkins, Sam, 151, 153
Weakley, Thomas Porter, 13, 158n7

Wesleyan University, Florence, Alabama, 2, 116, 156n5, 162n7, 164n13. *See also* LaGrange College
Wharton, John A., 81, 82, 83, 170n36, 185n51, 187n61
Wheeler, Joseph, 107, 110, 123, 125, 146, 192n13, 194n15, 199n23, 209nn18—19
Whitesides, Margaret Ann, 86, 108, 183n48
Whitman, Walt, 4
Williams, Thomas Jefferson, 147
Wilson, James H., 193n13
Wilson County, Tennessee, 158n9
Wilsons Creek, Missouri, battle of, 43, 169n31
Winston, Thomas Brown "Tom," 24, 27, 43, 48, 60, 67, 72, 74, 76, 79, 82, 86, 87, 88, 89, 95, 100, 104, 109, 113, 114, 115, 118, 123, 126, 131, 132, 133, 141, 143, 144, 154, 162n4, 164n13, 173n38, 182n44, 189n69, 191n7
Winston's School, Texarkana, Texas, 154
Wood, Alexander Hamilton, 182n42
Wood, Sterling Alexander Martin, 3, 4, 27, 29, 59, 62, 63, 73, 75, 76, 77, 78, 80, 84, 86, 87, 90, 103, 104, 109, 121–22, 125, 130, 156n6, 161n3, 177n19, 178n29, 181n42, 186n55, 187n61, 190n75, 197n19, 200nn28—30
Wood, William Basil, 8, 59, 84, 153, 175nn11–12, 177n17, 187n56, 188n63
Woodell, Margaret A., 18, 159n16

Yancey, William Lowndes, 3, 11, 13, 14, 157n6

www.ingramcontent.com/pod-product-compliance
Lightning Source LLC
Chambersburg PA
CBHW030516080526
44586CB00011B/218